Day by day method

spanish
with ease

Original text by

J. ANTON

Adapted for the use
of English speaking readers
by

John SMELLIE

Illustrated by J.L. GOUSSÉ

B.P. 25
94431 CHENNEVIERES S/MARNE Cedex
(France)

© ASSIMIL 1987   Nº I.S.B.N. 2-7005-0131-4

METHOD BOOKS

Bound books, lavishly illustrated, containing lessons and
exercises recorded on cassettes and CDs

Arabic with ease
Dutch with ease
New French with ease
Using French
Business French
German with ease
Hungarian with ease
Italian with ease
Spanish with ease
Using Spanish

guidelines, using an alphabet we already recognize. Certain sounds are described in a simplified form (e.g., the "th" sound that is found in most of Spain, but not in Latin America, is not featured as such in the pronunciation notes, but appears as an "s" sound). Spanish pronunciation is actually relatively simple. Every letter has a face value, and that face value never changes. The stress falls on the next-to-last syllable, and accents are only written when that basic rule is not applied.

Let these indications suffice for the time being. Remember that nobody speaks a language without making mistakes at first... Try and let it flow through you to begin with, a little each day, and in the end you'll feel more and more confident to make up your own Spanish sentences and answer back!

*The introduction above is essential reading. If you have not read it, read it now, so that you can fully understand the structure and procedure of this Spanish course. Even if you are not a beginner, the introduction will give you practical advice and basic explanations about how to use **Spanish With Ease**.*

LECCION PRIMERA (Pron. : lek'cion' priméra)

Un encuentro

1 — ¡Buenos días! Pablo. **(1)**
2 — ¡Ana! ¿Qué tal estás? **(2) (3)**
3 — Bien. Tú, en cambio, tienes mala cara. **(4)**
4 — Sí. Estoy un poco preocupado.
5 — ¿Sabes? Tenía ganas de verte. **(5)**
6 — Yo también.
7 — ¿Quieres comer conmigo?
8 — De acuerdo. Es una buena idea.

¡BUENOS DÍAS!

PRONUNCIACION (pronoun'ciacion'). oun' en'couen'tro. **1** ¡bouénoss diass! pablo. **2** ¡ana! ¿ké tal ésstass? **3** bién'. tou én' cam'bio tiénéss mala cara. **4** ésstoï oun poco préocoupado. **5** ¿sabéss? ténia ganas dé vérté. **6** yo tam'bién'. **7** ¿kiéréss comér con'migo? **8** dé acouérdo. éss ouna bouéna idéa.

EXERCISE : 1. Tú estás bien. 2. Tú tienes una idea. 3. Yo también. 4. Yo tenía ganas. 5. Tú quieres comer. 6. Es una buena idea. 7. Yo estoy de acuerdo.

LESSON ONE

The Spanish sentences given at the beginning of each lesson (left-hand page) are translated into English on the right-hand page. The English equivalent is given first, and the literal translation of the Spanish words is given (where applicable) in parentheses. Square brackets indicate words in English which are not necessary in Spanish.

A meeting (masculine)

1 — Hello (Good days) Pablo!
2 — Ana! How are you?
3 — Fine (Well). You, on the other hand (in exchange) don't look very well (have a bad face).
4 — Yes. I'm a little worried (preoccupied).
5 — Do you know? I wanted (had desires) to see you.
6 — Me too.
7 — Do you want to eat with me?
8 — OK. [It] is a good idea.

NOTES
(1) In Spanish, everything is pronounced. *Buenos* has three syllables, and the final *"s"* is always pronounced. The Spanish tend to run all the words in a sentence together.
(2) Verbs don't necessarily need to be accompanied by their subjects. Thus *estás* means "you are" (or "are you?"), and *es* can mean "he is", "it is", or simply "is".
(3) Since verbs in the question form (e.g., *¿estás?*) are identical to those in statement form (e.g., *estás*), there has to be some indication that a question is involved. In speech, asking a question involves changing the intonation of the sentence. In written language, the ¿ sign at the beginning of the question is the reader's signal that the sentence includes a question. The same is true of exclamation marks.
(4) The Spanish *r* is rolled. To roll an *r*, place the tip of your tongue on the ridge of the hard palate and then make it vibrate against the top front teeth. The *r* is rolled more at the beginning of words than in the middle, and the double *rr* is rolled even more than that. It's quite a difficult sound if you're not used to it : try saying *Henrique* ("Henry"). To start rolling the *r*, imagine there's a *d* between the *Hen-* and the *-rique*.
(5) *V* and *b* are pronounced identically in Spanish. They both sound like a slightly softer version of the English "b". The Spanish *automovil* is a good example : it also shows that the words "move" and "mobile" have the same root.

EXERCISE : 1. You are well. — **2.** You have an idea. — **3.** Me too. — **4.** I wanted to. — **5.** You want to eat. — **6.** It's a good idea. — **7.** I agree.

3 tres (tress)

EXERCISE
Ponga las palabras que faltan (**po**nga las pal**a**brass ké f**a**ltan)

(Fill in the missing words)
Each dot represents one letter.

1 *I am well.*

Yo . . . . . bien.

2 *You, on the other hand, are worried.*

Tú, ..., estás preocupado.

3 *Me too.*

Yo . . . .

4 *I wanted to eat / to see you.*

Yo . . . . . ganas de . . . . .

Yo . . . . . ganas . . . . .

****

LECCION SEGUNDA (Pron. : lekci**o**n ségo**u**nda)

In this lesson, we will start using personal pronouns.

1 — Yo v**o**y a casa. **(1)**
2 — ¿Vienes conmigo?

PRONUNCIACION (pronoun´ciacion´). **1** yo voï a cassa. **2** ¿vién**é**ss
con´migo?

5 *You are with me / You agree.*

Tú . . . .

Tú . . . . .   de   . . . .

THE MISSING WORDS : **1** estoy. **2** en cambio. **3** también. **4** tenía - comer / tenía - de verte. **5** estás conmigo / estás - acuerdo.

Later, we will look at the rules for accents in Spanish. By and large, accents are only written on words when the stress does **not** fall on the next-to-last syllable, but the whole story is a bit more complicated than this. For now, just look at *lección* and *pronunciación*, both of which are pronounced with the stress on the final syllable. (In this book, accents are never written on capital letters).

Re-read the lesson when you have been through the notes. Pay particular attention to the stress patterns, and say the words out loud.

There may seem to be a lot to remember in the notes, but don't worry! In the first few lessons, there's a lot of basic groundwork. When that's out of the way, things will be a lot easier.

****

LESSON TWO

1 — I'm going (to) home.
2 — Are you coming with me?

NOTES
(1) *En la casa* (with the feminine article *la*) means "in the house". When *casa* means "home", it doesn't need the article.

3   Estamos muy lejos. **(2)**
4   Tengo un problema.
5   El viene mañana. **(3)**
6   Nosotros vamos a comer.
7   Ella está cansada. **(4)**
8   Hoy tengo una cita.
9   Ellos están contentos.
10   Vosotros coméis en el restaurante.

3 ésstamoss moui léHoss. 4 tén'go oun' probléma. 5 él viéné magnana. 6 nossotross vamoss a comér. 7 él/a éssta can'ssada. 8 oï ten'go ouna cita. 9 él/oss ésstan' con'tén'toss. 10. vossotross coméiss én' el résstaourante.

* * * * *

EXERCISE :   1. Yo estoy contenta. 2. Tú quieres comer. 3. El viene mañana. 4, Nosotros estamos cansados. 5. Ellos están lejos. 6. Ella viene conmigo. 7. Vosotros coméis.

The most important thing to do at this stage is to concentrate on pronouncing each word or sentence correctly. Don't try to analyze the structure of each sentence – and don't be surprised if you can't find an adequate English translation for each Spanish word.

Spanish nouns can be either masculine or feminine. Masculine nouns use the definite article *el* : feminine nouns use the definite article *la*.

EXERCISE
Ponga las palabras que faltan (ponga las palabrass ké faltan)

(Fill in the missing words)

1 *I'm going to eat / I'm going to eat tomorrow at home.*

. .   . . . .   comer

. .   . .   comer   . . . . . .   en   . . . .

3   We are very far [away].
4   I have a problem.
5   He is coming tomorrow.
6   We are going to eat.
7   She is tired.
8   I have an appointment.
9   They are happy.
10   You (plural) eat at the restaurant.

(2) The *j* sound in Castilian is a harsh sound that exists in the Scottish "lo**ch**". Certain Spanish speakers pronounce the *j* more like a heavily aspirated "h" sound. In the pronunciation notes, you'll find the sign H. The Spanish *g* is pronounced the same way before an *e* or an *i*.

(3) The accent on the *ñ* is called a *tilde*. It turns the pure *n* into a composite sound similar to the one found in the middle of the two-syllable word "onion". In the pronunciation notes, this sound is depicted as **gn**. Example : *mañana* (pron. magnana).

(4) The *ll* sound is somewhere between an ordinary English "l" and the English "y" as in "you". Thus *millón* is pronounced "mil**yo**n". *Ll* is treated as a separate letter in dictionaries.

EXERCISE : **1.** I am happy. – **2.** You want to eat. – **3.** He is coming tomorrow. – **4.** We are tired. – **5.** They are far away. – **6.** She is coming with me. – **7.** You (plural) are eating.

We saw in the last lesson that verbs can be used without their personal pronouns. Personal pronouns are usually only used for added emphasis.

Remember! *Tú* and *él :* "you" and "he" are written with accents to distinguish them from the possessive *tu* and the masculine article *el : tú vienes* = "you are coming" ; *tu casa* = "your house" ; *él tiene* = "he has" ; *el problema* = "the problem".

Lección 2

7 siète (siété)

2 *Today you (plural) are eating at the restaurant.*

. . .   .   coméis   . .   el restaurante.

3 *She is coming with us / She is coming with us tomorrow.*

. . . . .   viene con   . . . .

. . . . .   viene con   . . . .

4 *You have an appointment / a problem.*

. .   tienes una   . . . .

. .   tienes un   . . . .

* *

LECCIÓN TERCERA. (Lek'cion' tercéra)

¿Qué tal está ?

1 — ¿Usted fuma?
2 — Muy poco.
3 — ¿Quiere un cigarro? **(1)**
4 — Sí. Gracias.
5 — El tabaco rubio, en España, es caro.
6 — Tiene usted razón. **(2)**

PRONUNCIACION (pronoun'ciacion'). ¿ké tal éssta? 1 ¿oussté fouma?
2 moui poco. 3 ¿kiéré oun cigarro? 4 si graciass. 5 el tabaco roubio én'
éspagna éss caro. 6 tiéné oussté raçon.

Words ending in *d* (usted, Madrid) are stressed on the final
syllable. The *d* itself is only very slightly pronounced, and
sounds more like the English "th" as in "with".

5 *He is very far away/He is very tired.*

. .   está muy   . . . . .

. .   está   . . .   .

*****

****

LESSON THREE

How are you?

1 — Do you smoke?
2 — Very little.
3 — Do [you] want a cigarette?
4 — Yes. Thank you.
5 — (The) light (blond) tobacco in Spain is expensive.
6 — You are (You have) right.

*****

NOTES
(1) Castilian Spanish is full of "th" sounds. Whenever a Spanish *c* comes before an *e* or an *i*, it is pronounced "th" as in "thank you". In parts of Southern Spain, and throughout Latin America this "th" sound is replaced by a simple "s" sound. In our pronunciation notes, we use the letter *c* or *ç*. Remember the rule : *c* before *e* or *i*, and *z*'s everywhere, are pronounced "th". Example : *Gracias* (pron. gra'cias) ; *razón* (pron. ra'çon).
(2) *Tienes razón* means "you are right", but *tienes* actually means "you have". *Tiene hambre :* "he his hungry" is a similar expression : literally "he has hunger".

7 — El tabaco negro cuesta mucho menos. (3)
8 — Y no fumar es todavía más barato.

7 él tabaco négro couéssta
mou'tcho ménoss. 8 y no foumar éss todavía mass barato.

So far we have been using the *tú* form of "you". This is the familiar form. For greater respect, the *usted* form should be used. *Usted* (pronounced oussté**th**) is the contracted form of *vuestra merced* : "your Grace" and the verb must be in the third person ("Is your grace coming?"). Both *tú* and *usted* are singular. When talking to several people, the familiar form becomes *vosotros* (or *vosotras* if all the people you are addressing are feminine) and the respectful form *usted* becomes *ustedes* (third person plural).

* * * * *

EXERCISE :   1. ¿Quiere usted fumar? 2. El tabaco es caro. 3. Tienes razón. 4. El fuma muy poco. 5. Todavía tengo un cigarro. 6. No es caro. 7. Es más barato.

EXERCISE
Ponga las palabras que faltan (ponga las palabrass ké faltan)

(Fill in the missing words)

1 *I smoke very little/I smoke a lot.*

Yo fumo   . . .   .

Yo fumo   . . . . .

2 *You are right/You have a cigarette.*

. .   tienes   . . . . .

. .   tienes un   . . . .

* *

7 — (The) black tobacco costs much less.
8 — And not smoking (not to smoke) is even cheaper.

(3) *Mucho* ("much", "many", "a lot of") changes its ending when it refers to feminine and plural nouns : *mucha alegría :* much happiness ; *muchas personas :* many people ; *muchos hombres :* a lot of men .

EXERCISE : **1.** Do you want to smoke? – **2.** Tobacco is expensive. – **3.** You are right. – **4.** He smokes very little. – **5.** I still have one cigarette. – **6.** It isn't dear. – **7.** It's cheaper.

3 *Tobacco is cheap / expensive.*

El tabaco . . . .

El tabaco . . . .

4 *The house is still far away.*

La casa está . . . .

5 *Light tobacco costs less.*

El tabaco . . . .

THE MISSING WORDS : **1** muy poco / mucho. **2** tú - razón / tú - cigarro. **3** es barato / es caro. **4** todavía lejos. **5** rubio cuesta menos.

****

LECCION CUARTA (Lek'cion' couarta)

Masculino y femenino (1)

1 El niño bebe el agua. **(2)**
2 La madre coge una llave.
3 La casa está lejos.
4 La cafetería está cerca de la panadería.
5 Tengo una amiga francesa. **(3)**
6 Tienes un transistor español. **(3)**
7 El vaso está lleno. **(4)**
8 La taza está vacía. **(4)**

PRONUNCIACION (pronoun'ciacion'). masscoulino y féménino. **1** el nigno bébé el agoua. **2** la madré coHe ouna //avé. **3** la cassa éssta' léHoss. **4** la cafétéria éssta cerca dé la panadéria. **5** tén'go ouna amiga fran'céssa. **6** tiénéss oun tran'ssisstor esspagnol. **7** el vasso éssta //eno. **8** la taça éssta vacia.

EL VASO ESTÁ VACÍO

EXERCISES : **1.** El niño tiene una llave. **2.** Mi amiga vive en Francia. **3.** El vaso está vacío. **4.** La casa es grande. **5.** La taza es pequeña.

LESSON FOUR

Masculine and feminine

1   The child drinks (the) water.
2   The mother takes a key.
3   The house is far [away].
4   The bar (café) is near the baker's.
5   I have a French friend (fem.).
6   You have a Spanish transistor.
7   The glass is full.
8   The cup is empty.

NOTES
(1) A rule of thumb for recognizing the gender of certain nouns : those ending in -o are masculine (e.g., *el vaso* : "the glass"), and those ending in -a are feminine (e.g., *la casa* : "the house"). There are (you guessed it!) several notable exceptions, such as *el problema* : the problem, *la mano* : the hand.
(2) *Agua* (pronounced in two syllables) is **not** an exception to the rule in note 1. For phonetic reasons, feminine nouns beginning with a stressed *a* use the masculine article *el*.
(3) *Un* and *una* are the masculine and feminine indefinite articles ("a", "an"), and become *unos* and *unas* in the plural ("some", "a few").
(4) Adjectives ending in -o in the masculine change to -a in the feminine : *un vaso lleno* : "a full glass" ; *una taza llena* : "a full cup".

* * * * *

For the pronunciation of *coge* in sentence 2, refer back to note (2) on Lesson 2.

EXERCISE : 1. The child has a key. – **2.** My friend (fem.) lives in France. – **3.** The glass is empty. – **4.** The house is big. – **5.** The cup is small.

EXERCISE
Ponga las palabras que faltan (ponga las palabrass ké faltan)

(Fill in the missing words)

1 *The child takes a key/a glass.*

. . niño ' . . . . llave.

. . niño . . . . vaso.

2 *The house is far away/near.*

. . casa está . . . . .

. . casa está . . . . .

****

LECCION QUINTA (Lek'cion' kin'ta)

Antes del viaje

1 Ahora, estamos en Burgos. **(1)**
2 Mañana, vamos a Madrid. **(2)**
3 — ¿Sabes? Ultimamente, me canso mucho.
4 — Deberías trabajar menos.
5 — La vida en la ciudad es demasiado agitada.
6   Antes de ir a París, quiero consultar al
    médico.

PRONUNCIACION (pronoun'ciacion'). an'téss del viaHé. **1** aora ésstamoss én' bourgoss. **2** magnana vamoss a madri(d) **3** ¿sabéss? oultimamén'té mé can'sso moutcho. **4** débériass trabaHar ménoss. **5** la vida én' la ciouda éss démassiado aHitada. **6** an'téss dé ir a pariss kiéro con'soultar al médico.

3 *I have a friend (masc.)/a good idea.*

Yo tengo . . amigo.

Yo tengo . . . . idea.

4 *The mother goes to the baker's.*

. . . madre va . . . panadería.

5 *The cup is full/empty.*

. . taza . . . .

. . taza . . . .

THE MISSING WORDS : **1** el - coge una / el - coge un. **2** la -lejos / la - cerca. **3** un / una buena. **4** la - a la. **5** la - está llena / la - está vacía.

* *

LESSON FIVE

Before the trip

1	Now we are in Burgos.
2	Tomorrow, we are going to Madrid.
3 —	Do you know? Lately I am getting very tired (I tire myself a lot).
4 —	You should work less.
5 —	(The) life in the city is too busy (agitated).
6	Before going (before of to go) to Paris, I want to see (consult) (to) the doctor.

NOTES
(1) The preposition *en* indicates position. Thus *estoy en Burgos* means "I am in Burgos".
(2) The preposition *a* indicates movement here : *Voy a Madrid* : "I'm going to Madrid". But *a* also has other uses : it introduces direct objects **when they are people.** To say "I see Pedro", for example, we must put in the preposition *a*, thus : *veo a Pedro.* We find the *a* again in sentence (6), *quiero consultar al médico* (*al* is the contracted form of *a el*).

Lección 5

7 — Yo conozco a un médico muy simpático.(3)
8 — ¿Puedes telefonearle?
9 — ¡Claro que sí! (4)

7 yo conoçco a oun médico moui sim'patico.
8 ¿pouédéss téléfonéarlé? **9** ¡claro ké si!

EXERCICE : 1. Ahora vamos a casa. 2. Puedes ir a París.
3. Tengo un amigo muy simpático. 4. Voy a Burgos. 5.
Estoy en París. 6. Nosotros estamos en la ciudad. 7.
Estás demasiado cansado. 8. Yo conozco a un médico.
9. Tú puedes telefonearle.

EXERCISE
Ponga las palabras que faltan (ponga las palabrass ké faltan)

(Fill in the missing words)

1 *Now I'm getting very tired / not getting very tired.*

. . . .   mucho.

. . . .   poco.

2 *We are in London / in England.*

Estamos   . .   Londres

Estamos   . .   Inglaterra

3 *He is going to Italy / to the baker's.*

El va   .   Italia.

El va   .   la   . . . .

4 *Before going to the café.*

. . . . .   de ir   .   . .   cafetería.

* *

7 — I know (to) a very nice doctor.
8 — Can you phone (to) him?
9 — Of course!

(3) Here we find the *a* used to introduce a person (direct object). *Simpático* means "nice" or "friendly" (**not** "sympathetic").
(4) *¡Claro que sí!* and *¡claro que no!* are expressions you will hear a lot in Spain. They mean : "of course!" and "of course not!".

EXERCISE : 1. Now we are going home. — **2.** You can go to Paris. — **3.** I have a very nice friend. — **4.** I am going to Burgos. — **5.** I am in Paris. — **6.** We are in the city. — **7.** You are too tired. — **8.** I know a doctor. — **9.** You can phone him.

5 *Can you come home with me?*

¿ . . . . . venir . casa . . . .?

¿ . . . . . venir . casa . . . él?

THE MISSING WORDS : **1** ahora me canso / ahora me canso. **2** en / en. **3** a / a - panadería. **4** antes - a la. **5** puedes - a - conmigo / puedes - a - con.

* * * * *

The *h* in Spanish is always silent.

Ahora ("now") is made up of *a + hora*, where *hora* means "hour" or "time" : literally : "at (the) time".

* *

LECCION SEXTA (Lek'cion' sessta)

Tener - Haber (1)

1. Ahora tengo hambre.
2. Hoy tienes una cita.
3. Ellos tienen un coche rojo.
4. Nosotros no tenemos ganas.
5. Vosotras tenéis un apartamento bonito.
6. Ella tiene un perro pequeño.
7. Yo he ido al cine.
8. ¿Has comido bien?
9. Él no ha venido todavía.
10. Nosotros hemos ganado la partida.
11. Vosotros habéis conocido a su hermana.
12. Ellas han telefoneado a su madre.

PRONUNCIACION (pronoun'ciacion'). téner - aber. **1** aora tén'go am'bré. **2** oï tiéness ouna cita. **3** él/oss tiénén' oun co'tche roHo. **4** nossotross no ténémoss ganass. **5** vossotrass téniaiss oun apartamén'to bonito. **6** él/a tiéne oun pérro pékégno. **7** yo é ido al cine. **8** ¿ass comido bién'? **9** él no a vénido todavia. **10** nossotross émoss ganado la partida. **11** vossotross abéiss conocido a sou érmana. **12** él/ass an' téléfonéado a sou madré.

USTEDES TIENEN UN APARTAMENTO BONITO

EXERCISE : 1. Tengo un coche. 2. Has comido. 3. Habéis ido al cine. 4. Tenemos hambre. 5. Has ido conmigo. 6. Han telefoneado. 7. Todavía no ha venido.

LESSON SIX

1 Now I'm hungry (I have hunger).
2 Today you have an appointment.
3 They have a red car.
4 We don't feel like it (don't have desires).
5 You have a nice apartment.
6 She has a small dog (dog small).
7 I have gone to the cinema.
8 Have you eaten well?
9 He has not come yet.
10 We have won the match.
11 You have known (to) his sister.
12 They (fem.) have phoned (to) their mother.

NOTES
(1) The verb "to have" has two different forms in Spanish, depending on whether it is the auxiliary (as in "I have eaten") or the transitive verb of possession (as in "I have a car").

The auxiliary *haber* is conjugated like other verbs (but it is irregular). It cannot stand alone : it needs a past participle after it : *has ido :* "you have gone" ; *hemos llegado :* "we have arrived".

Tener que + an infinitive is the Spanish for "I have to" : *tengo que ir a casa :* "I have to go home".

*****

EXERCISE : 1. I have a car. — **2.** You have eaten. — **3.** You (pl.) have gone to the cinema. — **4.** We are hungry. — **5.** You have gone with me. — **6.** They have phoned. — **7.** He has not come yet.

EXERCISE

Ponga las palabras que faltan (ponga las palabrass ké faltan)

(Fill in the missing words)

1 *I have a car/I am hungry.*

Yo . . . . coche.

Yo . . . .

2 *We have phoned his sister.*

Nosotros . . . . a . . her-

mana.

* *

LECCION SEPTIMA (lek'cion sép'tima)

LESSON SEVEN

Revisión y notas (révission y notass)

1. We're going to stop here and go over the points we've seen so far.

The first six lessons in the course will have given you an overall idea of how each lesson is made up. The sentences will start to get longer soon, and they'll be a bit more complicated... but not just yet!

3 *He hasn't come with us / He hasn't come yet.*

El   . .   . .   venido con   . . . .

El   . .   . .   venido   . . . .

4 *Have you eaten? / Have you an appointment?*

¿. . .   comido?

¿. . . . . .   una cita?

5 *They (fem.) have a dog / a nice apartment.*

. . . . .   tienen un   . . . . .

. . . . .   tienen un   . . . .

THE MISSING WORDS :   **1** tengo un / tengo hambre. **2** hemos telefoneado - su. **3** no ha - nosotros / no ha - todavía. **4** has / tienes. **5** ellas - perro / ellas - apartamento bonito.

****

But don't forget what we've done so far. The Spanish dialogues that we've studied are very common in everyday life.

*****

We have already picked up some basic points of grammar, too. Learning the rules of grammar is not as important as being able to speak : as we go along, there will be fewer and fewer grammatical notes, but more and more opportunities to use Spanish in practical applications. The exercises are very important, since they are designed so you can use **real** Spanish in **real** sentences.

2. **Pronunciation :** Spanish pronunciation is quite easy, because everything is pronounced, and each sound has just one value. The rules are much clearer than in English or French, for instance. All new sounds are difficult to imitate at first, but with practice they will become second nature to you.

There are no "in-between" vowel sounds in Spanish : all the vowels are pronounced as short, open sounds. Example : *mañana* (man'ya'na), which has three identical *a* sounds.

Just two consonants change sound depending on the vowel that follows : these are : *c* and *g*. The table below gives a summary of the Spanish consonants.

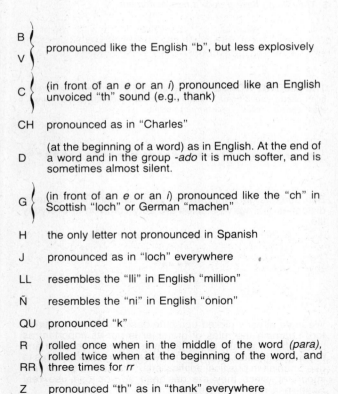

B V	pronounced like the English "b", but less explosively
C	(in front of an *e* or an *i*) pronounced like an English unvoiced "th" sound (e.g., thank)
CH	pronounced as in "Charles"
D	(at the beginning of a word) as in English. At the end of a word and in the group -*ado* it is much softer, and is sometimes almost silent.
G	(in front of an *e* or an *i*) pronounced like the "ch" in Scottish "loch" or German "machen"
H	the only letter not pronounced in Spanish
J	pronounced as in "loch" everywhere
LL	resembles the "lli" in English "million"
Ñ	resembles the "ni" in English "onion"
QU	pronounced "k"
R RR	rolled once when in the middle of the word *(para)*, rolled twice when at the beginning of the word, and three times for *rr*
Z	pronounced "th" as in "thank" everywhere

3. **Stress.** Here again, the rules are very clear in Spanish.

Words ending in vowels are stressed on the next-to-last syllable.
(e.g., *amigo, llave, mañana, vaso, tengo,* etc.).

Whenever the stress pattern is different from this, the word carries a written accent where the stress should fall. (e.g., *médico, está, razón, París,* etc.).

Words ending in a consonant generally take the stress on the last syllable, except with *n* and *s,* in which case the stress is on the next-to-last syllable. Examples (stressed vowel in **bold print**) : us**te**d, ve**nir**, a**mi**gos, **com**pran.

The only double letters in Spanish are *cc, ll, nn,* and *rr.* We have seen *ll* and *rr* in the table above ; *cc* and *nn* are both pronounced as if the two letters were separate : *lección* (lék'cion) and *innegable* (in'negablé).

4. Check the use of *a* and *en* in notes (1) and (2) of Lesson 5.

5. Check the **definite articles** *(el, la, los* and *las),* and the indefinite articles *(un, una, unos* and *unas)* (See Lesson 4.). The definite article is very often needed where English would leave it out.

6. **Plurals** are easy : add *-s* if the the ending is not stressed, or add *-es* if it is stressed. Examples : *llave, llaves ; casa, casas, bonito, bonitos.* And *razón, razones, ciudad, ciudades.*

7. Second Wave Exercises

Compare the sentences below with the Spanish in paragraph 8 opposite. Notice the Spanish word order. When you reach what is called the "second wave" or active phase of the learning process (See Lesson 50) you will have to try to give a **written** translation of the sentences in these exercises.

1   How are you? - Very well. And you?
2   Do you want to eat with me tomorrow? - Alright. It's a good idea.
3   Before going to Burgos, I want to phone my friend.
4   Have you eaten? - No, and I'm hungry.
5   Do you want a cigarette? - No, thank you. I don't smoke.
6   Now I want to go to the cinema. We have an appointment, you know.
7   Do you know my friend? - Yes. He's very nice.

****

LECCION OCTAVA (Lek'cion' octava)

Por favor. ¿Puede indicarme...?

1 — Por favor. ¿Sabe usted si hay una gasolinera por aquí? (1)

2 — ¿No es usted de aquí, verdad?

3 — No, y estoy un poco perdido.

PRONUNCIACION (pronoun'ciacion'). por fabor. ¿pouédé in'di-carmé...? **1** por favor ¿sabé oussté -- aï -- gaçolinéra -- --? **2** ¿-- éss oussté -- -- vérda? (The final d can be pronounced, but only very slightly). **3** -- -- ésstoï -- poco pérdido.

8. **Translation :**

1   ¿Qué tal estás ? - Muy bien. ¿Y tú?
2   ¿Quieres comer mañana conmigo? - De acuerdo.
    Es una buena idea.
3   Antes de ir a Burgos quiero telefonear a mi amiga.
4   ¿Has comido? - No, y tengo hambre.
5   ¿Quieres un cigarro? - No gracias, no fumo.
6   Ahora tengo ganas de ir al cine. - ¿Sabes que
    tenemos una cita?
7   ¿Conoces a mi amigo? - Sí, es muy simpático.

****

LESSON EIGHT

Please. Can you tell me...

1 — Please. Do you know if there is a petrol station near
      here (by here)?
2 — You are not from here, are you (true)?
3 — No, and I am a little lost.

NOTES
(1) *Hay* means "there is" or "there are". It also means "is there?"
or "are there?" if we change the intonation. It is the
impersonal form of the auxiliary verb *haber* (to have).

Lección 8

4 — No se preocupe, hay una muy cerca de aquí.

5 ¿Dónde tiene usted el coche?

6 — Es el rojo que está aparcado detrás del blanco. (3)

7 — Muy bien. La más próxima no está lejos.

8 ¿Ve usted el semáforo?

9 Para llegar a la gasolinera, tiene que girar a la derecha después del semáforo. (4)

10 — Muchas gracias por la información. Adiós. (5)

4 -- sé préocoupé aï -- moui cerca -- aki. 5 ¿don'dé -- oussté -- co'tche? 6 -- -- roHo ké éssta aparcado détrass dél blan'co. 7 -- bién' -- -- prok'sima -- -- léHos. 8 ¿bé -- -- sémaforo. 9 para llegar -- -- gaçolinera -- ké Hirar -- -- déré'tcha despouéss del sémaforo. 10 mou'tchass graciass por -- in'formacion' adioss.

Pronunciation notes are not given for words that are simple to pronounce. All words in Spanish are pronounced at their face value. Once you've learnt these face values, there won't be any difficulties at all.

¿SABE USTED SI HAY UNA GASOLINERA POR AQUÍ?

EXERCISE : 1. Hay un coche en la calle. 2. ¿Dónde está Pablo? 3. No se preocupe. 4. El rojo es para Ana. 5. Muy bien. 6. El vaso está detrás del niño. 7. Por aquí.

4	—	Don't worry (don't preoccupy yourself). There is one very close to here.
5		Where is your car? (where do you have your car?)
6	—	It is the red [one] that is parked behind the white [one].
7	—	Very well. The closest [one] is not far.
8		Do you see the traffic light? (semaphore)
9		(In order) to arrive at (arrive to) the petrol station, you have to (you have that) turn to the right after the traffic light.
10	—	Thank you very much for the information. Goodbye.

(3) Adjectives can be used with articles to replace "one". Thus *el blanco* means "the white one" (replacing a masculine noun), and *la más próxima* means "the nearest one" (feminine).

(4) *Para* with an infinitive means "in order to". Elsewhere, it translates the English "for" when there is a sense of destination.

(5) When there is a sense of **cause, exchange,** or **length of time,** "for" is translated by *por*. Here, for example, *Gracias por la información* implies that you offer thanks "in exchange for" the information. Everywhere else, we use *para*. See note (2) above.

* * * * *

There may seem to be a lot of details, but don't try to remember them all. Anything important is repeated several times in different situations. Relax and enjoy it!

Just remember this :

- put more stress on the syllables in bold print (tonic accent) than on the rest of the word ;
- all vowels must be pronounced ;
- *rr* should be rolled more than *r* (See page 21) ;

* * * * *

EXERCISE : 1. There is a car in the street. – **2.** Where is Pablo? – **3.** Don't worry. – **4.** The red one is for Ana. – **5.** Very well. – **6.** The glass is behind the child. – **7.** Near here.

EXERCISE
Ponga las palabras que faltan (ponga las palabrass ké faltan)

(Fill in the missing words)

1 *There is a petrol station near here.*

. . .   una gasolinera   . . . .   de   . . . .

2 *I am a little lost / very tired.*

Estoy   . .   . .

Estoy   . . .   .

3 *Don't worry.*

. .   . .   preocupe.

****

LECCION NOVENA (Lek'cion' novena)

La hora

1   **A**ntes de acostarse. **(1)**
2 — ¿Qué hora es?
3 — Son las diez y cuarto. **(2)**
4 — Voy a acostarme.
5 — ¿Mañana vas a madrugar? **(3)**

PRONUNCIACION (pronoun'ciacion'). la ora. **1** an'téss -- acosstarssé.
2 ¿ké ora --? **3** son' lass dièc -- couarto. **4** voï -- acosstarmé. **5**
¿magnana -- -- madrougar?

4 *Please / Thank you.*

. . . .

. . . . . .

5 *You are on the right / behind the car.*

Usted . . . . a . . . .

Usted . . . . coche.

6 *After eating / after you.*

. . . . comer.

. . . . de usted.

THE MISSING WORDS : **1** hay - cerca - aquí. **2** un poco perdido / muy cansado. **3** no se. **4** por favor / gracias. **5** está - la derecha / está detrás del. **6** después de / después.

****

LESSON NINE

The time (the hour)

1 — Before going to bed (to lie oneself down).
2 — What time is it? (What hour is it?)
3 — It is a quarter past ten (they are the tens and quarter).
4 — I'm going to bed (to lie myself down).
5 — Tomorrow are you going to get up early?

NOTES
(1) *Acostarse* is a reflexive verb. The *-se* on the end of the infinitive is the reflexive pronoun. It changes according to the subject of the verb, and, literally, means "oneself", "myself", "yourself", etc. Reflexive verbs are very common in Spanish.
(2) Except for one o'clock (one hour) we always say "they are" *(son)* with the feminine *las* referring to the hours. E.g., *son las ocho y media* = "it is half past eight" ("they are the eights and a half"). We'll come back to this later.
(3) *Madrugar* is a useful verb that means "to get up early". *La madrugada* is "the early morning" – between about 5 o'clock *(las cinco)* and 8 o'clock *(las ocho)*. The verb is a regular *-ar* verb *(yo madrugo, tú madrugas, etc.)*.

6 — Sí. ¿Puedes despertarme a las siete?
7 — ¿Por qué no pones tu despertador? (3)
8 — Porque el muelle está roto.
9 — Entonces, de acuerdo. Buenas noches.
10 — Buenas noches. Hasta mañana.

6 -- ¿pouédéss déspértarmé -- lass siéte?
7 ¿por ké -- ponéss -- déspértador? 8 porké -- mouélle -- roto (roulez fort le r). 9 én'ton'céss -- acouérdo. bouénass no'tchéss. 10 -- -- asta magnana.

EXERCISE : 1. ¿Qué hora es? 2. Antes de comer. 3. Ana va a madrugar. 4. Voy a irme a casa. 5. ¿Por qué no vienes al cine? 6. Porque no tengo ganas. 7. Son las cinco y cuarto.

EXERCISE
Ponga las palabras que faltan (ponga las palabrass ké faltan)

(Fill in the missing words)

1 *What time is it / please?*

¿ . . . . ?

¿ . . . . ?

2 *It's five past one. / It's half past one.*

. . la . . . .

. . la . . . .

3 *Why don't you come with me / tomorrow?*

¿ . . . . . . no vienes . . . . . . ?

¿ . . . . . . no vienes . . . . . . ?

4 *Because I can't. / I'm going with Ana.*

. . . . . . no . . . . .

. . . . . . voy . . . Ana.

6 — Yes. Can you wake me up at seven o'clock (at the sevens)?
7 — Why don't you set (put) your alarm clock?
8 — Because the spring is broken.
9 — Alright then, OK. Good night(s).
10 — Good night. See you tomorrow (Until tomorrow).

(3) *Por qué* : "why" ; porque (stress the *o*) : "because". You can see this in sentence 8.

EXERCISE : 1. What time is it? – **2.** Before eating. – **3.** Ana is going to get up early – **4.** I'm going to go home. – **5.** Why don't you come to the cinema? – **6.** Because I don't want to. – **7.** It is a quarter past five.

References : *If you find a sentence, or a word, or a point of pronunciation difficult to grasp, make a* **reference** *: underline the difficult passage, and then turn on a few pages and write the page number of the difficult passage in the margin. When you come to this lesson a few days later, we may have cleared up the problem, as we explain everything several times. If you still have the same difficulty when you come across the reference, write another reference a few lessons further on.*

5 *Alright, then, see you tomorrow/good night.*

. . . . mañana.

. . . . buenas . . . . . .

THE MISSING WORDS : 1 qué hora es / qué hora es por favor. **2** es - una y cinco / es - una y media. **3** por qué - conmigo / por qué - mañana. **4** porque - puedo / porque - con. **5** entonces hasta / entonces - noches.

LECCION DECIMA (Lek'cion' décima)

Ser - Estar (1)

1 Yo estoy contigo.
2 Tú estás cansada.
3 Hoy está ocupado.
4 Ellos están en la habitación.
5 Vosotras estáis con ellos.
6 Nosotros estamos en Barcelona.
7 Ya conocemos este tipo de construcción. Pero...
8 Yo soy francés.
9 Tú eres una mujer.
10 Es la una.
11 Nosotras somos jóvenes.
12 Vosotros sois inteligentes.
13 Las mesas son pequeñas.

PRONUNCIACION (pronoun'ciacion'). **1** -- -- con'tigo. **2** -- -- can'ssada. 3 oï -- ocoupado. 4 él/loss -- -- -- abitacion'. 5 vossotrass ésstaïss con' él/loss. 6 nossotross -- -- barcélona. 7 ya conocémoss éssté tipo -- con'strouk'cion'. péro... 8 soï fran'céss. 9 -- éréss -- mouHer. 11 -- somoss Hébénéss. 12 -- soïss in'teliHén'téss. 13 -- méçass sson' pékégnass.

EXERCISE : 1. Están contigo. 2. La taza es grande. 3. Yo soy joven. 4. Son las cuatro de la mañana. 5. Tú eres española. 6. Vosotros sois simpáticos. 7. Nosotras somos hermanas.

EXERCISE
Ponga las palabras que faltan (ponga las palabrass ké faltan)

(Fill in the missing words)

1 *I am busy / at home.*

Yo . . . . . . ocupada.

Yo . . . .

LESSON TEN

The two verbs "to be"

1   I am with you.
2   You are tired.
3   Today he is busy.
4   They are in the room (habitation).
5   You (familiar, fem. plural) are with them (masculine).
6   We are in Barcelona.
7   We already know this type of construction. But...
8   I am French.
9   You are a woman.
10   It is one o'clock (the one (fem.)).
11   We are young.
12   You (plural) are intelligent.
13   The tables are small.

NOTES

(1) There are two verbs "to be" in Spanish.

Ser expresses an essential characteristic with no indication of the circumstances of the subject : *soy inglés :* "I am English" ; *eres una mujer :* "you are a woman".

Estar, on the other hand, has to do with circumstances : it expresses situation in space or time, and physical or moral states, that **could** change into different states.

EXERCISE : 1. They are with you. − **2.** The cup is big. − **3.** I am young. − **4.** It is four o'clock in the morning. − **5.** You are Spanish (feminine). − **6.** You are nice. − **7.** We are sisters.

LA TAZA ES GRANDE

2 *You (familiar, fem. plural) are French/with them (masculine).*

Vosotras . . . . francesas.

Vosotras . . . .

3 *Have you gone?/Are you young?*

¿. . . . . .?

¿. . . . joven?

****

LECCION ONCE

Quiero hablar castellano

1   Ahora hablamos francés.
2   Queremos hablar también castellano.
3 — ¡Hola, Juan! **(1)**
4 — ¡Carmen! ¿Adónde vas? **(2)**
5 — Voy a clase. Me he puesto a estudiar francés.
6   El próximo verano quiero ir de vacaciones a Córcega.
7   ¿Tú no estudias ninguna lengua?
8 — Hablo un poco francés, pero con mucho acento.

PRONUNCIACION : kiéro ablar casstél/ano. 1 -- ablamos --. 2 kérémoss ablar -- casstél/ano. 3 ola Houan´. 4 ¡carmen´! ¿adon´dé --? 5 -- classé mé -- pouéssto -- éstoudiar --. 6 -- bérano -- vacacionéss -- corcéga. 7 -- éstoudiass nin´gouna lén´goua (évitez le son nasal en). 8 ablo -- acén´to.

4 *The house is white / in Barcelona.*

La casa . . . .

La casa . . . . . . Barcelona.

5 *We are nice / in the cafeteria.*

Nosotros . . . . . simpáticos.

Nosotros . . . . cafetería.

THE MISSING WORDS : **1** estoy / estoy en casa. **2** sois / estáis con ellos. **3** has ido / eres. **4** es blanca / está en. **5** somos / estamos en la.

****

LESSON ELEVEN

I want to speak Spanish (Castilian)

1 Now we speak French.
2 We also want to speak Castilian.
3 — Hello, Juan!
4 — Carmen! (To) where are you going?
5 — I'm going to class. I'm studying (I've put myself to) studying French.
6 (The) next summer I want to go on (of) holiday(s) to Corsica.
7 Don't you study any languages? (Don't you study no language?)
8 — I speak a little French, but with a lot of accent.

NOTES
(1) *Hola* is quite informal, and corresponds to "Hello". More formal greetings include *Buenos días :* "Good morning" (Good days) and *Buenas tardes :* "Good afternoon(s)". In Spain, the evening meal is often eaten as late as ten o'clock : this marks the end of *la tarde*.
(2) *Donde* (which we saw in the eighth lesson) refers to a fixed position : *¿Dónde estás? :* "Where are you?". *Adonde,* on the other hand, indicates movement : *¿Adónde va?* "Where is he going?". *Dónde* and *adónde* take an accent when they are in questions or in exclamations.

9 — ¿Por qué no vienes conmigo? Tengo un
buen profesor.
10 — Actualmente no tengo tiempo. **(3)**
11 Pero estudio un poco cada día en casa.

9 -- bouén´ proféçor. 10 ak´toualmén´té --. 11 péro
éstoudio -- cada día.

*From now on, we will only give pronunciation instructions for
new words. You will find pronunciation easier and easier as
you begin to recognize the words in Spanish. Remember that
the Spanish make very few breaks inside sentences, and
tend to run one word into the next.*

*****

EXERCISE :   1. Nosotros hablamos francés. 2. ¿Adónde
vas? 3. ¿Dónde estás? 4. Las vacaciones de verano. 5. No
tengo ninguna hermana. 6. Es un buen amigo. 7. Estudio
un poco cada día.

*****

It's too soon to start learning verb conjugations, but we
should start to look at the three different types of regular
verbs that exist in Spanish : the *hablar* (to speak) type, the
comer (to eat) type and the *vivir* (to live) type. These are the
models for each different type of infinitive : *-ar, -er* and *-ir*.

The "I" form (first person singular) in the present tense
always ends in *-o : yo hablo* (I speak) *yo como* (I eat) and *yo
vivo* (I live).

The "he, she or it" form (third person singular) in the present
tense ends in *-a* for *-ar* verbs, and in *-e* for all the others.
Remember that *usted*, the polite "you" form, is also in the
third person.

Spanish – like all languages – also has some irregular verbs.
A few of these are very common. We have already seen *yo
voy :* "I go".

But we'll come back to that.

9 — Why don't you come with me? I have a good teacher.
10 — At the moment I haven't time.
11 But I study a little every day at (in) home.

EXERCISE : 1. We speak French. – **2.** Where are you going? – **3.** Where are you? – **4.** The summer holidays. – **5.** I have no sister. – **6.** He is a good friend. – **7.** I study a little each day.

* * * * *

EXERCISE
Ponga las palabras que faltan (**po**nga las pal**a**brass ké f**a**ltan)

(Fill in the missing words)

1 *We want to speak with you (familiar, masc. plural) too/go.*

Queremos . . . . vosotros.

Queremos . . . . vosotros.

2 *Next summer, I want to study Castilian.*

. . . . quiero . . . . el

castellano.

3 *I haven't time/I don't want to.*

No . . . .

No tengo . . . . .

4 *Where are you?/Where are you going?*

¿. . . . estás?

¿. . . . . . vas?

****

LECCION DOCE

Entre vecinos

1   Esta familia está de vacaciones. **(1)**
2 — ¿Dónde viven ustedes?
3 — Vivimos aquí. Esta casa es la nuestra.
4 — ¿Tienen niños?
5 — Sí. Este niño es nuestro hijo Rafael.
6   Y la pequeña, que ustedes ven en el balcón, es nuestra hija Teresa.
7   ¿Quieren subir a tomar el café?
8 — Con mucho gusto. Además, Cecilia podrá hacer una amiga. **(2)**
9   Estamos de vacaciones y no conocemos a nadie aquí.

PRONUNCIACION: en'tré bécinoss. **1** éssta familia --. **2** -- vivén' --. **3** vivimoss -- nouéstra. **5** éssté -- nouéstro iHo rafael. **6** -- vén' -- balcon' -- iHa téréca. **7** kiéren' --. **8** -- gousto adémass cécilia podra acér --. **9** -- conocémoss -- nadié --.

NOTES
(1) Here we are introducing demonstrative adjectives (this, that, these, those). Take care not to confuse *esta* (feminine form of "this") with *está* ("he, she or it is"). *Esta* ("this") has no written accent and ends in a vowel, so the stress should be on the next-to-last syllable.

5 *You have no appointment / friend.*

No tienes . . . . cita.

No tienes . . . . . amigo.

THE MISSING WORDS : **1** hablar también con. / ir también con. **2** el verano próximo - estudiar. **3** tengo tiempo / ganas. **4** dónde / adónde. **5** ninguna / ningún.

✱✱

LESSON TWELVE

Amongst neighbours

1   This family is on holiday (of holidays).
2 — Where do you (polite, plural) live?
3 — We live here. This house is ours (the our).
4 — Have you (polite, plural) [any] children?
5 — Yes. This child is our son Rafael.
6   And the little [one] whom you see on the balcony is our daughter Teresa.
7   Do you want (polite, plural) to come up (go up) and have some coffee (take the coffee)?
8 — With pleasure (with much taste). Moreover, Cecilia will be able to make a friend.
9   We are on holiday and we don't know anybody (to nobody) here.

✱✱✱✱✱

NOTES
(1) Demonstrative adjectives : this, these : *este niño, esta familia :* "this child" (masculine), "this family" (feminine) ; *estos vasos, estas casas :* "these glasses" (masculine), "these houses" (feminine).
That, those : *ese balcón, esa mesa :* "that balcony", "that table" ; *esos cigarros, esas tazas :* "those cigarettes" (masculine), "those cups" (feminine).

Demonstrative pronouns : *esto :* "this" ; *eso :* "that".
(2) In the word *además :* "moreover", "besides", you will see *más :* "more".

10 — ¿Les molesta si nos tuteamos? (3)
11 — Al contrario, nosotros no estamos acos-
tumbrados a esas formalidades.
12 — Tanto mejor, nosotros tampoco. (4)

10 -- moléssta -- toutéamoss?
11 -- con'trario -- acosstoum'bradoss -- écass formalidadèss. 12
tan'to méHor -- tam'poco.

EXERCISE : 1. Estoy de vacaciones. 2. Esta mujer tiene
un hijo. 3. Este coche es rojo. 4. Nuestra hija está en
Francia. 5. No conocemos a nadie. 6. Esas mesas son
pequeñas. 7. Al contrario. 8. Tanto mejor. 9. Yo
tampoco.

* * * * *

EXERCISE
Ponga las palabras que faltan (ponga las palabrass ké faltan)

(Fill in the missing words)

1 *This child is our son Rafael.*

. . . . niño . . . . Rafael.

2 *So much the better, so are we/neither are we.*

. . . . , nosotros . . . .

. . . . , nosotros . . . .

3 *We live here/close to the petrol station.*

Nosotros . . . .

Nosotros . . . . de la gasolinera.

10 —	Do you mind if we call each other tú?
11 —	Not at all (on the contrary), we are not used (accustomed) to those formalities.
12 —	So much the better, neither are we (we neither).

NOTES
(3) *Molestar* (*-ar* verb) means "to bother". "Does it bother to them" (polite form of you, plural) would be a literal translation of this construction. *Tutear* (another *-ar* verb) means "to use the familiar form *tú* or *vosotros*". Here it is a reflexive verb.
(4) "So am I", "Neither do you", etc. in Spanish are constructions that need no verb.

EXERCISE : **1.** I am on holiday. – **2.** This woman has a son. – **3.** This car is red. – **4.** Our daughter is in France. – **5.** We do not know anybody. – **6.** Those tables are small. – **7.** On the contrary. – **8.** So much the better. – **9.** Neither am I.

ESTA FAMILIA ESTÁ DE VACACIONES

4 *Not at all, I don't mind / he is used to it.*

. . . . , . . . no me molesta.

. . . . , él . . . . acostumbrado.

5 *We do not know anybody here / We do not know his sister.*

Nosotros . . conocemos . . . .

Nosotros . . conocemos . . . hermana.

THE MISSING WORDS : **1** este - es nuestro hijo. **2** tanto mejor - también / tanto mejor - tampoco. **3** vivimos aquí / vivimos cerca. **4** al contrario, eso / al contrario, - está. **5** no - a nadie aquí / no - a su.

Lección **12**

LECCION TRECE

Un poco de todo

1 ¿Hay vino para cenar? **(1)**
2 He pagado veinte pesetas por la leche.
3 — Es la una y diez.
4 — No, son las dos y cuarto.
5 — ¿Por qué no vas?
6 — Porque José va a llegar ahora.
7 Eres un hombre.
8 Estás en la ciudad.
9 ¿Dónde estamos?
10 ¿Adónde vamos?
11 En esta calle, hay mucha circulación.
12 Esas camisas no son caras. **(2)**

PRONUNCIACION : 1 -- *bino.* 2 -- pagado -- pécétass -- lé'tché. 6 Hossé --. 7 om'bré. 11 circoulacion'. 12 -- camissass --.

EXERCISE : 1. Un poco de todo. 2. Son las cinco y cinco. 3. Esas casas son caras. 4. Eres joven. 5. ¿Por qué no vienes con nosotros? 6. He pagado quince pesetas. 7. ¿Hay muchos niños?

EXERCISE
Ponga las palabras que faltan (ponga las palabrass ké faltan)

(Fill in the missing words)

1 *I paid little / I paid thirteen pesetas.*

Yo . . . .

Yo . . . . pesetas.

2 *Those cars are expensive / red.*

. . . . coches . . . .

. . . coches . . . .

LESSON THIRTEEN

A little of everything

1	Is there any wine for dinner?
2	I paid twenty pesetas for the milk.
3 —	It is ten past one.
4 —	No, it is a quarter past two.
5 —	Why don't you go?
6 —	Because José is going to arrive now.
7	You are a man.
8	You are in the city.
9	Where are we?
10	Where are we going?
11	In this street, there is a lot of traffic.
12	Those shirts are not expensive.

EXERCISE : 1. A little of everything. – **2.** It is five past five. – **3.** Those houses are dear. – **4.** You are young. – **5.** Why don't you come with us? – **6.** I paid fifteen pesetas. – **7.** Are there many children?

EN ESTA CALLE, HAY MUCHA CIRCULACIÓN

NOTES
(1) *Cenar* is the verb "to dine" or "to have dinner". *La cena* is "the evening meal" or "supper".
(2) Remember the agreement of adjectives : *camisas* is feminine plural, so *caro* must change accordingly.

This lesson contains everything we have learnt so far. Read it through, trying to remember what you already know. The difficulties can be overcome, you see! If you do have any problems, though, look at the notes in previous lessons : for sentences 1 and 2 - see lesson 8 ; sentences 3, 4 and 5 - see lesson 9 ; sentences 7 and 8 - see lesson 10 ; sentences 9 and 10 - see lesson 11 ; sentences 11 and 12 - see lesson 12.

3 *You (familiar, singular) are French / at home.*

Tú   . . . .   francés.

Tú   . . . . casa.

4 *It is a quarter past one / a quarter to four.*

. . la . . . .

. . . las . . . . menos . . . . . .

****

LECCION CATORCE

LESSON FOURTEEN

Revision and Notes

1. **Diphthongs.** — *a, e* and *o* are "strong" vowels, and when two of them come together they form separate syllables (e.g. *poema*). A diphthong – that is, a continuous sound formed by two vowels in a **single** syllable – consists of one strong vowel and one weak vowel *(u, i, y),* or of two weak vowels. When there is one of each sort, the strong vowel takes more stress, unless a written accent indicates otherwise. Thus : *yo voy, hoy :* "I am going, today", or *el viaje, siete :* "the trip, seven", as opposed to *el día, todavía :* "the day, still".

When two weak vowels come together, slightly more stress falls on the second of the two : *muy :* "very" ; *viuda :* "widow".

And remember : two strong vowels make two separate syllables : *veo, creo :* "I see, I think" are two-syllable words.

5 *Where are you going now?/tomorrow?*

¿ . . . . . . vas . . . . ?

¿ . . . . . . vas . . . . ?

THE MISSING WORDS :   1 he pagado poco / he pagado trece. **2**
esos - son caros / esos - son rojos. **3** eres / estás en. **4** es - una y
cuarto / son - tres - cuarto. **5** adónde - a ir ahora / adónde - a ir
mañana.

*When you have finished reading each sentence, see if you
can repeat it without looking at it. This is an important
exercise, and will allow you, little by little, to* **think in Spanish.**

****

2. **Pronunciation.** — Now you know the sounds of Spanish.
We won't spend any more time on the basic sounds in the
revision lessons, but when there are exceptions to the rules
of pronunciation, we will give a note about it in the relevant
lesson. If you want to refresh your memory, look at note 2 in
Lesson 7.

3. *Para* in Spanish means "for" when there is a sense of
destination. *Un billete para Alicante :* "a ticket for Alicante" ;
este café es para usted : "this coffee is for you". *Para* is also
used with verbs to express "in order to" (purpose) : *Estoy
aquí para estudiar :* "I am here to study".
Por expresses cause, exchange, or length of time : *Estoy
aquí por unos días :* "I am here for a few days" ; *yo
contestaré por usted :* "I shall answer for you".

¿Por qué? = Why? (for what reason or cause?)
¿Para qué? =What for? (for what purpose?)

Por and *para,* like *ser* and *estar,* are difficult to grasp at the
beginning, but the distinction is usually quite clear. We won't
give you long lists of rules to memorize, but will comment on
these difficulties as we go along. It's always better to see
examples in real situations.

Reread notes 2 and 3 on lesson 8.

4. **The time.** — "It is a quarter past two" : *son las dos y cuarto.* "It is a quarter to three" : *son las tres menos cuarto.* "Twenty to" : *menos veinte.* "It is ten past four" : *son las cuatro y diez.*

For one o'clock, and all its variants, we use the singular *la una.* It is half past twelve : *son las doce y media.* For half past midnight, we add *de la noche :* "of the night". "At noon, at midnight", when the exact time is not given, is *a mediodía, a medianoche* in Spanish.

5. **Ser** and **estar** — Re-read the notes on lesson 10.
Remember this : *soy una mujer ; estoy cansado :* "I am a woman ; I am tired". In the first case, "I am" describes an essential quality that cannot change. In the second case, "tired" is only a phase I am passing through. Incidentally, in Spanish, *estoy casado* means "I am married", since this is not an essential quality of the subject, but simply his marital status.

So, *ser* describes inherent or permanent qualities. *Estar* is used for physical or mental circumstances – position or state.

There are one or two exceptions to this, but we'll deal with those when they come up.

Estoy has the stress on the final syllable, -toy. The rules of stress (lesson 7) apply here too, because the final *y* is considered as a consonant. (In fact it is a "semi-consonant").

6. **"Eleventh"** in Spanish is *undécimo.* Thus : *lección* (fem.) *undécima ;* "twelfth" = *doudécimo ;* "thirteenth" = *décimo tercero ;* "fourteenth" = *décimo cuatro,* and so on. Usually, however, it is rare to use these "ordinal numbers", and we use the cardinal numbers *once, doce,* etc. Thus, *el siglo*

décimo : "the tenth century" **but :** *el siglo quince :* "the fifteenth century" (the century fifteen) ; *el siglo veinte :* "the twentieth century" (the century twenty). The same is true of kings and queens : "Isabel II" : *Isabel segunda,* **but** "Alfonso XIII" : *Alfonso trece* ("Alfonso thirteen"). *Alfonso décimo tercero* would have been really too long!

* * * * *

7. **Writing in Spanish** (part two)

1   Is there much traffic now?
       Yes, because it's seven o'clock.
2   What time do you want me to wake you up tomorrow?
       At eight o'clock if you don't mind.
3   Today we are in Barcelona, and tomorrow we are going to Madrid.
4   Why don't you come with me?
       Because I am going to class.
5   Our son is in class with this girl.
       So is ours.
6   Is your house far?
       No, it is very close to here.

8. **Translation**

1   ¿Hay mucha circulación ahora? - Sí, porque son las siete.
2   ¿A qué hora quieres ir? - A las ocho, si no te molesta.
3   Hoy estamos en Barcelona y mañana vamos a Madrid.
4   ¿Por qué no vienes conmigo? - Porque voy a clase.
5   Nuestro hijo está en clase con esta niña. - El nuestro también.
6   ¿Tu casa está lejos? - No, está muy cerca de aquí.

LECCION QUINCE

Voy al mercado

1   Voy a hacer la plaza. **(1)**
2   Elena estudia en su habitación.
3 — Voy a hacer las compras.
4   ¿Necesitas algo? **(2)**
5 — Sí. ¿Quieres comprarme el periódico, por favor? **(3)**
6   Antes de irte, ¿puedes decirme dónde está el diccionario de inglés?
7 — Creo que está en el cuarto de estar.
8   Va a faltarme dinero.
9   ¿Puedes darme doscientas pesetas?
10 — Hay dinero en el cajón del armario.
11   ¿Puedes traerme también tabaco?
12 — Sí. Además tengo que comprar para mí. **(4)**
13   Hasta luego.

PRONUNCIACION: mércado 2 éléna 3 com'prass 4 nécessitass algo 5 com'prarmé --- périodico 6 irte - décirmé --- dikcionario in'gléss 8 faltarmé dinéro 9 darmé dosscien'tass 10 caHon' --- armario 11 traermé 13 louégo.

EXERCISE :   1. ¿Necesitas algo? 2. ¿Quieres hacerme esto? 3. Voy a decirte algo. 4. Tengo bastante dinero. 5. Además puedo comprarte un libro. 6. En el cuarto de estar hay un armario. 7. Hasta luego.

LESSON FIFTEEN

I am going to the market

1	I am going to (do) the market (place).
2	Elena studies in her room.
3	— I am going to do the shopping (the purchases).
4	Do you need anything?
5	— Yes. Will you buy me the newspaper, please?
6	Before you go, can you tell me where the English dictionary is?
7	— I think it's in the living room.
8	I'll need some more money (Money is going to lack to me).
9	Can you give me two hundred pesetas?
10	— There is [some] money in the drawer of the wardrobe.
11	Can you bring me [some] tobacco too?
12	— Yes. Moreover, I have to buy [some] for me.
13	See you later (Until then).

* * * * *

NOTES

(1) Traditionally, *la plaza :* "the town square" was where the market was held, and the expression *Voy a hacer la plaza :* "I'm going to do the market place" is still used even if the shopping is no longer done strictly at the market or on the main square. *Voy a hacer las compras* (sentence 3) is very common nowadays.

(2) *Necesitar :* "to need" ; *necesito :* "I need", *necesitas :* "you need", etc.

(3) When the verb is in the infinitive form (or imperative or gerund (-ing) form, as we shall see later), the object pronoun is written as part of the verb. These pronouns are known as conjunctive pronouns because they "join with" the verb in certain instances, thus : *decirme :* "(to) tell me" ; *traerme :* "(to) bring me". When there are two pronouns together, they can both join up with the infinitive (e.g., *puedes traermelo :* "can you bring me it", where *lo* is the direct object). We'll come back to this later.

(4) As we saw in Lesson 6, here's another example of *tengo que* + infinitive : "I have to...".

EXERCISE : 1. Do you need anything? – **2.** Will you do this for me? – **3.** I'm going to tell you something. – **4.** I have enough money. – **5.** I can buy you a book too. – **6.** There is a wardrobe in the living room. – **7.** See you later!

EJERCICIO DE CONTROL
Ponga las palabras que faltan

1 *I'm going to do the market/the shopping.*

. . . . la plaza.

. . . . las . . . .

2 *Will you buy me the newspaper?/some milk?*

¿ Quieres . . . . ?

¿ Quieres . . . . ?

3 *Do you need anything?*

¿ . . . . ?

****

LECCION DIECISEIS

El imperativo y el pronombre

1 Dame la mano. **(1)**
2 ¿Me das la mano? **(2)**
3 Date prisa. **(3)**
4 ¿Te das prisa?
5 Amaos los unos a los otros.
6 ¿Os amáis los unos a los otros?

PRONUNCIACION: im'pérativo pronom'bré. **1** damé ... mano. **3** daté priça **5** amaoss

4 *Can you leave me thirteen pesetas?*

¿ . . . . ?

5 *Do you have some money?/some tobacco?*

¿ . . . . ?

¿ . . . . ?

THE MISSING WORDS :   **1** voy a hacer. / voy a hacer - compras. **2** comprarme el periódico. / comprarme leche. **3** necesitas algo. **4** puedes dejarme trece pesetas. **5** tienes dinero. / tienes tabaco.

****

LESSON SIXTEEN

The imperative and the pronoun

1   Give me your (the) hand.
2   Will you (Do you) give me your (the) hand?
3   Hurry up (Give yourself haste).
4   Will you (Do you) hurry up?
5   Love one another (Love yourselves the ones to the others).
6   Do you love one another?

NOTES
(1) As we saw in the last lesson, the object pronoun is added to the end of the imperative. *Dame* (pronounced in two syllables) : "give me" ; *danos :* "give us". When there are two pronouns, we add them both to the imperative, thus : *damelo :* "give me it".
(2) *¿Me das? :* the pronoun comes before the verb here, because we are no longer using an imperative.

7 Déjeme este sitio. **(4)**
8 ¿Me deja este sitio?
9 Escríbannos mañana.
10 ¿Nos escriben mañana?

7 déHémé... sitio. 9 esscriban'nos.

* * * * *

EJERCICIO: 1. Dame mi taza, por favor. 2. Déjame el periódico. 3. Daos prisa. 4. Escríbenos mañana. 5. ¿Me dejas este sitio? 6. Mañana te veo. 7. Ahora no te dejan.

EJERCICIO DE CONTROL
Ponga las palabras que faltan

1 *Give me your hand / the glass.*

. . . .

. . . .

2 *Hurry up!*

. . . .

3 *Do you want to leave me a little room?*

¿Quieres   . . . . , ... ?

4 *Write to me tomorrow / Are you coming tomorrow?*

. . . .

¿ . . . . ?

* *

7	Leave me this place!
8	Will you leave (Do you leave) me this place?
9	Write to us tomorrow!
10	Will you write (Do you write) to us tomorrow?

(3) *Darse prisa* : "to give oneself haste" means "to hurry up". This is an example of a **reflexive verb.** A reflexive verb is one in which the direct or indirect object refers back to the subject of the verb. Examples : *despertarse* "to wake up" (lit. "to wake oneself") ; *sentarse* "to sit down" (lit. "to sit oneself"). The reflexive pronouns *(me, te, se, nos* and *os)* must be used with these verbs. Indeed, the reflexive pronouns can also be used with a large number of ordinary verbs to express reciprocity (e.g., *nos vemos hoy* : "we are seeing each other today") or to put the verb in the passive mood (e.g., *me llamo Juan* : "I am called Juan"). The meaning of certain other verbs can be modified by adding the reflexive pronouns (e.g., *dormir* : "to sleep" ; *dormirse* : "to go to sleep"). We'll be seeing more of these as we go along. Reflexive forms are very common in Spanish.

(4) *Deje* is the polite singular *(usted)* imperative form. The polite plural imperative would be *dejen.*

Sitio means "a place" (in a train, for example). It is also the word for "room" in the abstract sense of "Is there room?" (*¿Hay sitio?*).

EXERCISE 1. Give me my cup, please. – **2.** Leave me the newspaper. – **3.** Hurry up! (plural) – **4.** Write to us tomorrow. – **5.** Will you leave me this place? – **6.** I'll see you tomorrow. – **7.** Now they don't leave you.

* * * * *

5 *This place is for me.*

Este . . . .

THE MISSING WORDS : **1** dame la mano / dame el vaso. **2** date prisa. **3** dejarme un poco de sitio. **4** escríbeme mañana / vienes mañana. **5** - sitio es para mí.

* *

LECCION DIECISIETE

Yo soñaba... (1)

1 — ¿Qué hacías en el jardín?
2 — Miraba un pájaro y soñaba.
3 — ¿Soñabas?
4 — Sí, me imaginaba que tú y tus amigos llegabais volando.
5 — ¿Y qué hacíamos?
6 — Me hablabais y luego nos poníamos todos a jugar.
7 Y también comíamos y cantábamos.
8 — ¿Y no bebíamos?
9 — No me acuerdo muy bien, pero como tú también estabas
10 estoy segura de que debía de haber algo para beber. (2)
11 — ¡Ya está! tú y tus bromas. (3)
12 — En todo caso era un sueño muy bonito.

PRONUNCIACION: sognaba. **1** aciass ... Hardin'. **2** miraba .. paHaro **4** imaHinaba .. //égabaiss volan'do. **6** Hougar. **10** ségoura. **11** bromass . **12** souégno.

EJERCICIO: 1. Hacía una casa. **2.** Yo imaginaba que ibas a venir . **3.** Vosotros hablabais con ellos. **4.** No me acuerdo muy bien. **5.** Estoy seguro. **6.** ¡Ya está! **7.** En todo caso era bonito.

LESSON SEVENTEEN

I was dreaming...

1 — What were you doing in the garden?
2 — I was looking at a bird and I was dreaming.
3 — You were dreaming?
4 — Yes. I was imagining (to myself) that you and your
friends were arriving flying.
5 — And what were we doing?
6 — You were talking to me and then we all started (put
ourselves) to play.
7 And we were eating and singing too.
8 — Weren't we drinking?
9 — I don't remember very well, but as you were there
too (you too were there)
10 I'm sure that there must have been something (for)
to drink.
11 — I see! (That's it!) You and your jokes!
12 — In any case [it] was a very nice dream.

NOTES
(1) In this lesson we look at the imperfect tense. The imperfect is
the continuous past tense, and can very often be translated by
"was... ing", or "used to...". However, it is sometimes difficult
to draw the distinction between the imperfect and the simple
past ("I did"). In sentence (6) for example, "you talked to me"
must be in the imperfect in Spanish, because there is no
indication of the beginning or the end of the action of talking.

The imperfect ending for regular verbs is as follows : -ar
verbs : aba, abas, aba, ábamos, abais, aban ; -er and -ir verbs
both take the same ending : ía, ías, ía, íamos, íais, ían. Look
for these endings in the sentences above.

(2) Debía is the imperfect of deber : "must". Debía de haber
means "there must have been". Hay : "there is" is derived
from the verb haber, and is invariable ; hay tres libros : "there
are three books".

(3) Ya está is a very common expression, and means "OK" or
"Now I understand!" or "That's it!".

Don't forget :
- Learn the numbers as you go along : they're given at the
top of each page.
- Make a **reference** when you come across a word or a
construction that you find difficult. (See page 30).

EXERCISE : 1. He was making a house. – **2.** I thought that you
were going to come. – **3.** You were speaking with them. – **4.** I don't
remember very well. – **5.** I am sure. – **6.** That's it! – **7.** In any case it
was nice.

EJERCICIO DE CONTROL
Ponga las palabras que faltan

1 *What were you looking at?/What were you saying?*

¿ . . . . ?

¿ . . . . ?

2 *You arrived and I was playing.*

Vosotros . . . .

****

LECCION DIECIOCHO

Los otros pronombres personales

1 — Creo que no te ha entendido.
2 — Sin embargo, se lo he explicado. **(1) (2)**

PRONUNCIACION: 1 én'ten'dido. 2 explicado.

3 *There must be something to drink at home.*

Debe de . . . . para . . . . . en . . . .

4 *Before, I used to drink water.*

. . . . . yo . . . .

5 *I am sure it was very nice.*

. . . . de . . . .

THE MISSING WORDS : **1** qué mirabas / qué decías. **2** - llegabais y yo jugaba. **3** - haber algo - beber - casa. **4** antes - bebía agua. **5** estoy seguro - que era muy bonito.

****

LESSON EIGHTEEN

The other personal pronouns

1 — I think that he has not understood you.
2 — I have explained it to him, though.

NOTES
(1) *Sin embargo* means "however", "nevertheless", etc., and goes at the beginning of the phrase whenever possible.
(2) The perfect tense ("I have seen it") is used in Spanish in almost exactly the same way as in English.

Se lo he explicado : "I have explained it to him". *Lo* is the direct object pronoun ("it"), but you may be surprised to see *se* instead of *le* for the "to him" indirect object pronoun. Here, *se* is not the reflexive pronoun that we find in *entenderse* in the next sentence. When two object pronouns come together, the first one changes from *le* or *les* into *se*. You can see the full list of object pronouns in the table in Lesson 21. But don't worry : we'll be taking a closer look at them all soon.

3 — Por teléfono es más difícil entenderse.
4 — Tienes razón. Voy a ir a verle.
5   Me decías que ibas a venir.
6   Me lo decías ayer.
7 — ¿Nos puedes prestar las llaves?
8 — Os las voy a dar.
9   Voy a comprar una mesa.
10   La voy a comprar pasado mañana.
11 — La camisa de Juan está descosida.
12 — Se la coseré luego. **(3)**
13   El guitarrista tocaba una melodía. **(4)**
14   El niño le miraba.

PRONUNCIACION : 5 déciass 6 aiér 7 présstar 11 désscocida 12 cocéré 13 guitarrissta (the *u* is there to make the *g* hard ; the *rr* is rolled) tocaba -- mélodia.

EJERCICIO: 1. Me lo decías ayer. 2. No entiende. 3. Os las voy a dar. 4. ¿Puedes prestarme dinero? 5. Mi camisa está descosida. 6. El toca la guitarra. 7. También canta.

EJERCICIO DE CONTROL
Ponga las palabras que faltan

1 *However, he has not come.*

. . . . , ...

2 *I have told him/I have bought it.*

. . . . dicho.

. . . .

3 *I want to go to see him/to the restaurant.*

. . . .

. . . .

****

3 — By telephone it is more difficult to understand one another (oneself).
4 — You are (have) right. I'm going to see him.
5 You were telling me that you were going to come.
6 You were telling me (it) yesterday.
7 — Will you lend us the keys?
8 — I'm going to give them to you.
9 I'm going to buy a table.
10 I'm going to buy it the day after tomorrow.
11 — John's shirt is split (unsewn).
12 — I will sew it up for him (to him) later.
13 The guitarist was playing (was touching) a melody.
14 The child was looking at him.

(3) *Coseré* is the future of *coser*.
(4) *Tocar* means "to touch" and "to play" : *Yo tocaba la mesa* : "I was touching the table" ; *tú tocabas la guitarra* : "you were playing the guitar".

EXERCISE : 1. You were saying (it to) me yesterday. – **2.** He doesn't understand. – **3.** I'm going to give it to you. – **4.** Can you lend me some money? – **5.** My shirt is split. – **6.** He plays the guitar. – **7.** He sings too.

4 *John was playing the guitar.*

Juan . . . . . . : . . guitarra.

5 *Lend me your key.*

. . . .

THE MISSING WORDS : 1 sin embargo no ha venido. 2 se lo he / se lo he comprado. 3 quiero ir a verle / quiero ir al restaurante. 4 tocaba la. 5 préstame tu llave.

****

LECCION DIECINUEVE

Por teléfono

1 — Sí. Dígame.
2 — ¿Es usted la secretaria de la doctora Jiménez? (1)
3 — No. Soy su marido.
4 — Perdone. ¿Está la doctora?
5 — No. Está en el hospital. Acaba de salir. (2)
6   ¿Quiere dejarme el recado?
7 — Le telefoneaba para saber si esta tarde podía venir a ver a mi hijo.
8   Está enfermo y tiene mucha fiebre.
9 — De acuerdo. Se lo diré cuando vuelva.
10   Y usted no se inquiete, seguramente ha cogido frío;
11   los niños son fuertes y saben defenderse naturalmente.
12   ¿Quiere darme su dirección?
13 — Sí. Es: calle del Sabio número 3, tercero izquierda. (3)
14   Adiós y muchas gracias.

PRONUNCIACION : 1 digamé 2 sécrétaria .. doctora Himéneç 3 marido 4 perdoné 5 osspital acaba salir 6 récado 8 en'férmo .. fiébré. 9 .. vouélva 10 in'kiéte ségouramen'te .. coHido frio 11 .. fouértess .. défen'dérsé natouralmen'te 12 .. direk'cion' 13 ... sabio .. nouméro .. tercéro iskierda.

*****

The sentences in the lessons are starting to get longer. When you've finished reading each one, try and repeat it without looking at the text.

*The more you do this, the easier it will become to start **thinking in Spanish**.*

LESSON NINETEEN

On the (by) telephone

1 — Yes. Hello. (Tell me)
2 — Is that (Are you) Dr J's secretary?
3 — No. It's (I am) her husband.
4 — Excuse me. Is the doctor [in]?
5 — No. She is at (in) the hospital. She has just gone out.
6   Do you want to leave me the message?
7 — I was phoning her (for) to know if this evening she would be able to come to see my son.
8   He is ill, and has a (lot of) fever.
9 — Alright. I'll tell her when she comes back.
10   And you : don't worry, he has probably caught cold ;
11   children are strong, and they know [how] to defend themselves naturally.
12   Will you give me your address?
13 — Yes. It's : *calle del Sabio, numero 3* [3, Sage Street], third floor, left.
14   Goodbye and thank you very much.

NOTES

(1) *Doctora* is the feminine form of *doctor*. *Profesora* is the feminine form of *profesor* : "teacher".

(2) *Acabar de* is used in the present tense + infinitive to mean "I have just...". Thus, *acabo de comer* : "I have just eaten. *Acabar* on its own means "to finish".

(3) *Tercero izquierda* in this address means "third floor, door on the left". All addresses in apartment buildings include some similar indication, e.g., *1° dcha* : "1st floor, door on the right" *(derecha)*.

EJERCICIO: 1. ¿Está la doctora? **2.** Acaba de llegar. **3.** Han dejado un recado para ti. **4.** Se lo diré cuando vuelva. **5.** No te inquietes. **6.** Has cogido frío. **7.** Está enfermo.

EJERCICIO DE CONTROL
Ponga las palabras que faltan

1 *He has just gone out / eaten.*

. . . .

. . . .

2 *Do you want to leave me the message?*

¿ . . . . . .   usted   . . . . ?

3 *When she comes back, I'll tell her.*

. . . .   diré.

****

LECCION VEINTE.

Una buena noticia

1 — Tengo que anunciaros algo.
2 — Esperamos que no sea una mala noticia.
3 — No. Es una buena noticia.
4 — ¿De qué se trata? (1)
5 — Ya tengo el permiso de conducir.
6 — ¡Enhorabuena!
7   ¡Eso hay que celebrarlo! (2)

PRONUNCIACION: noticia. **1** anoun'ciaross algo **2** espéramoss **4** trata **5** pérmiço .. con'doucir **6** en'orabouéna **7** celébrarlo

EXERCISE : **1.** Is the doctor (fem.) in? – **2.** She has just arrived. – **3.** They have left a message for you. – **4.** I will tell her when she comes back. – **5.** Don't worry. – **6.** You have caught a cold. – **7.** He is ill.

4 *I have caught cold / I have taken the newspaper.*

. .   . .

. .   . .

5 *Can you give me your address?*

¿Puede usted   . . . . ?

THE MISSING WORDS :   **1** acaba de salir / acaba de comer. **2** quiere - dejarme el recado. **3** cuando vuelva se lo. **4** he cogido frío / he cogido el periódico. **5** darme su dirección.

****

LESSON TWENTY

Good news (A good news)

1 — I have to announce something to you.
2 — We hope that it is not (a) bad news.
3 — No. It's (a) good news.
4 — What is it? (What is it about?)
5 — (Already) I have my (the) driving license.
6 — Congratulations!
7 We must celebrate that! (It is necessary to celebrate it).

(See notes **(1)** and **(2)** page 64).

8   ¿Se lo has dicho a Juan?
9 — No, pero voy a telefonearle para decírselo.
        (3)
10 — Invítale a cenar.
11   Pásamelo cuando hayas terminado. **(4)**
12 — ¿Quién puede ocuparse de hacer las com-
        pras?
13 — Yo mismo.

8 ditcho .. 9
décírsélo 10 in'vitalé 11 paçamélo couan'do aïass terminado 12 kien'
13 mismo.

EJERCICIO: **1**. Voy a deciros algo. **2**. Es una buena
noticia. **3**. Se lo he dicho. **4**. Vamos a telefonearle. **5**.
Quiero decírselo. **6**. ¿De qué se trata? **7**. Yo mismo.

*****

EJERCICIO DE CONTROL
Ponga las palabras que faltan

1 *I must announce some bad news to you.*

. . . .   anunciaros   . . . .

2 *What about?*

¿ . . . . ?

3 *That must be celebrated.*

. . . .   celebrarlo.

4 *Have you already told her?*

¿ . . . .   ya?

****

8   Have you told John? (Have you said it to John?)
9 — No, but I'm going to phone (to) him (for) to tell him (it).
10 — Invite him to dinner (to have dinner).
11 Pass him to me (pass me him) when you have finished.
12 — Who can (busy himself to) do the shopping?
13 — I can (I myself).

NOTES

(1) *Tratarse* means "to be about". *¿De qué se trata?* : "What is it about"? But the verb is impersonal, and thus cannot have a subject. To express : "What is this book about?", we would have to say : *¿Se trata de qué en este libro?*

(2) *Eso* : "that" is the first word in the sentence, but we also find the object at the end of *celebra lo.* Very often in Spanish, the only way of stressing an important word is to put it at the beginning of the sentence and then repeat it later in the sentence.

(3) *Decírselo* is another example of two object pronouns attached to the end of an infinitive. See note (2) to Lesson 18, and note (1) to Lesson 16.

(4) *Cuando* : "when" takes the present subjunctive when the action has not yet taken place. *Hayas* is the *tú* form of the present subjunctive of *haber.* See also sentence **9** from Lesson 19 *(vuelvas* is the present subjunctive of *volver).* Seems complicated? Don't worry! We'll come back to this many times later on.

EXERCISE : **1.** I'm going to tell you (fam. plural) something. – **2.** It's good news. – **3.** I have told him. – **4.** We' re going to phone him. – **5.** I want to tell him. – **6.** What's it about? – **7.** Myself.

5 *I'm going to invite him to dinner/to eat with us.*

. . . .

. . . .

THE MISSING WORDS :   1 tengo que - una mala noticia. 2 de qué se trata. 3 eso hay que. 4 se lo has dicho. 5 voy a invitarle a cenar / voy a invitarle a comer con nosotros.

****

LECCION VEINTIUNA

LESSON TWENTY-ONE

Revisión y notas

1. Throughout the last six lessons, we have been paying particular attention to **pronouns.** We have covered a lot of ground quickly, and you have already come across many of the difficulties encountered with Spanish pronouns.

We have introduced you to the form of the pronouns themselves, and you have seen that their position in the sentence is also very important. It takes a long time to have everything on the tip of your tongue at the right time, but little by little, we'll get there in the end!

* * * * *

2. **Pronouns,** as you know, stand in place of nouns. They can replace a subject, a direct object, or an indirect object, and their form changes accordingly. If a pronoun is accompanied by a preposition *a, para, por, con,* etc. the form is different yet again.

Object pronouns cannot stand alone after the verb. They are placed **before** the verb, or, if the verb is in the infinitive, imperative, or gerund form, they can be attached to the end of the verb. Only if the pronoun is "strengthened" by a preposition can it figure as a separate word after the verb.

When two object pronouns are in the third person, the indirect object *le* or *les* becomes *se*. Thus "I have given it to him" becomes *se lo he dado,* and "I'm going to tell him (it)" becomes *voy a decírselo.* The same principle applies for imperatives (e.g., *dámelo, escríbannos),* and for gerunds, as we shall see later.

The two tables overleaf are for reference. Don't try to learn the different forms by heart, because the most efficient way of remembering them is by using them in context. If you're stuck on an exercise, and can't remember which pronoun form to use, refer to the tables. After a while, the commonest ones will come to mind automatically, but there's no hurry, so don't worry! We won't let you forget your pronouns.

Lección 21

PERSON	SUBJECT	OBJECT WITHOUT PREPOSITION		OBJECT WITH PREPOSITION	OBJECT WITH *con*
		direct	indirect		
1 singular	yo	me	me	mí	conmigo
2 singular	tú	te	te	ti	contigo
3 singular	él ella usted	lo(le) (1) la lo(le), la	le le le	él ella usted	con él con ella con usted
1 plural	nosotros/as	nos	nos	nosotros/as	con nosotros/as
2 plural	vosotros/as	os	os	vosotros/as	con vosotros/as
3 plural	ellos ellas ustedes	los(les) (1) las los(les), las	les les les	ellos ellas ustedes	con ellos con ellas con ustedes
reflexive		se	se	sí	consigo

(1) It is quite common to use the pronoun *le* in place of the pronoun *lo* as a direct object (in brackets in the table), but there is some confusion on this point.

The **Real Academia** accepts that the pronoun *lo* may be used as a direct object referring to persons. Thus we can say either *No lo conozco* or *No le conozco :* "I don't know him". (In the feminine, the use of *la* is prescribed : *No la conozco :* "I don't know her"). At the same time, however, the Academia recommends that speakers avoid this usage as much as possible.

direct object indirect object without preposition		object preceded by a preposition	object preceded by the preposition *con*
He loves me	He gives me a present (He gives it to me)	to me	and he sings with me
Me ama	*Me da un regalo (me lo da)*	*a mí*	*y canta conmigo*
te ama	*te lo da*	*a ti*	*y canta contigo*
le (1) ama	*se lo*	*a él*	*y canta con él*
la ama	*se lo*	*a ella*	*y canta con ella*
le (1) ama	*se lo*	*a usted*	*y canta con usted*
nos ama	*nos lo*	*a nosotros / as*	*y canta con nosotros / as*
os ama	*os lo*	*a vosotros / as*	*y canta con vosotros / as*
los ama	*se lo*	*a ellos*	*y canta con ellos*
las ama	*se lo*	*a ellas*	*y canta con ellas*
los ama	*se lo*	*a ustedes*	*y canta con ustedes*
se ama	*se lo da*	*a sí (mismo)*	—
se aman	*se lo dan*	*a sí (mismos)*	—

Lección 21

3. In the first lessons of this course, we have concentrated on the present indicative tense. In Lesson 17 we introduced the imperfect indicative. The table below gives the imperfect endings for all three groups of regular verbs : -ar, -er, and -ir.

cantar	comer	vivir
cantaba	comía	vivía
cantabas	comías	vivías
cantaba	comía	vivía
cantábamos	comíamos	vivíamos
cantabais	comíais	vivíais
cantaban	comían	vivían

You will notice that the endings are the same for second and third conjugation verbs (-er and -ir).

****

LECCION VEINTIDOS

Se bañaron

1 — La semana pasada acampamos junto al mar. **(1)**
2 — Tuvimos cuatro días de vacaciones y aprovechamos para ir a descansar.

PRONUNCIACION: bagnaron. **1** sémana ... acam'pamoss joun'to ... mar **2** touvimoss ... aprovétchamoss ... descan'sar.

4. **Writing in Spanish**

1   I'm going to do the market. Do you want me to buy you anything?
2   Do you want to leave me the newspaper? I'm in a big hurry.
3   I had a feeling you were going to come. I told you so.
4   I told him before I left.
5   My son has a high fever. Are you going to call the doctor?
6   Phone him up and tell him so.

5. **Translation**

1.   Voy a hacer la plaza. ¿Quieres que te compre algo?
2.   ¿Quieres dejarme el periódico? Tengo mucha prisa.
3.   Me imaginaba que ibas a venir. — Te lo había dicho.
4.   Se lo había dicho antes de irme.
5.   Mi hijo tiene mucha fiebre. — ¿Vas a llamar al médico?
6.   Telefonéale para decírselo.

****

LESSON TWENTY-TWO

They went swimming (They bathed themselves)

1 — Last week we camped next to the sea.
2 — We had four days (of) holiday(s) and took advantage [of them] to go and relax.

NOTES

(1) Here we start using the preterite (simple past) tense. You'll see most of the different forms in the lessons that follow. Don't try to remember them all yet. Just concentrate on **when** to use the preterite : in verbs referring to finished actions taking place at a **given time.** Example : *ayer fui al cine* ("yesterday I went to the cinema"), where *fui* is the preterite of the irregular verb *ir* ("to go"). Compare this use with the imperfect (See Note 1 to Lesson 17).

3   A la vuelta, visitamos algunos pueblos de la provincia de Santander.

4 — ¡Claro! Ahora me lo explico.

5   El miércoles os telefoneé a mediodía y pensé que vuestro teléfono no funcionaba.

6 — Sí, nos fuimos el martes al salir del trabajo. **(2)**

7 — ¿Hizo buen tiempo? **(3)**

8 — Hizo un tiempo estupendo.

9   Yo me paseé mucho por la costa.

10   Elvira contempló mucho la playa y el mar.

11   Y no vimos a nadie.

12 — ¿Os bañasteis?

13 — Todas las mañanas a la salida del sol.

3 vouélta viçitamoss algounoss pouébloss ... provin'çia .. san'tan'der. **5** miércoless ... médiodia ... pén'sé ... foun'cionaba **6** fouimoss ... martéss. **7** içó **8** ésstoupen'do **9** passéé ... cossta. **10** élvira con'tem'plo ... plaïa **12** bagnasstéiss **13** salida ... sol.

EJERCICIO: 1. A la vuelta, nos vimos en su casa. **2.** ¿Hizo buen tiempo? **3.** Me paseé mucho. **4.** Ahora me lo explico. **5.** Vino el miércoles a comer. **6.** No había nadie en la playa. **7.** Todas las mañanas voy a hacer las compras.

3   On the way back (At the return), we visited some
     villages in (of) the province of Santander.
4 — Of course! Now I understand (Now I explain it to
     myself).
5   On (The) Wednesday, I phoned you at midday and
     thought that your telephone was not working.
6 — Yes, we left on (the) Tuesday after (at the exit of
     the) work.
7 — Was the weather good? (Did it make good weather?)
8 — It was lovely weather (It made a weather lovely).
9   I walked (myself) a lot on (by) the coast.
10   Elvira contemplated a lot the beach and the sea.
11   And we didn't see (to) anyone.
12 — Did you swim? (Did you bathe yourselves?)
13 — Every morning when the sun came out (at the exit of
     the sun).

NOTES
(2) *Al* + **infinitive** makes a time clause. *Al comer* means "when I
was eating" or "when I ate" or "on eating", and can thus
replace *cuando comía* or *cuando comí. A la salida* is the same
idea, and is an alternative to *al salir* ("when I went out" or "on
going out").
(3) A few adjectives can come before the nouns they describe.
Bueno ("good") is one of these, and it drops its final *-o* before
masculine singular nouns. Other examples of this rule include
primero : "first", and *malo* : "bad".

* * * * *

EXERCISE : 1. When we came back, we met (saw ourselves) at
his house. – **2.** Was the weather good? – **3.** I walked (myself) a lot.
– **4.** Now I understand. – **5.** He came to eat on Wednesday. – **6.**
There was nobody on the beach. – **7.** Every morning I go to do the
shopping.

Lección 22

EXERCISE
Ponga las palabras que faltan (ponga las palabras ké faltan)

1 *Last week I ate with him in the restaurant.*

. .   . .   comí   . . .   .
. . . .

2 *When I came back I went to see him.*

.   . .   .

****

LECCION VEINTITRES

Vamos a su casa (1) o pequeños detalles

1 — Hace una semana que no he visto a los
       Soley. (2)
2 — ¡Claro! El lunes pasado se fueron a Holanda.
       (3)
3 — ¿Llevaron también a los niños?
4 — Sí, porque ya no tenían colegio. (4)
5 — ¿Sabes cuándo vuelven? (5)
6 — No estoy segura, pero creo que pronto
       estarán de vuelta.

PRONUNCIACION: déta//es **1** soléï **2** lounéss ... olan´da **4** coléHio **6**
pron´to

3 *I went swimming in the sea.*

. .   . .

4 *We saw him when we came out of the cinema.*

Lo   . . . . .   visto   . .   . .   cine.

5 *Yesterday the weather was very good.*

. . . .

THE MISSING WORDS :   **1** la semana pasada - con él en el restaurante. **2** a la vuelta he ido a verlo. **3** me bañé en el mar. **4** - hemos - al salir del -. **5** ayer hizo muy bueno.

✳✳✳✳✳✳✳✳✳✳✳✳✳✳✳✳✳✳✳✳✳✳✳✳✳✳✳✳✳✳✳✳✳✳✳✳✳✳

LESSON TWENTY-THREE

Let's go to his house, or small details

1 — I haven't seen the Soley[s] for a week (It makes a week that I haven't seen the Soleys).
2 — Of course! (The) Last Monday they went to Holland.
3 — Did they also take the children?
4 — Yes, because they (already) didn't have school.
5 — Do you know when they are coming back?
6 — I'm not sure, but I think that soon they will be back.

NOTES
(1) *A casa de Juan* means "to John's house" ; *en casa de Juan* means "at John's house, or at John's".
(2) To express "for" in Spanish time clauses, we have to use the verb *hacer :* "to do" or "to make", and a construction such as *hace una semana que no te he visto,* that could be literally translated : "that makes a week that I haven't seen you". Note that in the past (I hadn't seen you for a week) the verb *hacer* goes in the imperfect, thus : *hacía una semana que no te había visto.*
(3) The different meanings of the verb "to leave" have different words in Spanish. We've already seen *dejar :* "to leave" (objects). Now we have the intransitive "to leave" as in "we left yesterday", which is often expressed by the reflexive verb *irse* ("to go away").
(4) *Ya* ("already") is also used in the negative to mean "no longer" : *Ya no sé :* "I no longer know".
(5) *Volver* means "to come back" or "to go back". *La vuelta* is the noun from *volver : estoy de vuelta* means "I'm back".

7   Han ido solamente para hacer una visita a la madre de Anni, que estaba enferma. **(6)**

8 — ¿Sabes si es grave?

9 — No creo, pero para las personas mayores una operación es siempre delicada.

10 — ¿Quieres que vayamos a ver si han vuelto?

11 — Me parece una buena idea. **(7)**

12 Además, sé que tenían idea de ir luego de vacaciones a España.

13 — Entonces es posible que ya se hayan ido.

14 — Me extraña que lo hayan hecho tan rápido, pero es posible.

7 solamén'té ... viçita 8 grabé 9 perçonass maïoress ... opéracion' ... délicada 10 vaïamoss 14 extragna ... aïan' étcho tan' rapido.

EJERCICIO : 1. Hace una semana que no le veo. 2. Lo llevaron al colegio. 3. No estoy segura. 4. Vamos a hacerle una visita. 5. Me parece una buena idea. 6. Se han ido. 7. Eso me extraña.

EJERCICIO DE CONTROL
Ponga las palabras que faltan

1 *Haven't you seen her?*

¿ No · · . .   . . ?

2 *Tomorrow we will be back at five o'clock.*

. . . .

. . . . .

3 *I'm going to go to John's at the end of (on leaving) (the) class.*

. . . . Juan   . .   . .   . . , . . .

. .   . .

4 *I have been ill for two days.*

. . . .

7 They have only gone to visit Anny's mother, who is ill.

8 — Do you know if it's serious?

9 — I don't think [so], but for old people an operation is always delicate.

10 — Do you want us to go (that we should go) to see if they have come back?

11 — I think it's a good idea (That seems a good idea to me).

12 Moreover, I know that they had [the] idea of going (later) on holiday (of holidays) to Spain.

13 — Then it's possible that they have already left.

14 — I'm surprised (it surprises me) that they (should) have done it so fast, but it's possible.

---

(6) *Hacer una visita a,* literally "to make a visit to" is the Spanish for "to visit (someone)".

(7) *Parecer* : "to appear", "to seem". Idiomatically, it is frequently used in phrases like *¿Qué te parece? :* "What do you think of it?" (literally "What does it appear to you?").

EXERCISE : 1. I haven't seen him for a week. – **2.** They took him to school. – **3.** I'm not sure. – **4.** Let's go and visit him. – **5.** I think it's a good idea. – **6.** They have left. – **7.** I'm surprised at that.

5 *What do you think of it?*

¿ . . .   . ?

THE MISSING WORDS :   **1** la has visto. **2** mañana estaremos de vuelta a las cinco. **3** voy a ir a casa de - a la salida de clase. **4** hace dos días que estoy enfermo. **5** qué te parece.

Lección 23

LECCION VEINTICUATRO

Antes de comer

1 — ¿Qué estás haciendo? (1)
2 — Estoy jugando con Alicia.
3 — ¿A qué jugáis?
4 — Estamos jugando al ajedrez.
5 — ¿Y tú, qué haces?
6 — Estoy preparando la comida.
7 — ¿Qué has comprado para hoy?
8 — Carne, arroz, tomates, pepinos y berenjenas. ¿Qué te parece?
9 — ¡Ya se me hace la boca agua!
10 — Pero... tendrás que esperar porque todavía no está listo. (2)

11 — ¿Cuánto tiempo?
12 — Una hora, más o menos.
13 — Bueno, entonces date prisa porque tengo mucho hambre.
14 — Perdona Alicia. ¿A quién le toca jugar ahora? (3)

PRONUNCIACION: 2 Hougan'do aliçia 3 Hougaiss 4 aHédreç 6 préparan'do 8 carné arroç tomatéss pépinoss ... béren'Hénass 9 boça 10 ten'drass ... lissto 14 kién'.

LESSON TWENTY-FOUR

Before eating

1 — What are you doing?
2 — I'm playing with Alicia.
3 — What are you playing (at)?
4 — We are playing (at) chess.
5 — And (you), what are you doing?
6 — I'm preparing the meal.
7 — What have you bought for today?
8 — Meat, rice, tomatoes, cucumbers and aubergines [eggplants]. What do you think of that?
9 — My mouth is watering already! (Already the mouth makes itself water to me).
10 — But you will have to wait because it still isn't ready.
11 — How long?
12 — An hour, more or less.
13 — Good! Hurry up then because I'm very hungry.
14 — I'm sorry, Alicia. Whose turn is it to play now?

*****

NOTES
(1) The present participle *(-ando, -iendo)* is used with *estar* in the present continuous tense, exactly as in English. Thus, *estoy trabajando* means "I am working (at this very instant)", while *trabajo en Madrid* means "I (usually) work in Madrid".
(2) *Listo* is one of a small number of adjectives that changes meaning when the verb changes from *ser* to *estar*. *Es listo* means "he is clever", while *estoy listo* means "I am ready".
(3) In Lesson 18, we came across the two meanings of the verb *tocar* ("to touch" and "to play (music)"). Here's another use of the verb : *Me toca a mí :* "It's my turn".

EJERCICIO : **1**. Estoy trabajando. **2**. ¿Qué te parece? **3**. Todavía no estamos listos. **4**. ¿Cuánto tiempo hace? **5**. Tres semanas más o menos. **6**. Date prisa porque tengo que irme. **7**. Te toca a ti.

EJERCICIO DE CONTROL
Ponga las palabras que faltan

1 *What are you eating / doing?*

¿ . . .   . ?

¿ . . .   . ?

2 *Is she ready? / Is she playing?*

¿ . . . . ?

¿ . . . . ?

****

LECCION VEINTICINCO

Me gusta el castellano (1)

1 — Quisiera aprender bien el castellano.
2 — ¿Por qué no vas a España?
3 — Probablemente iré el año que viene, pero no sé todavía qué región elegir.
4 — El mejor castellano se habla en Burgos y en Valladolid: en Castilla la Vieja.
5 — Creía que era en Madrid.

PRONUNCIACION: goussta. **3** probabléménte... réHion' éléHir. **4** valladoli ... casstilla ... vieHa. **5** créia.

EXERCISE : 1. I am working. – **2.** What do you think about it? – **3.** We are not yet ready. – **4.** How long is it? – **5.** About three weeks. – **6.** Hurry up because I have to leave. – **7.** It's your turn.

3 *Today we are going to eat meat with rice.*

. . .

4 *We have waited about two hours.*

. . . . . esperado . . . . . .

5 *It's your turn.*

. . . . . .

THE MISSING WORDS : **1** qué estás comiendo / haciendo. **2** está lista / está jugando. **3** hoy vamos a comer carne con arroz. **4** hemos - dos horas más o menos. **5** te toca a ti.

****

LESSON TWENTY-FIVE

I like Spanish (Castilian pleases me)

1 — I would like to learn Spanish well (learn well Castilian).
2 — Why don't you go to Spain?
3 — I will probably go next year (the year that comes), but I still don't know which (what) region to choose.
4 — The best Castilian is spoken (speaks itself) in Burgos and in Valladolid : in Old Castile.
5 — I thought it was in Madrid.

NOTES
(1) *Gusto* : "taste". *Gustar* is also very commonly used impersonally to express "to like" : *me gusta* (literally "it pleases me"). Thus, "Do you (polite sing.) like this meal?" : *le gusta (a usted) esta comida?*

6 — En Madrid, se habla bien pero el idioma del pueblo no es tan puro. (2)

7 Sin embargo, si vas a Madrid encontrarás una vida más movida y una gran cantidad de espectáculos.

8 — ¿Y dónde se habla el peor castellano?

9 — Es difícil de decir y... no creo que se pueda hablar así. (3)

10 Casi todas las provincias tienen su acento propio y se encuentra en toda España gente que habla correctamente.

11 Cataluña, el País Vasco, Galicia, el País Valenciano, tienen su idioma propio y además sus habitantes hablan el castellano. (4)

12 En Andalucía, se habla el castellano pero con un acento particular.

13 — Entonces ... España es un conjunto muy rico de pueblos.

14 — En efecto, es una tierra de una riqueza insospechada.

6 idioma ... pouro. 7 en'con'trarass ... movida ... gran' can'tidad (vous pouvez prononcer légèrement le d final) ... ésspectacouloss. 8 péor. 9 dificil ... décir ... pouéda açi. 10 caçi ... propio ... Hén'té ... correctamén'té. 11 cataloungna, païss vassco, galiçia ... valén'çiano ... abitan'tèss. 12 an'dalouçia ... particoular. 13 con'Houn'to ... rico. 14 éfécto ... tierra ... rikéça in'ssosspétchada.

*****

EJERCICIO : 1. Me gusta viajar. 2. Probablemente iré mañana. 3. Creía que no ibas a venir. 4. Esta comida es peor que la de ayer. 5. Es difícil de decir. 6. El idioma es un ser viviente. 7. En esta región, la gente tiene mucho acento.

6 —	In Madrid, they speak (it speaks itself) well, but the language of the people is not so pure.
7	However, if you go to Madrid, you will find a busier life and a large quantity of attractions (spectacles).
8 —	And where is the worst Spanish spoken?
9 —	It's difficult to say, and... I don't think one can talk like this (thus).
10	Almost all the provinces have their own accent, and one meets all over Spain (in all Spain) people who speak correctly.
11	Catalonia, the Basque Country, Galicia, and the Valencia area have their own languages, and their inhabitants speak Castilian also.
12	In Andalucia, Castilian is spoken, but with a particular accent.
13 —	So... Spain is a very rich mixture (assembly) of people.
14 —	Indeed, it is a land of (an) unsuspected richness.

NOTES
(2) *El idioma* (masc.) means "the language" ; *la lengua* means "the tongue" in both senses of the word. *El pueblo* is both "the village" and "the people".
(3) *No creo que* ("I don't think that...") takes the present subjunctive.
(4) *Su idioma propio* is in the singular, because the regions only have one *idioma propio* each.

ME GUSTA VIAJAR

EXERCISE : 1. I like to travel. – **2.** I will probably go tomorrow. – **3.** I thought you were not going to come. – **4.** This meal is worse than yesterday's. – **5.** It is difficult to say. – **6.** Language is a living being. – **7.** In this region, the people have a strong accent.

EJERCICIO DE CONTROL
Ponga las palabras que faltan

1 *I like (the) good cinema/I like to travel.*

.. .. buen ....

.. ..

2 *I speak (well) French and Castilian.*

....

....

****

LECCION VEINTISEIS

Un regalo

1 — Me gusta lo que haces. ¿Qué es? **(1)**
2 — Estoy haciendo una lámpara y esto será el pie. **(2)**
3 — ¿En madera tallada?
4 — Sí, me encanta trabajar la madera. Cuando la tallo siento que me habla. Es una materia noble.
5 — ¿Esta es la pantalla?

PRONUNCIACION: régalo. **2** lam'para ... pié. **3** madéra tal/ada. **4** en'can'ta ... sién'to ... matéria noble. **5** pan'tal/a.

3 *The language of the people is very rich.*

. . . .

4 *For a Scotsman the "jota" is easy to say.*

. . . .

. . . .

5 *I like your accent.*

. . . .

THE MISSING WORDS : **1** me gusta el - cine / me gusta viajar. **2** hablo bien el francés y el castellano. **3** la lengua del pueblo es muy rica. **4** para un escocés, la "jota" es fácil de decir. **5** tu acento me gusta.

****

LESSON TWENTY-SIX

A gift

1 — I like what you are making. What is it?
2 — I'm making a lamp, and this will be the stand (foot).
3 — In carved wood?
4 — Yes. I adore working wood (To work wood delights me). When I carve it, I feel that it talks to me. It is a fine (noble) material.
5 — Is this the lampshade?

NOTES
(1) *Lo que haces* : "what you are making", or literally, "that which you are making". If you can replace the word "what" with "that which", you must use *lo que* in Spanish. Remember that *hacer* means "to make" and "to do".
(2) In Lesson 12, we saw the demonstrative adjectives *este* and *esta* ("this"), and *estos* and *estas* ("these"). Here we are introducing demonstrative pronouns : *Esto* refers to something indeterminate (*¡Dame esto!* : "Give me this!"), but if we want to say "Give me this one", when referring to somebody or something specific, the demonstrative pronoun takes the gender of the person or object it is replacing. Example : *¡Dame ésta!* : "give me this one (fem.)". Note the written accent to differentiate the pronoun from the feminine demonstrative adjective *esta* : this (fem.).

6 — Sí. ¿Te gusta?

7 — Mucho. ¿Dónde la vas a poner?

8 — No es para mí. Quiero hacer un regalo. (3)

9   A las personas a las que quiero mucho me gusta regalarles algo hecho con mis propias manos.

10 — Es bonito lo que dices.

11 — Eso no tiene importancia. Es simplemente un gesto que me gusta hacer.

12 — ¿Para quién es el regalo?

13 — Para ti.

14 — Nunca me habían hecho un regalo como éste.

9 régalarless ...
propiass manoss. 11 im'portan'sia ... Hessto 14 noun'ca.

EJERCICIO: 1. Esto me gusta. 2. Me encanta ir al campo. 3. Este regalo es para ti. 4. Lo que haces es bonito. 5. ¿Te gustan sus manos? 6. He hecho esto para ella. 7. Nunca había venido hasta aquí.

EJERCICIO DE CONTROL
Ponga las palabras que faltan

1 *What you say is not true.*

. . . .

2 *It's my gift / It's my brother.*

. . . .

. . . .

3 *This lamp is for me.*

. . . .

6 — Yes. Do you like it?
7 — A lot. Where are you going to put it?
8 — It isn't for me. I want to make a gift.
9 — To the people (to those) who[m] I love a lot, I like to give (to them) something made with my own hands.
10 — What you're saying is nice (It's nice that which you say).
11 — That is unimportant (doesn't have importance). It's simply a gesture that I like to make.
12 — For whom is the gift?
13 — For you.
14 — Never have they made a present like this [one].

NOTES
(3) *No es para mí :* "it isn't for me". *Mí* (with an accent on the i) is the personal pronoun "me". Without the accent, *mi* is the possessive adjective "my". *Para mí :* "for me" ; *mi casa :* "my house".

EXERCISE : 1. I like this. – **2.** I adore going to the country. – **3.** This gift is for you. – **4.** What you are making is nice. – **5.** Do you like its hands? – **6.** I have made this for her. – **7.** I had never come as far as here.

NUNCA HABÍA TRABAJADO LA MADERA

26

4 *I like his gestures.*

. .   . .

5 *I had never worked wood.*

. . . .

THE MISSING WORDS :   **1** lo que dices no es verdad. **2** es mi regalo / es mi hermano. **3** esta lámpara es para mí. **4** me gustan sus gestos. **5** nunca había trabajado la madera.

LECCION VEINTISIETE

Mañana iremos de campo (1)

1 — ¿Qué haremos mañana? Tenemos el día libre.
2 — Mañana no es hoy. Yo no sé lo que querré.
3 — Tú tendrás que llamar a Roberto y estoy casi seguro de que pasaréis el día estudiando.
4 — No me acordaba de que le había prometido llamarle para preparar el examen juntos.
5 — ¿Crees que estará ahora en casa?
6 — No lo sé. ¿ Por qué me lo preguntas ?
7 — Porque se me acaba de ocurrir una idea. (2)
8 — ¿Qué te parece si vamos de campo?
9 — Tú y Roberto podréis estudiar si queréis y yo jugaré a la pelota con los niños.
10 — Me gusta tu idea.
11 — Habrá que madrugar para aprovechar todo el día.
12 — Voy a llamar a Roberto para ver si está de acuerdo.

PRONUNCIACION: irémoss ... campo. 1 arémoss 2 kérré 3 tén'drass ... robérto ... paçaréiss 4 acordaba ... prométido ... éxamen' 5 ésstara. 6 prégoun'tass 7 ocourrir 9 podréiss ... Hougaré ... pélota 11 abra.

If you want to see in greater detail how to form the Spanish future, turn to Lesson 28 (Paragraphs 6 and 7).

LESSON TWENTY-SEVEN

Tomorrow we'll go to the country

1 — What will we do tomorrow? We have the day free.
2 — Tomorrow is not today. I don't know what I will want.
3 — You will have to call Roberto, and I am almost certain that you'll spend the day working.
4 — I didn't remember that I had promised (to him) to phone (to) him (for) to prepare the exam together.
5 — Do you think that he'll be now at home?
6 — I don't know. Why do you ask (me it)?
7 — Because I have just had an idea (an idea has just occurred to me).
8 — What do you think of going to the country? (What does it seem to you if we go to the country?)
9 — You and Roberto will be able to study if you (will) want and I will play (at the) ball with the children.
10 — I like your idea (Your idea pleases me).
11 — It'll be necessary to get up early (for) to take advantage of the whole day (all the day).
12 — I'm going to call Roberto (for) to see if he agrees (is of agreement).

HE GUSTA TU IDEA

NOTES
(1) *El campo :* "the field" and "the country". *Ir de campo :* "to go to the country".
(2) A particularly Spanish construction : things often "do themselves" to people. Another example is *olvidar :* "to forget" : the commonest way of saying "I have forgotten" is *se me ha olvidado :* literally, "it has forgotten itself to me". Thus *olvidarse* is a sort of reflexive verb.

EJERCICIO: 1. Hoy tengo el día libre. **2.** Estaba casi seguro de que no ibas a venir. **3.** No me acordaba. **4.** No tengo ni idea. **5.** Se me acaba de ocurrir. **6.** ¿Jugarás con nosotros? **7.** Nosotros lo haremos.

*****

EJERCICIO DE CONTROL
Ponga las palabras que faltan

1 *Will you be at home tomorrow?*

¿ . . . . ?

2 *He will go tonight to the cinema.*

. . . .

****
LECCION VEINTIOCHO
LESSON TWENTY-EIGHT
Revision y notas
1. **The preterite** (simple past). (See note 1, Lesson 22). The difference between the preterite and the imperfect : the preterite expresses a complete action, which has taken place at a particular time (e.g., *Pasó tres horas en el baño* : "he spent three hours in the bath"). The imperfect, on the other hand, concentrates on the duration of the action, without specifying its beginning or its end (e.g., *¿Qué decías?* : "What were you saying?" ; *Vivían en Burgos* : "They lived (used to live) in Burgos".

The preterite endings are as follows :
-ar verbs : stem + *-é, -aste, -ó, -amos, -asteis, -aron*
er and *-ir* verbs : stem + *í, iste, ió, imos, isteis, ieron*

You will notice that certain first person plural forms are the same in the preterite as they are in the present tense. The meaning depends on the context (Sometimes, the word *ya* : ("already") is added before the verb in the preterite (cf. American usage : Did you see it already?).

EXERCISE : 1. Today I have the day free. – **2.** I was almost certain that you were not going to come. – **3.** I didn't remember. – **4.** I have no idea. – **5.** It has just occurred to me. – **6.** Will you play with us? – **7.** We will do it.

3 *I have just had an idea.*

. . . .

4 *Will you go to the country tomorrow?*

¿ . . . . ?

5 *Will you play with the children?*

¿ . . . . ?

THE MISSING WORDS : **1** estarás en tu casa mañana. **2** irá esta noche al cine. **3** se me acaba de ocurrir una idea. **4** iréis de campo mañana. **5** jugarás con los niños.

****

Examples of *-ar* verbs in the preterite tense : *tomé el tren :* "I took the train" ; *jugaste con él :* "you played with him" ; *habló poco :* "he/she/you spoke little" ; *cantamos :* "we sang" ; *ayer fumasteis mucho :* "you smoked a lot yesterday" ; *telefonearon tarde :* "they/you phoned late".

Examples of *-er* and *-ir* verbs in the preterite tense : *escribí ayer :* "I wrote yesterday" ; *saliste pronto :* "you went out early" ; *volvió solo :* "he/she/you came back alone" ; *creímos en él :* "we believed in him" ; *prometisteis venir :* "you promised to come" ; *lo vieron :* "they/you/saw him".

Read the examples above. They will help you recognize and use the preterite tense, and they also contain some useful vocabulary. We have already seen all these verbs in previous exercises. Have you forgotten some of them? That's quite natural, and you shouldn't worry if you have, because we'll be using them all again soon. For the time being, just try to become familiar with these verbs in their different tenses.

Lección 28

2. **Country names** : most country names are used without definite articles (e.g., *Bélgica* (pron. belHica) : Belgium ; *Suiza* : Switzerland ; *Francia* : France ; *Inglaterra* : England ; *Escocia* : Scotland ; *Italia* : Italy ; *Rusia* : Russia ; *Holanda* : Holland ; *Argelia* : Algeria ; *Marruecos* : Morocco ; *Europa* : (pron. éouropa) Europe ; *Norteamérica* : North America ; *Sudamérica* (or just *América*) : South America : *América latina* : Latin America). .

Certain exceptions, however, take a definite article (e.g., *el Japon, la Argentina, el Perú, los Estados Unidos* (the United States), *El Salvador*, etc.).

When a country name is qualified, however, it always takes the article : *la Francia del siglo XVIII (dieciocho)* : 18th Century France ; *la España de Carlos V (quinto)* : Charles the Fifth's Spain.

3. **The present participle** (see Note 1 to Lesson 24). (Also called the gerundive) Corresponding exactly to the *-ing* form in English, the present participle is used with *estar* to express the present continuous tense : *estoy hablando* : "I am speaking".

**Form : *-ar* verbs : stem + *-ando* ;
-er and *-ir* verbs : stem + *-iendo*.**

Examples : *cantar* : *cantando* ; *beber* : *bebiendo* ; *vivir* : *viviendo*.

4. **Demonstratives** (see Note 2 to Lesson 26 and Note 1 to Lesson 12). There are three demonstratives in Spanish : *este, ese,* and *aquel*. They can be adjectives or pronouns. Like other adjectives, demonstratives change form when qualifying feminine and/or plural nouns (see table below). Both masculine and feminine demonstrative pronouns carry a written accent.

Demonstrative pronouns :

Masculine	Feminine	Neuter
éste *éstos*	*ésta* *éstas*	*esto*
ése *ésos*	*ésa* *ésas*	*eso*
aquél *aquéllos*	*aquélla* *aquéllas*	*aquello*

éste : "this one" (replacing a masculine noun).

ésta : "this one" (replacing a feminine noun)
esto : "this" (indeterminate ; invariable)

ése : "that one" (replacing a masculine noun)
ésa : "that one" (replacing a feminine noun)
eso : "that" (as opposed to "this" : something close at hand)

aquel : "that one" (replacing a masculine noun)
aquella : "that one" (replacing a feminine noun)
aquello : "that" ("that over there, yonder").

Demonstrative adjectives :

Masculine	Feminine
este *estos*	*esta* *estas*
ese *esos*	*esa* *esas*
aquel *aquellos*	*aquella* *aquellas*

Remember that tables are for reference only. You shouldn't try to memorize these tables, as the words are all taken out of context. The tables will help you realize what demonstratives are and where to use them. Concentrate on the examples given in the lessons, but if you have a problem, refer back to these tables.

5. **Lo que...** "that which". *Dime lo que estas haciendo* : "Tell me what (that which) you are doing". *Lo* is the "neuter article" and is used when there is no reference to a specific noun. If, on the other hand, we are talking about a book, for instance, we use the ordinary masculine article, thus : *Dame el que te gusta"* : "give me the one you like". The same applies to feminines and/or plurals : *la que, los que, las que.*

Lección 28

6. The future tense.
The future endings are as follows :

all verbs (-ar, -er, -ir) : infinitive + é, ás, á, emos, éis, án

Examples : *tomaré el tren :* "I shall take the train" ; *jugarás con él :* "you will play with him" ; *hablará poco :* he / she / you will speak little ; *cantaremos :* "we shall sing" ; *fumaréis mucho :* "you will smoke a lot" ; *telefonearán tarde :* "they / you will phone late".

Remember that the endings given above are added to the infinitive, and not to the stem as in other tenses. (The stem is the infinitive without -ar, -er, -ir).

7. Negatives.
The simplest negative form is *no,* which always comes before the verb, thus : *no tengo tiempo :* "I haven't time".

Other negative words include *nunca, jamás :* "never", (sentence 14, Lesson 26) ; *nada :* "nothing" ; *nadie :* "nobody" (sentence 11, Lesson 22) ; *tampoco :* "neither" ; *ninguno :* "none" ; *ni :* "neither / nor" (sentence 4, Lesson 24). These words can be used before the verb, in which case they stand alone, or after the verb, in which case they need the *no* before the verb.

In Spanish, two negatives **don't** make a positive. Example : *No hemos nunca visto a nadie :* "We have never seen anybody" (literally : we haven't never seen nobody).

8. **Writing in Spanish** (second wave)

1   Was the weather good last Sunday? - Yes, we went to the beach.
2   He had been back for a week when he phoned me.
3   What are you doing? - I'm playing with the children.
4   I don't know if you will like this meal (food). - I think I'll like it.
5   You had never told me what you told me today.
6   Tomorrow I will have to get up early because I have to go on a trip. - I'll accompany you to the station.

9. **Translation**

1   ¿Hizo buen tiempo el domingo pasado? - Sí, y fuimos a la playa.
2   Hacía una semana que había vuelto cuando me telefoneó.
3   ¿Qué estás haciendo? - Estoy jugando con los niños.
4   No sé si te gustará esta comida. - Creo que me gustará.
5   Nunca me habías dicho lo que me has dicho hoy.
6   Mañana tendré que madrugar porque tengo que salir de viaje. - Te acompañaré a la estación.

Lección 28

LECCION VEINTINUEVE

Calado hasta los huesos

1 Pablo e Isabel se han dado cita a la salida del trabajo.
2 Quieren volver a casa juntos.
3 Como llueve y no tiene paraguas, Isabel decide entrar a tomar un té con Miguel en un bar. (1)
4 — Me extraña que Pablo se retrase, es siempre tan puntual...
5 — Habrá tenido, seguramente, un problema a última hora.
6 — Además, con este tiempo no se puede esperar fuera.
7 — En fin, esperemos que venga pronto.
8 — ¡Mírale! Allí llega. Parece que me busca.
9 — Sí. Es él, voy a salir a decirle que estás aquí.
10 ¡Pablo...! Isabel está dentro; como no venías, hemos entrado a tomar algo.
11 Habéis hecho bien. Yo creía que no iba a terminar nunca.
12 Empezaba a preocuparme porque no podía advertir a Isabel y no podía, tampoco, dejar el trabajo.
13 ¡Cómo llueve, estoy calado!
14 — Ven a tomar algo caliente.

PRONUNCIACION: calado ... ouéçoss 1 dado 2 volver 3 llouèvé ... paraguass ... décidé en'trar ... tomar ... miguel ... bar. 4 rétracé poun'toual 5 oultima 6 espérar fouéra. 7 fin' espérémoss ven'ga 8 miralé a/li ... bousca. 9 aki 10 den'tro ... véniass ... en'trado 11 iba terminar. 12 em'pésaba préocouparmé ... advértir. 14 calien'té.

NOTES

(1) *Paraguas* : "umbrella", the word is made up of *para-*, from the verb *parar* : "to stop" + *-aguas* : "waters". Compare *parasol*. Note the pronunciation of *Miguel* : the *u* is there to harden the *g*.

LESSON TWENTY-NINE

Soaked to the skin (soaked to the bones)

1   Pablo and Isabel have arranged to meet (have given each other appointment) after work.

2   They want to go home together.

3   As it is raining and they don't have [an] umbrella, Isabel decides to go in to take a tea with Miguel.

4   — I'm surprised (It surprises me) that Pablo is late, he's always so punctual...

5   — He will probably have had a last-minute problem.

6   Moreover, with this weather, one cannot wait outside.

7   — Anyway, let's hope that he comes (might come) soon.

8   — Look (at him)! Here he comes (There he arrives)! He seems to be looking for me (It seems that he looks for me).

9   Yes. It's him. I'm going to go out and tell him that you're here.

10   Pablo...! Isabel is inside ; as you weren't coming, we have come in for a drink (to take something).

11   — You have done well. I thought I was never going to finish.

12   I was starting to worry (myself) because I couldn't warn Isabel, and I couldn't leave (the) work either.

13   How it's raining! I'm soaked.

14   — Come to take something hot.

EJERCICIO: 1. Queríamos pasearnos juntos. **2.** Me extraña. **3.** A última hora no pude venir. **4.** Dentro hace más calor que fuera. **5.** Habéis hecho bien. **6.** Empezaba a preocuparme. **7.** Estoy calado.

EJERCICIO DE CONTROL
Ponga las palabras que faltan

1 *We want to go back together/early.*

Queremos . . . .

Queremos . . . .

2 *I'm surprised he hasn't arrived yet.*

. . . . que no haya . . . .

3 *I'm going to go out and tell him.*

Voy . . . . para . . . .

4 *You have done well/You have done what I wanted.*

. . . . bien.

. . . . quería.

5 *As he hadn't come, we left.*

. . . . nos . . . . ido.

****

LECCION TREINTA

Hacer su casa

1 — Los alumnos que he tenido este año quieren hacer una fiesta de fin de curso.

PRONUNCIACION: 1 aloum'nos ... ténido ... agno ... fiéssta ... courço

EXERCISE : **1.** We wanted to go for a walk together. – **2.** I'm surprised. – **3.** At the last minute I couldn't come. – **4.** It's warmer inside than outside. – **5.** You have done well. – **6.** I was starting to worry. – **7.** I am soaked.

* * * * *

THE MISSING WORDS :   **1** volver juntos. / volver pronto. **2** me extraña - llegado todavía. **3** a ir fuera - decírselo. **4** habéis hecho / habéis hecho lo que. **5** como no venía - hemos.

* * * * *

You will notice that the language we are using is gradually becoming more idiomatic. The literal translations of the Lessons are becoming very un-English... And you'll notice that Spanish word order is rather different from English.

Spanish verbs tend to come as soon as possible in the sentence. *(Terminada la lección, nos fuimos tomar el té :* "When the lesson was finished, we all went for tea." *Trabaja mucho mi padre :* "My father works a lot".

LESSON THIRTY

Doing up one's house

1 —   The pupils that I've had this year want to have (do)
an end-of-year (end-of-course) party.

2 Les he propuesto hacerla en nuestra casa. ¿Qué te parece?

3 — Muy bien, pero no olvides que esta semana tenemos todos los días ocupados.

4 — ¿Tanto tenemos que hacer?

5 — Si queremos que la casa esté terminada antes de irnos de vacaciones, tendremos que trabajar mucho este mes.

6 — Mañana, domingo, tenemos que raspar las dos habitaciones del segundo piso.

7 El lunes habrá que ir a comprar la madera para terminar la escalera.

8 El martes podemos pintar la cocina y una habitación. (1)

9 El miércoles la otra habitación y comenzar la escalera.

10 El jueves terminar la escalera y arreglar la chimenea.

11 El viernes estaría bien poder limpiar y ordenar un poco todo.

12 Y el sábado... el sábado todo estaría listo para hacer la fiesta.

13 — Creo que es un buen programa y, además, será la ocasión para celebrar el fin de los trabajos. (2)

14 — Pues... ¡Manos a la obra! (3)

2 propouéssto acerla 3 olvidéss 5 éssté términada ... irnoss ... tén'drémoss 6 ... domin'go ... rasspar ... ségoun'do piço 7 ésscaléra. 8 podémoss pin'tar ... cocina 9 comen'sar 10 Houévéss ... arréglar ... tchiménéa 11 viernéss ésstaria ... poder lim'piar ... ordénar 12 sabado ... lissto 13 ... programa ... ocacion ...14 obra.

NOTES
(1) Have you noticed that the definite article is used when we name the days of the week? But we don't use the article with *mañana* : "tomorrow", *ayer* : "yesterday", *pasado mañana* : "the day after tomorrow", or with *anteayer* : "the day before yesterday".
(2) *Un buen programa* : "a good programme". *Programa* is masculine despite its final -a, and the preceding adjective *bueno* therefore drops its final -o. See note 3 to Lesson 22.

2   I have proposed to them to do it in our house. What do you think of that?

3 — Very good (Very well), but don't forget that this week we have every day (all the days) occupied.

4 — Do we have so much to do?

5 — If we want the house to be (that the house be) finished before we go on holiday, we will have to work a lot this month.

6 — Tomorrow, Sunday, we have to scrape the two rooms on the second floor.

7   On (The) Monday it will be necessary to go to buy the wood to finish the stairs.

8   On Tuesday we can paint the kitchen and one room.

9   On Wednesday [we can do] the other room and begin the stairs.

10   On Thursday [we can] finish the stairs and fix the fireplace.

11   On Friday it would be good (well) to be able to clean and tidy up a little.

12   And on Saturday... on Saturday everything would be ready to have (to do) the party.

13 — I think that it's a good programme, and, moreover, it will be the occasion to celebrate the end of work(s).

14 — Right then! All hands to the pump (Hands to the work)!

NOTES
(3) *Pues* is a useful little word that is often impossible to translate. Used as a conjunction, it means "so" (with a sense of purpose), but it is often used just to cover hesitation.

EJERCICIO: 1. Los alumnos han tenido un examen. **2.** No olvides tu trabajo. **3.** Acabo de terminar de leer el libro. **4.** Mañana, sábado, tomaré un día de descanso. **5.** Esta chimenea calienta mucho. **6.** Hoy, voy a limpiar mi habitación. **7.** No voy a dejar pasar la ocasión.

EJERCICIO DE CONTROL
Ponga las palabras que faltan

1 *My friends have done up a house / My friends have had a party.*

. . . . han . . . .

. . . . han . . . .

2 *I finished the classes a month ago / a week ago.*

. . . . que . . . . cursos.

. . . . que . . . .

. . . . . .

****

LECCION TREINTA Y UNA
Las cuatro estaciones (1)

1 En primavera, la naturaleza se viste de colores.
2 Los árboles están en flor.
3 La vida resucita en los campos y los jardines florecen.
4 Los pájaros, como los niños, parecen despertarse.
5 Los armarios se vacían y se rellenan.

PRONUNCIACION: esstacioness. **1** primavéra ... natouraléça ... vissté ... coloréss **2** árboless ... flor **3** réçoucita ... Hardiness floréssen. **5** ré*ll*énan'.

EXERCISE : 1. The pupils have had an exam. – **2.** Don't forget your work. – **3.** I have just finished reading the book. – **4.** Tomorrow, Saturday, I will take a day's rest. – **5.** This fireplace heats a lot. – **6.** Today, I am going to clean my room. – **7.** I am not going to miss the opportunity (let the opportunity pass).

3 *On Wednesday it'll be necessary to go buy the paint.*

. . . . que . . . .

. . pintura.

4 *This week there is a good cinema programme.*

. . . . de

cine.

5 *Tell me (it)/Tell him so.*

. . . . . .

. . . . . .

THE MISSING WORDS : **1** mis amigos - hecho una casa / mis amigos - hecho una fiesta. **2** hace un mes - terminé los. / hace una semana - terminé los cursos. **3** el miércoles habrá - ir a comprar la. **4** esta semana hay un buen programa. **5** dímelo / díselo.

****

LESSON THIRTY-ONE

The four seasons

1   In (the) spring, nature dresses in (of) colours.
2   The trees are in flower.
3   (The) life comes back (resuscitates) in the fields and the gardens flower.
4   The birds, like the children, seem to wake (themselves) up.
5   The cupboards empty [themselves] and fill [themselves].

NOTES
(1) *Estación* has two meanings : "station" and "season".

6 El verano es la estación en la que la tierra ofrece al hombre sus frutos.
7 Es la época de la cosecha en los campos y de la recolección de la fruta. **(2)**
8 Los días son. más largos. El sol se levanta más pronto y se pone más tarde. **(3)**
9 En las ciudades, se aprovecha para coger las vacaciones. **(4)**
10 En otoño, el vino llega a las bodegas.
11 Los árboles dejan caer sus hojas.
12 Los colegiales vuelven a tomar el camino de la escuela.
13 En invierno, la vida es más lenta. La nieve reviste la tierra de blanco.
14 Todo parece reposar y, en silencio, se espera el nuevo ciclo.

6 *bé*rano... tié*rra* ofré*ce*... **o**m'bré... frou*toss* 7 **é**poca... cossé*tcha*... récolék'ción. 8 largoss... lé*van'*ta... pron'to 10 otogno... bo*dé*gass 11 caér... **o**Hass 12 ésscolaress... camino... ésscou*é*la 13 in'*bi*erno... len'ta niè*vé* révissté 14 répo*çar*... silen'cio... nou*é*bo ciclo.

*****

EJERCICIO: 1. Hoy me voy a vestir de blanco. 2. Estos árboles tienen muchas hojas. 3. Los pájaros vuelan. 4. Este verano hace mucho calor. 5. La cosecha ha sido muy buena. 6. El sol se levanta y se pone. 7. La fruta me gusta.

EJERCICIO DE CONTROL
Ponga las palabras que faltan

1 *This year, the harvest will take place (will have place) early.*

. . . . , . . cosecha tendrá lugar . . . .

6	(The) summer is the season in which the land offers to (the) man its fruits.
7	It is the period of the harvest in the fields and of the picking (collection) of the fruit.
8	The days are longer. The sun rises earlier and sets later.
9	In the towns, one takes advantage [of it] to take (the) holidays.
10	In autumn, the wine arrives in the (to the) cellars.
11	The trees lose (let drop) their leaves.
12	The schoolchildren take the road to school again.
13	In winter (the) life is slower. The snow dresses the land in (of) white.
14	Everything seems to rest and, in silence, we await a new cycle (a new cycle awaits itself).

EXERCISE : 1. Today, I am going to dress (myself) in (of) white. –
2. These trees have a lot of leaves. – **3.** Birds fly. – **4.** This summer it is very hot. – **5.** The harvest has been very good. – **6.** The sun rises and sets. – **7.** I like fruit.

NOTES

(2) *Fruta* (fem.) applies to the fruit we eat. *Fruto* means fruit in the sense of "result", as in *el fruto de mi trabajo* : "the fruit(s) of my work.

(3) The sun "gets up" like people, with the reflexive verb *levantarse*. But it doesn't "lie down", it "puts itself" : *el sol se levanta y se pone. La puesta del sol* : "the sunset".

(4) Spanish has two verbs "to take" : *coger* and *tomar*. The sense of *coger* is more physical ("to take hold of" or "to catch"), while *tomar* is more often used in phrases like *tomar un vaso de vino* : "to take a glass of wine".

(5) *Vuelvan a tomar* : "they take again". The verb *volver* can be used with any other verb to express repetition.

2 *The trees. (in) of my garden are in flower.*

. . . . de mi . . . .

3 *Today, the sun has set later than yesterday.*

. . . . se ha puesto . . . . que . . . .

4 *Each season lasts three months.*

Cada . . . . dura . . . .

* *

LECCION TREINTA Y DOS

Los puntos cardinales

1   Me gustaría conocer un poco más España.
2   He hecho un amigo que me cuenta muchas
         cosas.
3   Hoy quiero hacerle algunas preguntas sobre
         la situación geográfica de ese país, que
         tanto me hace soñar. **(1)**
4 — ¡Hola Marcos! Te estaba esperando. **(2)**
5 — He venido en cuanto he podido y te traigo
         algunos mapas. Si quieres, podemos ojear-
         los juntos. **(3)**

PRONUNCIACION: poun'tos cardinaless. **1** gousstaria. **2** couen'ta **3** prégoun'tass sobré sitouacion Héografica ... sognar. **4** marcoss ... éssphéran'do **5** podido ... traigo ... mapas ... oHéarloss.

5 *In winter it is cold / In summer it is hot.*

. .   . .   frío.

. .   . .

THE MISSING WORDS :   **1** este año la - más pronto. **2** los árboles - jardín están en flor. **3** hoy el sol - más tarde - ayer. **4** estación - tres meses. **5** en invierno hace. / en verano hace calor.

★★★★★★★★★★★★★★★★★★★★★★★★★★★★★★★★★★★★★★★

LESSON THIRTY-TWO

The cardinal points

1   I would like to know Spain a bit more.
2   I have made a friend who tells me many things.
3   Today I want to ask him questions (make questions to him) on the geographical situation of that country that makes me dream so much.
4 — Hello Marcos! I was waiting for you.
5 — I came (have come) as soon as I could (have been able) and I bring you some maps. If you want, we can look at them together.

NOTES
(1) *Hacer una pregunta :* "to ask a question" (lit. "to make a question"). We can also say *poner una pregunta :* "to put a question", e.g., *¿Puedo ponerte una pregunta? :* "Can I put a question to you?"
(2) The stress falls on the word *Marcos.*
(3) The verb *ojear* (derived from *el ojo :* "eye") means "to have a look at". *Echar una ojeada :* "to glance" (lit. "to cast a glance").

Lección 32

6 — De acuerdo. Con los mapas, será más fácil hacerme una idea.

7 — España y Portugal forman la península Ibérica.

8 En líneas generales, podemos decir que España limita:

9 Al norte con Francia y el mar Cantábrico. (4)

10 — ¿El mar Cantábrico?

11 — Sí, el mar Cantábrico es el nombre que dan los españoles

12 a esa parte del Atlántico.

13 Al sur, España limita con el mar Mediterráneo y África en general.

14 Al este, con el Mediterráneo y al oeste, con Portugal y el océano Atlántico.

6 fassil **7** portougal forman' ... penin'soula ibérica **8** linéass Hénéraless ... limita **9** ..norté ... fransia .. can'tabrico **11** nom'bré ... ésspagnoless **12** parté ... atlan'tico. **13** sour ... méditérranéo ... africa. **14** oéssté.

EJERCICIO: 1. He hecho un amigo en la playa. 2. Quería hacerle algunas preguntas. 3. He venido en cuanto he podido. 4. Vamos a echar una ojeada. 5. Me gustaría comprar algunos mapas. 6. Los puntos cardinales son: norte, sur, este y oeste.

EJERCICIO DE CONTROL
Ponga las palabras que faltan

1 *Give (fam.) me a little more money ∕ Give (pol.) me a little more money.*

. . . . de dinero.

. . . .

2 *We want to give him a present (make a present to him).*

. . . . un . . . .

6 — OK. With the maps it will be easier to get (give me) an idea.

7 — Spain and Portugal form the Iberian peninsula.

8 By and large (in general lines) we can say that Spain borders (limits) :

9 To the north with France and the Cantabrican Sea.

10 — The Cantabrican Sea?

11 — Yes. The Cantabrican Sea is the name that the Spanish give

12 to that part of the Atlantic.

13 To the south, Spain borders (limits) with the Mediterranean Sea and Africa in general.

14 To the east, with the Mediterranean and to the west, with Portugal and the Atlantic Ocean.

NOTES
(4) In ordinary Spanish, *mar* is a masculine noun *(el mar Rojo :* "the Red Sea"). But for sailors and fishermen living by the sea, it is feminine *(Alta mar, baja mar :* "high tide, low tide").

EXERCISE : 1. I have made a friend on the beach. — **2.** I wanted to ask him/you some questions. — **3.** I came as soon as I could. — **4.** Let's have a look. — **5.** I would like to buy some maps. — **6.** The cardinal points are : north, south, east and west.

3 *He came as soon as he could.*

. . . . en . . . .

4 *If you go (towards the) north, you will find the sea.*

Si . . . . encontrarás . . . . .

****

LECCION TREINTA Y TRES

Un año

1 Enero es el primer mes del año. A menudo, decimos:

2 Estamos a principios de año. **(1)**

3 Febrero es el mes más corto del año.

4 En marzo, se cierra el primer trimestre y comienza la primavera.

5 En abril, aguas mil. **(2)**

6 Mayo es el mes de las flores.

7 Junio: comienzo del verano, vacaciones escolares y fin del primer semestre.

8 Julio tiene dos significados en castellano. **(3)**

9 Agosto es el mes de la cosecha. De ahí viene la frase: "Hacer su agosto". **(4)**

10 El otoño comienza en septiembre.

11 En octubre, el tiempo es ya más gris.

12 La vida nocturna disminuye en noviembre. El año va apagándose.

13 En diciembre, entramos en invierno y nos preparamos para

14 festejar el fin de año y el año nuevo.

PRONUNCIACION: 1 énéro ... primér mess ... ménoudo décimoss. **2** prin'cipioss **3** fébréro... corto **4** março ciérra ... trimesstré ... comien'ça **5** abril ... mil. **6** maïo **7** Hounio ... sémesstré. **8** Houlio ... siHnificadoss. **9** agossto ... aï ... frassé **11** octoubré ... griss. **12** noctouna dissminouïe ... no*b*iem'bré ... apagan'doçé **13** dissiem'bré en'tramoss ... préparamoss **14** fesstéHar.

5 *It's hotter in the (to the) south than in the (to the) north.*

. . . . calor . . . . . que al . . . . .

THE MISSING WORDS : 1 dame un poco más. / déme (ou dadme) un poco más de dinero. 2 queremos hacerle - regalo. 3 vino - cuanto pudo. 4 vas hacia el norte - el mar. 5 hace más - al sur - norte.

****

LESSON THIRTY-THREE

A year

1　January is the first month of the year. Often, we say :
2　We are at [the] beginning(s) of [the] year.
3　February is the shortest month of the year.
4　In March the first quarter closes (itself) and the spring begins.
5　"April showers"
6　May is the month of the flowers.
7　June : start of the summer, school holidays and end of the first semester.
8　July has two meanings in Spanish.
9　August is the month of the harvest. From there comes the phrase *"Hacer su agosto"*
10　The autumn starts in September.
11　In October the weather is already greyer.
12　Night life diminishes in November. The year carries on extinguishing itself.
13　In December, we enter winter and prepare ourselves (for) to
14　celebrate the end of (the) year and the New Year.

NOTES
(1) *Principio* means both "beginning" and "principle".
(2) *En abril, aguas mil* is a proverb. A literal translation would be "In April, waters thousand (waters by the thousand)".
(3) *Julio* is also a boy's name.
(4) *Hacer su agosto* : "to get rich" (lit. "to do one's August").

EJERCICIO: 1. Fiestas de principios de año. 2. Este trimestre me ha parecido corto. 3. Dicen que en abril llueve mucho. 4. Este semestre tendremos más vacaciones 5. Esta ciudad tiene mucha vida nocturna 6. Aquel invierno fue más frío. 7. Fiestas de fin de año.

EJERCICIO DE CONTROL
Ponga las palabras que faltan

1 *Last winter it snowed often/it was very cold.*

. . . . nevó . . . .

. . . . hizo . . . .

2 *We have just started the new year.*

. . . . de comenzar . . . .

3 *This summer it has been very hot.*

. . . . mucho . . . . .

4 *Will you be able to come next summer?*

¿ . . . . el . . . . ?

5 *We will do the end-of-year party together.*

Haremos . . . . de . . . .

****

LECCION TREINTA Y CUATRO

El color

1 — Háblame de los colores.
2 — Haremos una frase para cada color y tú los combinarás luego. (1)

PRONUNCIACION: 1 ablamé. 2 arémoss ... com'binarass.

EXERCISE : **1.** Beginning of the year celebrations. – **2.** This quarter has seemed short to me. – **3.** They say that in April it rains a lot. – **4.** This semester we will have more holidays. – **5.** This town has a lot of night life. – **6.** That winter was colder. – **7.** End-of-year parties.

THE MISSING WORDS :   **1** el invierno pasado - a menudo. / el invierno pasado - mucho frío. **2** acabamos - el nuevo año. **3** este verano ha hecho - calor. **4** podrás venir - verano próximo. **5** la fiesta de fin - año juntos.

* *

LESSON THIRTY-FOUR

(The) colour

1 — Talk to me of (the) colours.
2 — We will make a sentence for each colour and you will put them together after(wards).

NOTES
(1) The use of *tú* here is to add emphasis. As we saw in Lesson 2, Spanish personal pronouns are only ever used for added emphasis.

3   En **Africa**, hay una mayoría negra.

4   El color de la sangre de todos los hombres es rojo.

5   La esperanza se representa con el color de los árboles: el verde. **(2)**

6   Amarillo es el color del sol.

7   Gris el del tiempo de lluvia.

8   "La vida en rosa" **(3)** es una canción de Edith Piaf.

9   El color castaño, es el que generalmente llamamos marrón,

10   palabra que se ha convertido en un galicismo muy empleado

11   en todas las partes de España. **(4)**

12   Tus ojos tienen el color del cielo y el mar: son azules.

13   La nieve es blanca.

14   La lista de los colores es inmensa, pero puedes obtener muchos mezclando los que hemos enumerado. **(5)**

3 maïoria. 4 san'gré 5 esspérança ... répréçen'ta ... vérdé. 6 amaril/o 7 l/ouvia. 8 roça ... can'cion. 9 casstagno ... marron'. 10 palabra con'bértido ... galicissmo ... ém'pléado. 12 oHoss ... ciélo ... açuless. 14 in'men'sa ... obténer ... méç'clan'do ... énoumérado.

NOTES

(2) Reflexive verbs are commonly used to replace the passive. "It is represented" thus becomes *se representa* : literally "it represents itself". From now on, we will no longer explain this every time. See also sentence 10 : *se ha convertido* : "has been converted".

(3) This is a translation of the original French title of the song "La vie en rose". By rights, "pink" in Spanish should be *de color de rosa.* The word *de* translates the English "in" in sentences like "I have painted the table in blue" : *he pintado la mesa de azul.*

* * * * *

EJERCICIO: 1. Tú ves siempre todo de color de rosa. **2.** Este gris no me gusta. **3.** No bromees. **4.** Tenemos que elegir un color. **5.** Yo prefiero el verde o el amarillo. **6.** Dame mi camisa azul. **7.** Mezclando el rojo y el blanco he obtenido el rosa.

3   In Africa there is a black majority.
4   The colour of (the) blood of all men is red.
5   Hope is represented (represents itself) by (with) the colour of the trees : (the) green.
6   Yellow is the colour of the sun.
7   Grey the one of (the) rainy weather.
8   "La vie en rose" is a song by (of) Edith Piaf.
9   The colour chestnut is the one that we generally call *"marrón"* (brown)
10   [a] word that has been converted into a very common gallicism
11   all over Spain.
12   Your eyes have the colour of the sky and the sea : they are blue.
13   The snow is white.
14   The list of the colours is huge (immense), but you can obtain many [of them] [by] mixing the ones that we have enumerated.

NOTES
(4) *En todas las partes* : everywhere.
(5) *Mezclando* : "mixing". The present participle can be used as a complete phrase (e.g., by mixing, while mixing, on mixing, etc.), without adding a preposition.

EXERCISE : 1. You always see everything in pink. – 2. I don't like this grey. – 3. Don't joke. – 4. We have to choose a colour. – 5. I prefer green or yellow. – 6. Give me my blue shirt. – 7. By mixing red and white, I have obtained pink.

Lección 34

EJERCICIO DE CONTROL
Ponga las palabras que faltan

1 *Nature is a symphony of colours.*

. . . . sinfonía   . .

. . . . . .

2 *In spring many fruits are still green.*

. .   . .   muchas   . . . .

. . . .

****

LECCION TREINTA Y CINCO

LESSON THIRTY-FIVE

Revisión y notas

1. **Pronunciation.** Remember the rule for the letter *c* : when it comes before an *e* or an *i*, it is pronounced like the "th" sound in "thank you". Everywhere else it is hard, like a "k". Practice with the following examples : *lección, tercera, cinco, conocer, decimos, principio, vacaciones, hacer, fácil*. The letter *z* is always pronounced like a "th". *Zaragoza, calzados*. This lisping sound is peculiar to Castilian Spanish, and exists neither in the South of Spain, nor in Latin America, where it is replaced by the straightforward "s" sound.

2. **The infinitive is preceded by the word *a*** after a verb of movement. Thus, "I am going to buy a book" becomes *voy a comprar un libro,* since *ir* is a verb of movement. In other cases, there are no absolute rules for which preposition to use.

3 *I like the colours of your house.*

. .   . . , ...

4 *What colour are you going to paint your room?*

¿ . .   . .   pintar   . .

. . . . ?

5 *I'd like to paint it white.*

Quisiera   . . . .   de   . . . . .

THE MISSING WORDS :   **1** la naturaleza es una - de colores. **2** en primavera - frutas están todavía verdes. **3** me gustan los colores de tu casa. **4** de qué color vas a - tu habitación. **5** pintarla - blanco.

* *

A MÍ, ME GUSTAN LAS MANZANAS ROJAS

3. Acabar : "to finish", synonymous with *terminar*. Recently, we've seen sentences containing this verb followed by the preposition *de*. In these cases, the verb means "to have just...", thus : *acabo de llegar :* "I have just arrived", *acabamos de terminar :* "we have just finished".

Lección 35

4. Direct object with *a*. When the direct object is a person (or a personified thing), it must be preceded by *a*. Thus, *espero a un amigo* : "I am waiting for a friend", but *espero un tren* : "I am waiting for a train".

Querer means "to want" when it is used without the *a* : *mi amiga quiere un niño* ; but is means "to love" when used with the direct person object *a* : *quiere a los niños*. ("he / she / you love(s) children").

5. Numbers. Have you been reading the page numbers? If so, you will already know how to count beyond a hundred! There are a number of peculiarities : *ciento* ("a hundred") drops the final *-to* when it comes before a noun, or before *mil* ("thousand"), or before *millon* ("million"). "200, 300...", on the other hand, retain their endings, and the endings agree with the nouns they are qualifying, thus : *doscientos libros* ("200 books"), *cuatrocientas pesetas* ("400 pesetas").

    500 : *quinientos*
    700 : *setecientos*

    1,000 : *mil,* but *millares de aviones :* thousands of planes.
1,000,000 : *un millón*

6. En cuanto... (see sentence 5, Lesson 32)
Cuanto usually means "how much" or "how many" : *¿Cuanto le debo? :* "How much is that?" (lit. "How much do I owe you?"). However, in certain expressions, the word *cuanto* is used idiomatically, e.g., *en cuanto he podido :* "as soon as I could".

7. Writing in Spanish (second wave)

1   Will you come to wait for me after work if it isn't raining?
2   This month, I haven't gone out of my house often. - Neither have I.

* *

3 Do you want us to go see the sunset together?
4 I'd like to ask you (polite, sing.) some questions. Do you agree?
5 This quarter I have been very tired. - So have I.
6 This fruit is green. - I like red apples.

8. Translation

1 ¿Vendrás a esperarme a la salida del trabajo si no llueve?
2 Este mes, no he salido a menudo de mi casa. - Yo tampoco.
3 ¿Quieres que vayamos a ver la puesta de sol juntos?
4 Quisiera hacerle algunas preguntas. ¿Está de acuerdo?
5 Este trimestre me he cansado mucho. - Yo también.
6 Esta fruta está verde. - Me gustan les manzanas rojas.

*****

Every day we introduce something new. But we always go back over what we've seen (especially in the second wave). In this way, you will find it easier to remember what you've learnt in each lesson, and it'll all fall into place in the end!

*****

So far we've done thirty-five lessons. Your knowledge of Spanish is probably still a bit sketchy, but don't worry. Rome wasn't built in a day!

****

LECCION TREINTA Y SEIS

Después del viaje

1 — ¿Os habéis fijado en el paisaje? **(1)**
2 — Acabamos de llegar y todavía no hemos visto gran cosa.
3 Pero lo poco que hemos visto desde el coche, nos ha parecido maravilloso.
4 — Yo, como conducía, no me he fijado mucho.
5 — ¿Es la primera vez que venís aquí?
6 — Sí. No conocíamos esta región.
7 — Si no estáis demasiado cansados del viaje, podemos ir a dar un pequeño paseo. **(2)**
8 — Me han dicho que cerca de aquí hay un manantial.
9 — ¿Podrías acompañarnos hasta allí?

¡FÍJATE EN LO QUE COMES!

10 — ¡Claro que sí! Además no está muy lejos.
11 De paso, os enseñaré la gruta.¡Ya veréis, es fantástica! **(3)**
12 Esperad un momento, voy a coger mi linterna.
13 La gruta es muy oscura y quiero que veáis el río subterráneo.
14 ¡Ya está! ¡En marcha!

PRONUNCIACION: viaHé **1** fiHado ... païçaHé **3** parécido maravi/oço **4** con'doucia **5** priméra beç ... béniss **6** conociamoss **7** démassiado ... passéo **8** ditcho ... manan'tial **9** podriass acom'pagnarnoss **11** passo ... en'ségnaré ... grouta ... véréiss ... fan'tastica **12** esspéra (d) ... momen'to ... lin'térna **13** oscoura ... véaiss ... rio soubtérranéo **14** martcha.

LESSON THIRTY-SIX

After the trip

1 — Did you pay attention to the countryside?
2 — We have just arrived and have still not seen much (great thing).
3 — But the little (that) we have seen from the car has seemed marvellous to us.
4 — As I was driving, I didn't see much.
5 — Is it the first time that you come here?
6 — Yes. We didn't know this region.
7 — If you're not too tired by (of) the trip, we can go for a little walk.
8 — They have told me that close to here there is a spring.
9 — Could you (Would you be able to) accompany us (until) there?
10 — Of course! Besides, it isn't very far.
11 — On the way (On passing), I will show you the grotto. You will see (already) - it's fantastic!
12 — Wait a moment, I'm going to get (take) my torch.
13 — The grotto is very dark and I want you to see (that you might see) the underground river.
14 — OK! Off we go!

*****

NOTES
(1) *Fijarse* is commonly used in the sense of "to look" or "to pay attention" (see sentence 4). Another common expression is ¡*fíjate!* : "fancy that" or "would you believe it!" (lit. "look!").
(2) *El paseo* is a Spanish institution : the late afternoon walk, very often taken on *el paseo* (the main stretch or promenade). Notice that the verb *dar* : "to give" is used with this word : thus, "to go for a walk" is *dar un paseo* (or *pasearse*).
(3) *Enseñar* has three meanings : "to show", "to teach" and "to learn".

EJERCICIO: 1. ¿Te has fijado? **2.** Acabamos de llegar. **3.** ¿Quién conducía? **4.** Vamos a dar un paseo. **5.** De paso, te enseñaré el jardín. **6.** Esperad un momento. **7.** ¡En marcha!

EJERCICIO DE CONTROL
Ponga las palabras que faltan

1 *Pay attention to what you say.*

. . . . . . en . . . . . . dices.

2 *On Sunday, you were driving a red car.*

. . . . tú . . . .

3 *I am too tired to go for a walk.*

. . . . a

. . . .

****

LECCION TREINTA Y SIETE

Voy a poner la mesa

1 — ¿Cuántos seremos hoy a comer?
2 — Cinco o seis, porque no sé si Eduardo ha invitado a una amiga de clase.
3 — Bueno, voy a poner seis cubiertos por si acaso viene su amiga. **(1)**
4 — Pon el mantel que está sobre la silla, está recién planchado. **(2)**

PRONUNCIACION: 1 sérémoss **2** édouardo **3** coubiértoss ... acaço **4** pon' ... man'tél ... si/la ... récién' plan'tchado

*****

EXERCISE : 1. Have you seen? – **2.** We have just arrived. – **3.** Who was driving? – **4.** We are going for a walk. – **5.** On the way past, I'll show you the garden. – **6.** Wait a moment. – **7.** Off we go!

* * * * *

4 *They (had) told me that you weren't going to come.*

Me . . . . no . . . . . venir.

5 *If you (fam. plural) are not in a hurry, wait a moment.*

Si no . . . . , ...

THE MISSING WORDS : **1** fíjate - lo que. **2** el domingo - conducías un coche rojo. **3** estoy demasiado cansado para ir - pasearme. **4** habían dicho que - ibas a. **5** tenéis prisa, esperad un momento.

* *

LESSON THIRTY-SEVEN

I am going to set the table

1 — How many will we be today to eat?
2 — Five or six, because I don't know if Eduardo has invited a schoolfriend (friend of class).
3 — Good, I'm going to set six places (covers) just in case his friend comes.
4 — Put [on] the tablecloth that is on the chair. It has just been ironed.

NOTES
(1) *Por si acaso :* "just in case".
(2) *Recién,* the contracted form of *recientemente* ("recently") is used before past participles. Notice that the meaning is the same as *acabar de...* We'll see more about this in the next revision lesson.

5   Voy a preguntarle a Jerónimo si quiere ayudarte; así, todo estará listo enseguida.

6 — Yo voy a ir poniendo los platos. (3)

7 — ¡Jerónimo! ¿Quieres llevar al comedor seis cuchillos, seis tenedores y seis cucharillas?

8   Marcelo está poniendo la mesa y necesita ayuda.

9 — Voy a coger la bandeja y, de paso, llevaré los vasos y el pan.

10   Dile a Marcelo que las servilletas están en el cajón de la derecha.

11 — Creo que sólo falta el agua y el vino.

12 — Inés ha ido a buscar algunas flores y dos velas.

13 — Me gusta comer en una mesa preparada con gusto.

14 — Y tienes razón, la comida es mejor.

5 Héromino ... aïoudarté ... en´séguida 6 poniénˊdo ... platoss. 7 //évar ... comédor ... coutchi//oss ... ténédoréss ... coutchari//ass 8 marcélo 9 bandéHa panˊ 10 dilé ... servi//étass 11 solo falta 12 inéss ... bélass 13 goussta 14 raçon.

EJERCICIO: 1. ¿Quieres poner la mesa? 2. ¿Cuántos cubiertos pongo? 3. Pon el mantel y las servilletas rojas. 4. Esas flores están recién cogidas 5. Telefonéame antes por si acaso no puedo venir. 6. ¿Quieres ayudarme? 7. Esta mesa está puesta con mucho gusto.

EJERCICIO DE CONTROL
Ponga las palabras que faltan

1 *How many of us are invited to the party?*

¿ . . . . de entre . . . .

. . . . ?

5   I am going to ask (to him) (to) Jerónimo if he wants to help you ; thus, everything will be ready straight away.

6 — I am going to carry on putting on the plates.

7 — Jerónimo! Will you (Do you want to) bring to the dining room six knives, six forks and six teaspoons?

8   Marcelo is setting the table and needs help.

9 — I'm going to get the tray, and, on the way past, I'll bring the glasses and the bread.

10   Tell (him) (to) Marcelo that the napkins (serviettes) are in the right-hand drawer.

11 — I think that only the water and the wine are missing.

12 — Inés has gone to look for some flowers and two candles.

13 — I like to eat on a table prepared with taste.

14 — And you are right, the meal is better.

NOTES
(3) *Ir* followed by a gerundive can express continuation of actions or movements.

EXERCISE : 1. Will you set the table? – **2.** How many places do [should] I set? – **3.** Put on the tablecloth and the red napkins (serviettes). – **4.** These flowers have just been picked. – **5.** Phone me beforehand, just in case I can't come. – **6.** Will you help me? – **7.** This table is set with a lot of taste.

Lección 37

2 *The knives and forks (covers) are in the left-hand drawer.*

. . .   .

. .   . .

3 *Will you help me (to) carry the chairs?*

¿ . . . . llevar   . . .   . ?

****

LECCION TREINTA Y OCHO

En el mercado

1 De vez en cuando, me gusta ir al mercado. **(1)**

2 Hay un ambiente muy particular y muy diferente del que se encuentra en las tiendas de cada barrio.

3 Olores y voces se entremezclan formando un todo muy animado. **(2)**

4 Pero... allí oigo vocear a una pescadera. Voy a ver qué pescado tiene. **(3)**

5 — ¡Sardinas frescas! ¡Recién llegadas esta mañanita! **(4)**

PRONUNCIACION: 2 am'bien'té ... diféren'té ... tien'dass ... barrio. **3** oloréss ... vocéss ... en'trémeç'clan' ... animado. **4** oïgo vocéar ... pesscadéra **5** sardinass frésscass ... magnanita

*****

4 *Only you were missing.*

Sólo . . . .

5 *The meal that you had prepared us was very good.*

. . . . tú nos . . . .

. . . .

THE MISSING WORDS : **1** cuántos - nosotros han sido invitados a la fiesta. **2** los cubiertos están en el cajón de la izquierda. **3** quieres ayudarme a - las sillas. **4** faltabas tú. **5** la comida que - habías preparado estaba muy buena.

****

LESSON THIRTY-EIGHT

At the market
1 From time to time I like to go to the market.
2 There is a very special atmosphere, very different from the one that is found in the shops of each neighbourhood.
3 Smells and voices mix (themselves) together forming a very lively (animated) whole.
4 But... there I hear a fishwife shouting. I'm going to see what fish she has.
5 — Fresh sardines! Just arrived this morning!

NOTES
(1) *De vez en cuando :* "from time to time".
(2) *Voces :* "voices" ; *la voz :* "the voice" ; *vocear* (sentence 4) : "to shout something out" *(vocear los periódicos :* lit. "to shout out the newspapers"). *No deis voces :* "don't shout".
(3) *Oír :* "to hear" ; *oigo :* "I hear". The imperative ¡*oiga!* is used when making telephone calls (lit. "hear [me]"), the response being ¡*diga!* ("tell [me]"). Note that verbs of perception (seeing, hearing, feeling, etc.), followed by the "-ing" form in English are followed by the straight infinitive in Spanish. Example : "I saw you coming" : *Te vi venir.* Also, "I can't hear you" would most commonly be "I don't hear you" in Spanish : *no te oigo.* *Pescado* is the word for a fish once it has been caught. Otherwise, use *pez* (masc.)
(4) Remember the use of *recién* with a past participle. We'll go over this again in Lesson 42.
Esta mañanita : "early this morning" (familiar). Almost any noun can take the diminutive ending *-ito* or *-ita.*

6 ¡Buenos días, señor! ¿Qué desea? ¡Todo es fresco!

7 — Quisiera medio kilo de anchoas y una raja de merluza. **(5).**

8 Luego iré a la carnicería y a la charcutería pero antes voy a comprar huevos y fruta.

9 — Buenos días, señora. Quisiera medio kilo de naranjas y tres o cuatro limones.

10 — ¿Algo más?

11 — Sí, un kilo de uvas y unos trescientos cincuenta gramos de cerezas para hacer un pastel.

12 Eso es todo. ¿Cuánto es?

13 — Trescientas veintisiete pesetas.

14 — Adiós y gracias.

15 — A usted.

6 deçea 7 médio kilo ... an'tchoass ... raHa ... merlouça 8 carniçéria ... tcharcoutéria ... ouévoss 9 naran'Has ... limonéss 11 ouvass ... tresscien'tass cin'couen'ta gramoss ... céréçass ... passtél.

EJERCICIO: 1. Vamos a verle de vez en cuando. 2. En su barrio, hay muchas tiendas. 3. Me gusta el olor de estas naranjas. 4. No te oigo bien. 5. ¿Algo más? 6. Eso es todo. 7. ¿Cuánto es?

EJERCICIO DE CONTROL
Ponga las palabras que faltan :

1 *From time to time you go to see them / we eat fish.*

. . . .

. . . .

2 *In your neighbourhood there is a lot of atmosphere.*

. . . .

3 *The market is always very animated.*

. . . . . . está siempre . . . .

| 6 | | Good day, sir. What do you wish? Everything is fresh. |

6   Good day, sir. What do you wish? Everything is fresh.

7 — I would like half [a] kilo of anchovies and a slice of hake.

8   Afterwards (Then) I will go to the butcher's and to the pork butcher's but before [hand] I am going to buy [some] eggs and [some] fruit.

9 — Good day, Madam. I would like half [a] kilo of oranges and four lemons.

10 — Anything else?

11 — Yes, a kilo of grapes and about three hundred [and] fifty grammes of cherries to make a cake.

12   That is all. How much is it?

13 — Three hundred [and] twenty-seven pesetas.

14 — Goodbye and thank you.

15 — Thank you (To you).

NOTES
(5) *Quisiera* is a useful way of saying "I would like". We could also say *me gustaría* ("it would please me"), but *quisiera* is more common and more elegant. In fact it is the imperfect subjunctive of *querer :* "to want".

* * * * *

EXERCISE : **1.** We go to see him from time to time. — **2.** In his neighbourhood there are lots of shops. — **3.** I like the smell of these oranges. — **4.** I can't hear you well. — **5.** Anything else? — **6.** That is all. — **7.** How much is it?

4 *Do you wish anything else?*

¿ . . . . ?

5 *How much is that?*

¿ . . . . ?

★★

LECCION TREINTA Y NUEVE

Vestirse

1 — ¿Qué hace ahí toda esa ropa ? **(1)**
2 — No te preocupes por todo ese desorden.
3 Como empieza a hacer frío, he comenzado a sacar la ropa de invierno. **(2)**
4 Esta tarde lavaré y guardaré una parte de la ropa de verano.
5 Y mañana iremos a comprar unos pantalones para ti, que... ¡buena falta te hacen! **(3)**
6 — Yo prefiero ir el domingo al Rastro para poder comprarlos más baratos. **(4)**
7 — Tú, siempre estás haciendo economías, pero tienes razón.
8 Si todos hicieran como tú, la vida no estaría tan cara.
9 Pruébate esta chaqueta, creo que ya no te vale. **(5)**

PRONUNCIACION: vésstirssé 1 ropa 2 déssorden' 3 em'piéça ... sacar 4 lavaré ... gouardaré ... parté. 5 pan'taloness 6 préfiéro ... rasstro 7 économiass 8 iciéran 9 prouébaté ... tchakéta ... valé

THE MISSING WORDS : **1** de vez en cuando, vas a verlos / de vez en cuando comemos pescado. **2** en tu barrio hay mucho ambiente. **3** el mercado - muy animado. **4** desea usted algo más. **5** cuánto es.

****

LESSON THIRTY-NINE

Dressing (oneself)

1 — What are all these clothes doing here?
2 — Don't worry about (for) all this mess (disorder).
3 As it's starting to be (to make) cold, I have begun to get out the winter clothes.
4 This afternoon I will wash [them] and I will put away some of the summer clothes.
5 And tomorrow we will go to buy some (pairs of) trousers for you... you could do with them! (that they make a good lack to you).
6 — I prefer to go to the Rastro on Sunday so that I can buy them cheaper.
7 — You're always making savings, but you're right.
8 If everyone did like you, (the) life wouldn't be so expensive.
9 Try this jacket, I don't think it fits you any more.

NOTES
(1) *Ropa :* "clothing". *El abrigo es ropa de invierno :* "the coat is winter clothing". *Ropa blanca :* "linen" ; *ropa de cama :* "bedclothes".
(2) *Empezar* and *comenzar* both mean "to start" or "to begin".
(3) *Un pantalon :* "a pair of trousers".
(4) *El rastro :* "the trace". Here, *El Rastro* is the name given to the fleamarket.
(5) *Valer* is a word with many meanings. Literally, it means "to be worth" (*¿Cuándo vale? :* "how much is it worth" or "how much is it?"). Here, however, it is used in the sense of "to be useful" (*No te vale :* "it's no use to you").
Remember also that the word *vale* is a very common way of saying "OK" or "that's right".

10 — Me está demasiado corta, pero no la tires.
  (6)
11   Se la voy a dar a Daniel y a Lidia ya que
     tienen la misma talla.
12 — ¿Te acuerdas de este vestido? Hace años
     que no me lo pongo.
13 — Póntelo, a mí me gusta mucho.
14 — Es una pena que no tenga zapatos y medias
     que vayan con él.

10 corta ... tiréss
11 daniél ... lidia ... ta//a. **12** vésstido ... pon'go **13** pon'télo **14** péna ...
ten'ga zapatoss ... vaïan'.

EJERCICIO: **1.** ¿Qué haces ahí? **2.** Estos días ha
comenzado a hacer más frío. **3.** He empezado a escribir a
Roberto. **4.** Pruébate esta camisa. **5.** Este vestido es
demasiado largo para mí. **6.** Prefiero comprar una talla
más pequeña **7.** Quiero unos zapatos negros.

EJERCICIO DE CONTROL
Ponga las palabras que faltan :

1 *Today I am going to dress in white.*

. . . .

2 *Tomorrow I have to wash a lot of clothes.*

. . . .

3 *My trousers are too long for you.*

. . . .

para ti.

4 *Later you will try the jacket that I have bought you.*

Luego te . . . .

comprado.

10 — It is too short for me (to me), but don't throw it away.
11 I'm going to give it (to them) to Daniel and to Lidia since they take (have) the same size.
12 — Do you remember this dress? I haven't worn it for years (It makes years that I don't put it on).
13 — Put it on, I like it a lot.
14 — It's a pity (a pain) that I don't have shoes and stockings that go with it.

NOTAS
(6) *Me está bien, mejor :* "it suits me well, better".

EXERCISE : 1. What are you doing there? – **2.** These days it has started to get colder. – **3.** I have started to write to Roberto. – **4.** Try on this shirt. – **5.** This dress is too long for me. – **6.** I prefer to buy a smaller size. – **7.** I want some black shoes.

5 *It's a pity that it's raining.*

. . . . que llueva.

THE MISSING WORDS : **1** hoy voy a vestirme de blanco. **2** mañana tengo que lavar mucha ropa. **3** mis pantalones son demasiado largos. **4** probarás la chaqueta que te he. **5** es una pena.

LECCION CUARENTA

La televisión

1 — ¿Qué lees?
2 — Estoy echando una ojeada al programa de televisión. (1)
3 — ¿Hay algo interesante?
4 — Hasta ahora, no·he encontrado nada que valga la pena. (2)
5 — Mira a ver lo que ponen en la cuarta cadena.
6 — ¡Hombre! Esta noche, ponen "Tiempos modernos" de Charlie Chaplin. (3)
7 — Ya la he visto pero me gustaría verla de nuevo.
8 — Me encantan las películas de Charlot. (4)
9 — Podemos telefonear a Susana, a Clemente y a Rosa y proponerles que cenemos juntos.
10 — Y luego, podríamos reunirnos con Vicente y ver la película en su casa.
11 — Muy bien. Un poco de "tele" no está tampoco mal.
12 — ¡Claro que no!

Inocencia

13 — Niños, apagad la televisión e id a acostaros.
14 — Mamá... por favor, deja que nos quedemos dos o tres muertos más.

PRONUNCIACION: téléviçion' 1 léess. 2 étchan'do. 3 in'téréçanté 4 balga. 5 cadéna. 6 modérnoss. 8 pélicoulass tcharlo. 9 souçana ... clémen'te ... proponerless ... cénémos. 10 réounirnos ... bicen'té 11 télé. inocen'cia. 13 apagad ... acosstaross. 14 kédémoss ... mouértoss.

LESSON FORTY

The television

1 — What are you reading?
2 — I'm having a look at the TV Times.
3 — Is there anything interesting?
4 — So far (Until now), I haven't found anything (nothing) that is worthwhile.
5 — Look what's on Channel Four (Look to see what they put on the fourth channel)
6 — Well! Tonight they're showing (they put) "Modern Times" by Charlie Chaplin.
7 — I've already seen it, but I'd like to see it again.
8 I adore the films of Charlie Chaplin.
9 — We can phone (to) Susana, (to) Clemente and (to) Rosa and propose (to them) that we dine together.
10 And afterwards, we could join up with Vicente and watch (see) the film at his house.
11 — Very well. A bit of "telly" isn't bad either.
12 — Of course it isn't!

Innocence

13 — Children, turn off the television and go to bed.
14 — Mummy... please, let us stay (let that we might stay) for two or three more dead men.

NOTES
(1) *Programa* : (masc.) "program", or "programme" in the sense of schedule. A TV programme can also be *una emisión de televisión.*
(2) *No vale la pena* : "it isn't worth the trouble". *No vale nada* : "it's worth nothing".
(3) *¡Hombre!* is a common exclamation, even when addressing women!
(4) *Charlot* : the popular name for Charlie Chaplin in Spanish (and other languages).

EJERCICIO: 1. ¿Qué leías ayer? **2.** ¿Ponen alguna película interesante? **3.** Hasta ahora no he tenido tiempo. **4.** Yo no he apagado la televisión. **5.** Quédate con nosotros. **6.** Me han propuesto un nuevo trabajo. **7.** Hoy he visto de nuevo a Juan.

EJERCICIO DE CONTROL
Ponga las palabras que faltan

1 *Tomorrow I will read the newspaper when I leave work.*

. . . .

. . . .

2 *I watched a very interesting programme on television.*

. . . . en la . . . .

. . . .

3 *Television is a means of communication.*

. . . .

. . . .

****

LECCION CUARENTA Y NUNA

Una carta

1 — Me parece que han llamado a la puerta. **(1)**
2 — Yo no he oído nada, pero es posible.

PRONUNCIACION: pouérta 2 oído

EXERCISE : 1. What were you reading yesterday? – **2.** Is there an interesting film on? – **3.** So far I haven't had time. – **4.** I haven't turned off the television. – **5.** Stay with us. – **6.** I have been offered a new job. – **7.** I saw Juan again today.

4 *Later you will realize.*

. . . .

5 *The film that we saw yesterday was very good.*

. . . .
. . . . .

THE MISSING WORDS : **1** mañana leeré el periódico a la salida del trabajo. **2** he visto - televisión un programa muy interesante. **3** la televisión es un medio de comunicación. **4** más tarde te darás cuenta. **5** la película que vimos ayer era muy buena.

****

LESSON FORTY-ONE

A letter

1 — I think (It seems to me) that someone (they) knocked (called) at the door.
2 — I didn't hear anything (nothing), but it is possible.

NOTES
(1) *Llamar :* "to call" ; *me llamo Juan :* "My name is Juan" or literally, "I am called Juan".

3   Tenemos que llamar al electricista para que
    venga a arreglarnos el timbre. **(2)**
4 — Voy a abrir.
5 — Buenas tardes. ¿Señores de Vázquez?
6 — Sí, aquí es.
7 — Esta carta certificada es para ustedes.
8   ¿Puede firmar aquí, por favor?
9 — Por supuesto, pase un momento, voy a
    coger un bolígrafo.
10 — ¿Quién es?
11 — El cartero, trae una carta para nosotros.
12 — ¿De dónde viene?
13 — No lo sé, ahora mismo lo miramos, pero
    antes voy a firmar porque el cartero está
    esperando en el pasillo.
14   ¡Vaya! Ahora no sé donde he dejado el
    bolígrafo.

3 élék'tricissta ... ben'ga ... tim'bré 4 abrir. 5 vaçkec 7 certificada 8 firmar 9 soupouessto paçé ... boligrafo 11 cartéro 13 passi//o 14 vaïa ... déHado.

EJERCICIO: 1. Llaman a la puerta. 2. Voy a abrir. 3. ¿Cómo firmas tú? 4. Pasad un momento. 5. Déjame un bolígrafo. 6. Tus cartas nos gustan. 7. Esperé en el pasillo.

EJERCICIO DE CONTROL
Ponga las palabras que faltan

1 *The electrician is going to come to repair the bell.*

. . electricista . . . .

. . . .

2 *Open the door.*

. . . .

3		We have to call (to) the electrician for him to come (so that he might come) to fix (for us) the bell.
4	—	I'm going to open [the door].
5	—	Good afternoon(s). Mr and Mrs (Messrs.) de Vasquez?
6	—	Yes, it's here.
7	—	This registered letter is for you.
8	—	Can you sign here, please?
9	—	Of course, come in (pass) a moment, I'll go and get (I'm going to get) a ballpoint pen.
10	—	Who is it?
11	—	The postman. He has brought (He brings) a letter for us.
12	—	Where is it from?
13	—	I don't know (it). We['ll] look at it right now, but first (before) I'm going to sign, because the postman is waiting in the corridor.
14		Damn! Now I don't know where I've put the biro.

NOTES

(2) *Arreglar* ("to fix") is connected with *una regla :* "a rule". (cf. "to put something straight"). *Reparar* also exists.

EXERCISE : 1. Someone's knocking at the door. – **2.** I'll go and open up. – **3.** How do you sign? – **4.** Come in a moment. – **5.** Give me a ballpoint pen – **6.** We like your letters. – **7** I waited in the corridor.

3 *I have received a registered letter.*

. .   recibido   . . .   .

4 *I have to buy myself a biro.*

. . . .   : . . . .

****

LECCION CUARENTA Y DOS

LESSON FORTY-TWO

Revisión y notas

1. **A verb is a verb,** and should never be split up by a personal pronoun. Thus, "You have seen" is *Usted ha visto,* and "Have you seen?" is the same, *¿Usted ha visto?* or *¿Ha visto usted?.* The pronoun would never go straight after the auxiliary as it does in English questions.

2. **The passive** is very often avoided in Spanish, and expressed with some imaginary agent or "doer of the action". We can do this in English, too : "they called me to tell me...", where "they" is the collective impersonal outside. *On* in French is used in the same way. The Spanish pronoun *se* can be translated by "one", but this "one" is, like "they"

5 *Sign here, please.*

. . . .

THE MISSING WORDS : **1** el - va a venir para arreglar el timbre. **2** ábreme la puerta. **3** he - una carta certificada. **4** tengo que comprarme un bolígrafo. **5** firme aquí, por favor.

* *

above, an undefined agent. (e.g., *se dice que tiene dos mujeres :* "they say he has two wives" (or "he is said to have [passive] two wives"). "One eats very well in this restaurant" or the more familiar "you eat very well here" would also be expressed in Spanish using *se : Se come bien aquí.* The English "one" used stylistically to replace "I" or "we" can be translated by the Spanish *uno* or *una.* One of the commonest ways of expressing the passive in Spanish involves using the third person plural. Thus, "I was robbed" [passive] becomes *me robaron* (literally "they robbed me"). "They" is thus used impersonally.

In some cases *se* joins up with the verb, and that verb then behaves like a reflexive verb. In *se dicen tantas cosas,* ("so many things are said" the *cosas* "say **themselves**", in the same way as things "forget themselves to us" and so on. This is one of the commonest ways of expressing the passive in Spanish.

We'll come across these forms and expressions a lot. For the time being just read through the revision notes, and remember where they are so you can refer back if need be.

3. **Recién :** (see sentences 4 in Lesson 37 and 5 in Lesson 38). This adverb is much used with past participles to mean "recently" or "just". *Están recién cogidas :* "they have just been picked". or "they're recently picked" In Latin America it is used with other parts of the verb : *recién llegamos :* "we just arrived" (cf. *acabamos de llegar). Los recién llegados :* "recent arrivals" (lit. "the recently arrived ones").

4. *Ir* **with a gerundive** indicates **progression**, e.g., *las nubes iban ocultando el cielo :* "the clouds were gradually hiding the sky".
When there is **a series of actions or movements** we can also use *ir* + gerundive : *El hombre conataba las ovejas que iban pasando :* "the man was counting the sheep that were passing (one by one)".
If the action is prolonged, we can use the verb *andar* followed by a gerundive, thus : *anduvo buscando todo el día :* "he went on looking all day".

****

LECCION CUARENTA Y TRES

Esperamos a un amigo

1 — ¿Adónde vas?
2 — Voy a la estación. Juan llega a las nueve y media y, probablemente, vendrá cargado.
3 — ¿Vas a ir en coche?
4 — No. Voy a coger el autobús. Hoy, hay demasiada circulación.
5 — ¿Quieres que te acompañe?
6 — Si no tienes nada que hacer y quieres venir, te espero.

PRONUNCIACION: 2 ven'dra cargado 4 aoutobous 5 acom'pagné

5. Writing in Spanish

1.   Is this the first time you've been here? - Yes, I didn't know this town.
2.   The tablecloth has just been ironed. - I'll set the table.
3.   Every now and then, I like to go to the garden. - So do I.
4.   Try on this shirt. I can't wear it any more.
5.   There's nothing here that's worthwhile.
6.   Did someone knock at the door? - I don't think so.

6. Translation

1.   ¿Es la primera vez que vienes aquí? - Sí, no conocía esta ciudad.
2.   El mantel está recién planchado. - Voy a poner la mesa.
3.   De vez en cuando, me gusta ir al jardín. - A mí también.
4.   Pruébate esta camisa. - Ya no me vale.
5.   Aquí no hay nada que valga la pena.
6.   ¿Han llamado a la puerta? - No creo.

* *

LESSON FORTY-THREE

We are waiting for a friend

1. — (To) Where are you going?
2. — I'm going to the station. Juan is arriving at half past nine, and he'll probably come with a lot of luggage (probably he'll come loaded).
3. — Are you going to go in [the] car?
4. — No. I'm going to catch the bus. Today there is too much traffic.
5. — Do you want me to come with you? (that I should accompany you?)
6. — If you don't have anything (nothing) (that) to do and you want to come, I'm waiting for you.

7 — De acuerdo. Voy a peinarme y nos vamos. (1)

8 — Entre los tres, podremos llevar todas las maletas,

9   y, si pesan demasiado, cogeremos un taxi.

10 — ¿Crees que vendrá muy cargado?

11 — No lo sé, pero, en su última carta, me decía que tenía intención de quedarse aquí unos meses. (2)

12   Creo que ha alquilado una casa vieja a quince kilómetros de aquí.

13 — ¿Y qué quiere hacer? (3)

14 — No tengo ninguna idea sobre sus planes.

PRONUNCIACION:

7 péinarmé 8 én'tré ... malétass 9 péçan ... coHérémoss ... tassi 11 in'ten'cion' ... kédarssé 12 alkilado ... kilométross 14 planéss.

EJERCICIO: 1. La estación no está lejos del centro de la ciudad. **2.** El autobús te dejará a la puerta de casa. **3.** Antes de ayer, había mucha circulación. **4.** Teresa iba a su casa muy cargada. **5.** La hemos ayudado los cuatro. **6.** Tengo la intención de hacerme una mesa. **7.** Todavía no tengo planes para el próximo año.

7 — OK. I['ll] comb my hair (myself) and we'll go.
8 — With three of us (Between the three) we'll be able to carry all the suitcases,
9 and, if they weigh too much, we'll catch a taxi.
10 — Do you think he'll come with a lot of luggage? (very loaded?)
11 — I don't know (it), but in his last letter he told me that he intended to stay here a few months.
12 I think that he has rented an old house (at) fifteen kilometers from here.
13 — And what is he going to do?
14 — I have no idea about (on) his plans.

NOTES
(1) See note 3 to Lesson 23.
(2) *Unos meses* : "a few months" ; *unas mesas* : "a few tables". *Algunos, algunas* also means "some" or "a few", but is rather more specific than *unos, unas*.
(3) Are you starting to recognize the different forms of this verb? *Yo hago* : "I do" or "I make" ; *yo hacía* : "I was doing/making" ; *yo haré* : "I will do/make" ; *hecho* : "done/made".

EXERCISE : 1. The station is not far from the town centre. – 2. The bus will leave you at the front door. – 3. The day before yesterday there was a lot of traffic. – 4. Teresa was going home with a lot of luggage. – 5. All four of us helped her. – 6. I intend to make myself a table. – 7. I still don't have plans for next year.

* * * * *

Now you're starting to get the idea of the sound of Spanish, the pronunciation guide given after the sentences is no longer very useful. However, we'll continue to give pronunciation notes for a few lessons more, but advise you to start trying to do without.
Only use the paragraph **PRONUNCIACION** *if you're in any doubt. If you want to refresh your memory on the general rules of pronunciation, refer back to lessons 7 and 35.*

Lección 43

EJERCICIO DE CONTROL
Ponga las palabras que faltan

1 *The last bus passes at one o'clock in the morning.*

. . . . pasa . . . .

. . . . . .

2 *Do you want to come with me?*

¿ . . . . ?

3 *I have to get dressed and comb my hair before I leave.*

. . . .

. . . .

****

LECCION CUARENTA Y CUATRO

Saldos

1 – Es fin de temporada. **(1)**
2   El inventario comienza a hacerse en los comercios.
3   Pronto será la época de las rebajas. **(2)**
4 — Si estás de acuerdo, mañana, podemos levantarnos pronto e ir a ver si compramos algo. **(3)**
5   Las rebajas han comenzado.
6 — Sí. Yo necesito zapatos ¿y tú?
7 — Yo quería hacer esta tarde una pequeña lista de lo que me parece más necesario.

PRONUNCIACION: saldoss 1 tem'porada 2 in'ven'tario ... comércioss
3 rébaHass

4 *I only have one suitcase.*

. . . .

5 *He intended to buy an old house.*

. . . .

. . . .

THE MISSING WORDS :   1 el último autobús - a la una de la mañana **2** quieres acompañarme **3** tengo que vestirme y peinarme antes de salir **4** tengo solamente una maleta. **5** tenía la intención de comprar una casa vieja.

****

LESSON FORTY-FOUR

[The] sales

1 It's [the] end of [the] season.
2 Businesses are starting to do inventories (The inventory is starting to be done in the businesses).
3 Soon it will be the period (epoch) of the reductions.
4 — If you agree, tomorrow we can get up early and go and see if we [can] buy something.
5 The reductions have started.
6 — Yes. I need shoes. And you?
7 — I would like to make this afternoon a small list of what (that which) I think is (seems to me) most necessary.

NOTES
(1) *Temporada :* "season". We have already seen the word *estación,* which means "season" in the sense "spring, summer, etc.".
(2) *Rebaja :* lit. "reduction". This word is in fact more common than *saldo :* "sale".
(3) Note that *y :* "and" becomes *e* when it appears before *i* or *hi*.

Lección 44

8 — De todas formas, no creo que necesitemos muchas cosas.

9 — En esta casa todos somos muy cuidadosos.

10 — Si no nos gastamos todo el presupuesto que hemos previsto,

11 me gustaría comprar unas cuantas planchas de madera de pino. (4)

12 — ¿Qué quieres hacer con ellas?

13 — Una biblioteca. (5)

14 — ¡Ah, sí! ya no me acordaba.

8 nécésitémoss 9 couidadossos 10 gasstamoss ... préçoupouéssto ... prévissto 13 bibliotéca.

EJERCICIO: 1. La nueva temporada de cine, todavía, no ha comenzado. 2. En ciertas zapaterías, hay ya rebajas. 3. De todas las formas, yo no podré ir. 4. Yo me gasto poco dinero en vestidos. 5. Tenemos un presupuesto de cinco mil pesetas. 6. José es muy cuidadoso. 7. Necesito unos zapatos.

EJERCICIO DE CONTROL
Ponga las palabras que faltan

1 *We will take [our] holidays out of season.*

. . . .   fuera de

. . . .

2 *Today I got up early.*

. . . .

3 *This month there are sales everywhere.*

. . . .

. . . . . .

8 — In any case (In all forms), I don't think that we need many things.

9 — In this house we are all very careful.

10 — If we don't spend all the budget that we have foreseen,

11 I would like to buy a few planks of (wood of) pine.

12 — What do you want to make with them?

13 — A bookcase.

14 — Oh yes! I'd forgotten already (Already I didn't remember).

NOTES

(4) *Unas cuantas* : "a few" : another way of saying *algunas* or *unas*, but with more insistence on the "not very many" aspect.

(5) *Una biblioteca* : "a library" and "a bookcase".

EXERCISE : **1.** The new cinema season has not started yet. – **2.** In certain shoe shops there are already sales. – **3.** In any case I won't be able to go. – **4.** I spend little money on dresses. – **5.** We have a budget of five thousand pesetas. – **6.** José is very careful. – **7.** I need some shoes.

4 *I need to go for walks often.*

. . . .

5 *This morning I have spent sixty francs.*

. . . . me he . . . . fran-

cos

THE MISSING WORDS : **1** tomaremos las vacaciones - temporada. **2** hoy me he levantado pronto. **3** este mes hay rebajas en todos los sitios. **4** necesito pasearme a menudo. **5** esta mañana - gastado sesenta.

Lección 44

LECCION CUARENTA Y CINCO
Un triste y banal fin

1   Sacado de un periódico, de la sección titulada:
2   "Eso no les pasa más que a los demás." **(1)**
3   El relato literal que leemos es el siguiente: **(2)**
4   Un carpintero y sus dos hijos se matan al caer de un balcón a la calle. **(3)**
5   Sevilla: - Ayer, a las cinco y cinco de la tarde, el señor R. Pérez, carpintero de profesión,
6   se hallaba en el balcón de su domicilio, **(4)**
7   situado en el cuarto piso del inmueble que habitaba,
8   teniendo en brazos a su hijo Joaquín de dos años de edad.
9   De pronto, el otro hijo del señor R. Pérez, cayó a la calle
10 y, al querer impedirlo, el desgraciado señor resbaló
11 al pisar una cáscara de plátano que se encontraba en el suelo;
12 el padre perdió el equilibrio y cayó también a la calle con el niño que tenía en sus brazos.
13 Los tres resultaron muertos en el acto.
14 La esposa y madre se ha vuelto loca. **(5)**

ME HE VUELTO DESCONFIADO

PRONUNCIACION: trissté ... banal 1 sacado ... sek'cion titoulada. 3 rélato litéral ... léémoss ... siguien'té 4 carpin'téro ... matan' 5 sévil/a ... péreç ... proféssion' 6 domicilio 7 in'mouéblé 8 braços ... Hoakin' édad (le d seulement esquissé) 9 caïo 10 im'pédirlo ... dessgraciado ... réssbalo 11 pissar ... casscara platano ... souélo 12 perdio ... ékilibrio 13 réçoultaron' ... ak'to 14 esspoça.

LESSON FORTY-FIVE

A sad and undramatic end

1 Taken out of a newspaper, from the section entitled :
2 "It only happens to others" (That doesn't happen more than to the others).
3 The true (literal) story that we are reading is the following (one) :
4 A carpenter and his two sons killed themselves by falling from a balcony to the street.
5 Sevilla : - Yesterday at five past five in the afternoon, Mr R. Pérez, carpenter by profession
6 was (found himself) on the balcony of his home,
7 (situated) on the fourth floor of the building where he lived
8 holding in [his] arms (to) his son Joaquín, (of) two years of age.
9 Suddenly, the other son of Mr R. Pérez, fell to the street
10 and, trying to stop (impede) him, the unfortunate man slipped
11 by treading on a banana skin that was (found itself) on the floor ;
12 the father lost his (the) balance and fell also to the street with the child that he was holding in his arms.
13 The three were killed instantly (resulted dead in the act).
14 The wife and mother has gone mad.

NOTES
(1) *Pasar :* "to happen" ; *¿Qué pasa? :* "What's happening?". *Los demás :* "other people, others".
(2) *Leamos,* from the verb *leer :* "to read". The *u* in *siguiente* is there to harden the *i*.
(3) *Al caer :* "on falling". Other examples of this construction can be found in sentences 10 and 11. See also Lesson 49, paragraph 1.
(4) "To find" : *hallar* or *encontrar.* When used reflexively *(hallarse, encontrarse),* these verbs are best translated by the English verb "to be". *Me encontraba en el pasillo :* "I was (I found myself) in the corridor". Note also the use of *situada* in sentence 7.
(5) *Se ha vuelto loca :* "she became (turned) mad". *¿Te has vuelto loco? :* "Have you gone mad?"

EJERCICIO: 1. Yo compro todos los días el periódico. 2. ¿Cuál es su profesión? 3. Estoy domiciliado en Córdoba. 4. Vivo en un inmueble nuevo. 5. Esta mañana, mi padre se ha caído en la calle. 6. Mi madre coge a mi hermano pequeño en brazos. 7. He encontrado un bolígrafo en el suelo.

EJERCICIO DE CONTROL
Ponga las palabras que faltan

1 *My brothers and I read the newspaper together.*

. . . .

. . . . . .

2 *Our address is the following.*

. . . .

3 *At my friends' house there are three balconies with flowers.*

. . . .

. . . .

****

LECCION CUARENTA Y SEIS

La familia

1 Mi abuela y mi abuelo, por parte de mi padre, son originarios del campo: son campesinos.(1)
2 La madre de mi madre, mi abuela, también nació en el campo. (2)
3 Mi otro abuelo murió durante la guerra. Yo no le he conocido.

PRONUNCIACION: 1 abouéla ... oriHinarioss cam'péçinoss 2 nacio 3 mourio douran'té guérra (u muet ; les rr roulés)

EXERCISE : 1. I buy the newspaper every day. – **2.** What is your job? – **3.** My home is in Córdoba. – **4.** I live in a new building. – **5.** This morning, my father fell in the street. – **6.** My mother takes·my little brother in her arms. – **7.** I have found a biro on the floor.

* * * * *

4 *I like bananas.*

. . . .

5 *I wanted to stop him.*

. . . .

THE MISSING WORDS : 1 mis hermanos y yo leemos el periódico juntos. **2** nuestra dirección es la siguiente. **3** en casa de mis amigos hay tres balcones con flores. **4** me gustan los plátanos. **5** quería impedirlo.

* *

LESSON FORTY-SIX

The family

1   My grandmother and my grandfather on my father's side (part) are from the country : they are farmers.
2   My mother's mother, my grandmother, was also born in the country.
3   My other grandfather died during the war. I haven't [ever] known him.

NOTES
(1) *Campesinos :* "people who work the land" or "peasants".
(2) The active intransitive verb *nacer* translates the English "to be born" (passive).

4   Yo soy el mayor de los nietos por parte de mis abuelos paternos. (3)

5   Los hijos e hijas de mis tías son mis primos y primas.

6   A mis abuelos, les gusta verse rodeados de sus nietos.

7   Algunos de mis primos tienen hijos.

8   Biznietos y bisabuelos juegan, a menudo, juntos como si tuvieran la misma edad.

9   Cuando se les observa, es muy fácil estar de acuerdo con el refrán que dice:

10 ''Los extremos se tocan''.

11 Personas mayores y niños dan, a menudo, el mismo tipo de alegrías y preocupaciones.

12 Las unas por su sabiduría,

13 y los otros por su vitalidad.

14 Para nuestros predecesores, así como para nuestros descendientes somos, a veces, espejos.

4 niétoss ... patérnoss
5 tiass ... primoss 6 verssé rodéadoss 8 biçniétoss ... biçabouéloss 9 obsserva ... réfran' 10 ésstrémoss 11 alégriass 12 sabidouria 13 bitalida(d) 14 prédécéçoress ... desscén'dien'tess ... esspéHoss.

LOS EXTREMOS SE TOCAN

EJERCICIO: 1. Mis abuelos son muy mayores. 2. Mis padres son hijos de campesinos. 3. Mi hermana es la mayor de la familia. 4. Nuestra casa está rodeada de jardines. 5. Hoy, he tenido una gran alegría. 6. Los niños tienen mucha vitalidad. 7. En tu casa, hay un gran espejo.

4   I am the eldest of the grandchildren on my paternal
        grandparents' side.
5   The sons and daughters of my aunts are my
        cousins (masc. and fem.).
6   My grandparents like to be surrounded by their
        grandchildren (To my grandparents it pleases to
        them to see themselves surrounded by their
        grandchildren).
7   Some of my cousins have children (sons and
        daughters).
8   Great-grandchildren and great-grandparents often
        play together as if they had (might have) the same
        age.
9   When one observes (to) them, it is very easy to
        agree with the proverb that says :
10   "The extremes touch themselves".
11   Elderly people and children often give the same
        type of happiness(es) and worries.
12   The former through their wisdom
13   and the latter through their vitality.
14   For our predecessors, (thus) as for our
        descendants, we are at times mirrors.

NOTES

(3) *Mayor* : "major" : *la mayoría* : "the majority" ; *el mayor* : "the
elder / eldest" ; *las personas mayores* : "elderly people". We
will see later how *mayor* can be used to form certain
comparatives and superlatives.

There are no particular difficulties in this lesson. The most
important thing to notice is the vocabulary, but, as in the next
revision lesson, we also see a lot of possessive adjectives.
Remember the ones we've already seen : *su casa* :
"his / her / your / their house" ; *vuestra amiga* : "your (fam.
plural) friend (fem.)" ; *su sabiduría* : "his / her / your / their
wisdom".

EXERCISE : 1. My grandparents are very elderly. – **2.** My parents
are children of country people. – **3.** My sister is the eldest in the
family. – **4.** Our house is surrounded by gardens. – **5.** Today I have
been very happy. – **6.** Children have a lot of vitality. – **7.** In your
house there is a big mirror.

EJERCICIO DE CONTROL
Ponga las palabras que faltan

1 *Peasants work the land.*

. . . .

2 *During the Spanish [Civil] War there were more than a million dead.*

. . . . hubo . . .

. . . . . millón . . . .

3 *I have never known my grandparents on my father's side.*

Yo . . . .

. . . .

****

LECCION CUARENTA Y SIETE

Cuestión de cartera

1 — Nuestro coche está averiado y no estará arreglado antes de diez días.
2   ¿Y el vuestro?
3 — El nuestro está en el garaje y nos han dicho que tienen para rato.
4 — ¿Y cómo vamos a hacer para ir a Suecia la semana que viene? (1)
5 — Tenemos muchas posibilidades, a saber: el avión, el tren, el barco, la moto, además de la bicicleta y del autostop.

PRONUNCIACION: 1 avériado 3 garaHé 4 souécia 5 possibilidadess...
avion' tren' barco bicikléta ... aoutostop

4 *Proverbs express the wisdom of the people.*

. . .   .   expresan   . .   . .

. . . . . .

5 *At times we look at ourselves in a mirror.*

.   . . .

* * * * *

THE MISSING WORDS :   **1** los campesinos trabajan la tierra. **2**
durante la guerra de España - más de un - de muertos. **3** no he
conocido a mis abuelos por parte de mi padre. **4** los refranes - la
sabiduría del pueblo. **5** a veces, nos miramos en un espejo.

* *

LESSON FORTY-SEVEN

[A] question of money (wallet)

1 — Our car is broken down and it won't be fixed for
(before) ten days.
2 And yours?
3 — Ours is in the garage and they have told us that it
will take a while (they have for while).
4 — And how are we going to go (how are we going to
do to go) to Sweden next week?
5 — We have many possibilities, namely : the plane, the
train, the boat, the motorbike, besides the bicycle
and hitch-hiking.

NOTES
(1) *La semana que viene* means the same as *la semana próxima.*

6 — ¿Y por qué no, también, el burro o el mulo?

7 — Yo había pensado que podíamos ir a pie.

8 — Sois muy graciosos, pero tenemos un problema y hay que resolverlo.

9 — Más vale reírse que enfadarse.

10 — El avión es más rápido que el tren y que el barco. **(2)**

11 — El avión es tan caro como el barco.

12 — Y el tren es menos caro que el avión y que el barco,

13 — y como nuestros monederos no soportan las alturas y se marean... **(3)**

14 — ¡Entonces... guiados por la voz de la razón... iremos en tren!

6 bourro ... moulo **8** gracioçoss ... réssolverlo **9** réirssé ... en'fadarssé **13** monédéross ... soportan' ... altourass ... maréan' **14** guiadoss (u muet) ... voç.

EJERCICIO: 1. Acabo de llevar el coche al garaje. **2.** Todavía tengo para un buen rato. **3.** No te enfades por tan poca cosa. **4.** Nuestra casa es más grande que la vuestra. **5.** Su hijo es más pequeño que el nuestro. **6.** Sus abuelos son tan mayores como los nuestros. **7.** En barco, me mareo.

EJERCICIO DE CONTROL
Ponga las palabras que faltan

1 *The car will not be ready for Monday.*

. .   . .

. . . . .

6 — And why not, also, the donkey and the mule?
7 — I had thought that we could go on foot (at foot).
8 — You are very funny (gracious), but we have a problem and we must (it is necessary to) solve it.
9 — It's better to laugh than to get angry.
10 — The plane is faster than the train and than the boat.
11 — The plane is as expensive as the boat.
12 And the train is less expensive than the plane and than the boat,
13 and as our purses don't stand (support) (the) heights, and get seasick...
14 — Well then!... guided by the voice of reason... we'll go by (in) train!

NOTES
(2) In sentences 10, 11 and 12 you can see the standard comparative construction. We'll go over this in the next revision lesson.
(3) *Me mareo :* "I feel sick". *Un mareo :* "seasickness" or "nausea". You can see the word *mar* in these expressions, but they refer to any sort of nausea, and not merely seasickness.

EXERCISE : 1. I have just taken the car to the garage. – **2.** I still have a while to wait. – **3.** Don't get angry for so little. – **4.** Our house is bigger than yours. – **5.** Your son is smaller than ours. – **6.** His grandparents are as elderly as ours. – **7.** I get seasick in boats.

2 *Excuse me, is there a garage near here?*

Perdone, ¿ . . . . ?

3 *Our neighbourhood is less lively than yours.*

. . . .

. . . .

4 *Last year it was colder than this one [this year].*

. . . . hizo . . . .

Lección 47

5 *My friends live as far [away] as you.*

. . . .

. . . .

****

LECCION CUARENTA Y OCHO

Lo nuestro (1)

1 — Este jersey, ¿es el mío o el tuyo?
2 — Ese es el mío.
3   Si quieres, póntelo pero te estará demasiado grande. (2)
4 — No, voy a buscar el mío.
5 — El tuyo se lo ha puesto Mayte esta mañana. (3)
6   Pero ponte el suyo, te irá muy bien con esa ropa.
7 — Después de todo... no es una mala idea.
8 — Es una ventaja que la ropa de unos sirva para otros. (4)
9 — Y que todos nosotros estemos de acuerdo para funcionar así.
10 — Es mejor que:
11   Lo mío mío y lo tuyo de entrambos. (5)

PRONUNCIACION: 1 Hersséi ... mio ... tuïo. 5 maïté. 8 ben'taHa ... sirba. 11 en'tram'boss.

*****

THE MISSING WORDS : 1 el coche no estará listo para el lunes. 2 hay un garaje cerca de aquí. 3 nuestro barrio es menos animado que el vuestro. 4 el año pasado - más que éste. 5 mis amigos viven tan lejos como vosotros (ou ustedes).

****

LESSON FORTY-EIGHT

Ours

1	—	Is this jersey mine or yours?
2	—	That one is mine.
3		If you want, put it on, but it will be too big for you.
4	—	No, I'll go and get mine (I'm going to look for mine).
5	—	Mayte put yours on this morning (Yours she has put it on herself Mayte this morning).
6		But put hers on, it will go very well with what you're wearing (it will go to you very well that clothing).
7	—	After all... it's not a bad idea.
8	—	It's an advantage that the clothes of some [people] are useful for other(s) [people].
9	—	And that we all agree to act (function) thus.
10	—	It's better that :
11		What's mine is mine and what's yours we share.

*****

NOTES
(1) *Lo nuestro* : "that which is ours" ; *lo importante* : "that which is important" (*lo más importante es el amor* : "the most important [thing] is love") See paragraph 5 in Lesson 28.
(2) See note 5 to Lesson 39. *Te estará bien* : "it will suit you well".
(3) Notice the word order. *Ponerse un vestido* : "to put a dress on (oneself)".
(4) Cf. *No sirve* : "it's useless" or "he's useless".
(5) Spanish proverb.

Refranes: (6)

1   No se ganó Zamora en una hora.
2   Por el hilo se saca el ovillo.
3   Quien mucho abarca, poco aprieta.

PRONUNCIACION: 1 çamora. 2 ilo ... *o*billo. 3 abarca ... apriéta.

EJERCICIO: 1. Mi jersey es menos bonito que el tuyo. 2. El suyo es más grande que el mío. 3. Después de todo ... creo que podré arreglarme. 4. Este pescado es mejor que aquél. 5. Este pantalón me está tan bien como ése. 6. Tengo que ir a buscar a los niños. 7. Yo, por mi parte, estoy de acuerdo.

EJERCICIO DE CONTROL
Ponga las palabras que faltan

1 *Put on these trousers and tell me if they suit you.*

. . . .

. . . .

2 *It is too big for me.*

. . . .

Proverbs

1 Zamora wasn't won in an hour. [Rome wasn't built in a day]
2 By the thread one takes out the ball.
3 [He] who embraces a lot, grasps little.

NOTES
(6) These three old Spanish proverbs have a particular rhyme and rhythm. A literal English translation is given. Can you think of equivalent English proverbs?

EXERCISE : 1. My jersey is less nice than yours. – **2.** His is bigger than mine. – **3.** After all... I think I will be able to straighten myself out. – **4.** This fish is better than that one. – **5.** This pair of trousers suits me as well as that one. – **6.** I have to fetch the children. – **7.** For my part, I agree.

*****

3 *I don't think it's any use.*

. . . . day . . . .

4 *Buy me some white thread and the newspaper.*

. . . .

5 *I like proverbs.*

. . . .

THE MISSING WORDS : 1 ponte este pantalón y dime si te está bien. 2 es demasiado grande para mí. 3 no creo que me sirva. 4 cómprame hilo blanco y el periódico. 5 me gustan los refranes.

LECCION CUARENTA Y NUEVE

LESSON FORTY-NINE

Revisión y notas

1. **Al caer :** "on falling" or "when I / you / he / etc. fell". This is a very common construction. Other examples include : *al despertarme :* "when I woke up" ("on waking myself up") ; *al salir de casa :* "when I left the house" ; *al llegar :* "when I arrived". See also note 2 to Lesson 22.

2. **A expresses movement ; en expresses position.** Thus, *voy a Madrid :* "I'm going to Madrid", but *estamos en México :* "We are in Mexico".

3. **The comparative :** see Lesson 47 (sentences 10, 11 and 12, and sentences 4, 5 and 6 in the *ejercicio).* To summarize the standard forms of the comparative, we have : **más... que** *(tu hijo es más joven que el mío :* "your son is younger than mine") ; **menos... que** *(el tren es menos rápido que el avion :* "the train is less fast than the plane") ; **tan... como :** *(los europeos son tan simpáticos como los americanos :* "Europeans are as nice as Americans").

As in English, however, there are a certain number of irregular comparatives : *malo - peor :* "bad - worse" ; *bueno - mejor :* "good - better" ; *pequeño - menor :* "small - smaller" ; *grande - mayor :* "big - bigger".

4. **Possessives :** in Spanish, there are two sorts of possessive adjective :

mi, mis : my	*nuestro, a, os, as :* our
tu, tus : your	*vuestro, a, os, as :* your
su, sus : his / her	*su, sus :* their

LESSON FORTY-NINE

mío, a, os, as : my, mine *tuyo, a, os, as* : your, yours *suyo, a, os, as* : his/her, his/hers	*nuestro, a, os, as* : our, ours *vuestro, a, os, as* : your, yours *suyo, a, os, as* : their, theirs

The adjectives in the first table are placed before the noun, while those in the second table are always placed after the noun. The words in table two, however, are much more commonly used as pronouns. In this case, they are preceded by the definite articles *el, la, los* or *las*. Example : *este coche es el mío* : "this car is mine" ; *¿Cuál es el tuyo?* : "Which [one] is yours?".

5. **Writing in Spanish** : (second wave)

1   I'm going to get the train. - Do you want me to come with you?
2   It's the time for end-of-season sales. - I'm going to buy.
3   What are you reading? - It's a book of proverbs.
4   My brother Juan is the oldest in the family. - How old is he?
5   Your work is as interesting as mine.
6   This pullover is mine but you can put it on.

6. **Translation**

1   Voy a coger el tren. - ¿Quieres que te acompañe?
2   Es la época de las rebajas de fin de temporada. - Voy a comprar.
3   ¿Qué lees? - Es un libro de refranes.
4   Mi hermano Juan es el mayor de la familia. - ¿Qué edad tiene?
5   Tu trabajo es tan interesante como el mío.
6   Este jersey es mío pero puedes ponértelo.

SECOND WAVE (segunda ola)

We have now reached the point where you can get the general meaning of each sentence without too much difficulty, even if you have to read the sentence twice.

It's perfectly natural that you will come across certain constructions or common words that seem strange, and certain verb forms that seem very different from their infinitives. Conjugating the regular verbs (like *comprar, vender* and *vivir*) doesn't pose any particular problem. But, as we will see in the lessons that follow, there are also irregular verbs. You've already seen some of them, and they're really not that difficult.

Remember : **¡No se ganó Zamora en una hora!**. Don't try to learn everything at the same time.

****

LECCION CINCUENTA

Un largo fin de semana

1 — Dentro de dos semanas, tendré un puente de cinco días. (1)

2 — Eso, más que un puente parece un acueducto. ¿Estás seguro?

3 — Sí. Nos hemos arreglado entre los compañeros de trabajo.

4 — Entonces, podríamos ir a esquiar. (2)

*From now on, no pronunciation notes are given. From time to time, however, we will point out certain words that may need special attention. Just remember : every letter has a particular role. Spanish spelling is **systematic,** so it is a good deal easier than English spelling.*

Now you are going to start the **active phase** of the learning process. This phase will involve increased accuracy on your part.

From Lesson 50 onwards, when you have finished the day's lesson, you should review a lesson from the early part of the course (starting at the very beginning!). The procedure is as follows :

— Read the lesson out loud (after listening to the cassettes, if you have them), and check the meaning of each sentence you are unsure of by looking at the literal English translation given opposite.

— Translate the English sentences back into Spanish. Don't work in silence : you must accustom your tongue, lips, mouth and ears to the sounds and shapes of Spanish.

— Check your version against the Spanish original.

* * * * *

If you find it easier to remember things if you write them down, you can complete the second wave exercises by writing them down after you've spoken them out loud.

* *

LESSON FIFTY

A long weekend

1 — In two weeks, I will have a break (bridge) of five days.
2 — That, more than a bridge sounds (seems) [like] an aqueduct. Are you sure?
3 — Yes. We have worked it out with (arranged ourselves between) the friends (companions) at (of) work.
4 — Well, then, we could (would be able) go skiing (to ski).

NOTES
(1) *Dentro de :* "inside" or "within" ; *ahí dentro :* "in there".
Un puente : "a bridge". When a public holiday falls, say, on a Tuesday, the weekend can be prolonged by making "a bridge" over the Monday.
(2) No word in Spanish begins with *s* + a consonant. Remember *estupido, estupendo, estación,* etc.

5 — Es una buena ocasión para que me mues-
tres el refugio del que me has hablado. **(3)**

6 — ¿A partir de qué momento estarás libre ?

7 –– Del jueves por la tarde al miércoles por la
mañana.

8 — Perfecto. Podemos coger el tren de las diez
de la noche,

9   y así llegaremos al amanecer al pueblecito
del que te he hablado.

10   Podemos desayunar allí y hacer las compras
para los cinco días. **(4)**

11 — Como las mochilas son grandes, no habrá
problema.

12 — A dos kilómetros del pueblo, comienza el
camino de montaña,

13   y como en esta época hay mucha nieve,
podremos ponernos los esquíes.

14 — No olvides que yo no he hecho mucho esquí
de fondo.

EJERCICIO: 1. La semana que viene hay un puente de
cuatro días. **2.** Dentro de una hora, tengo una cita. **3.** Me
he arreglado con mis amigos. **4.** ¿Me harás conocer a tu
familia? **5.** Mi mochila es muy pesada. **6.** Conozco un
camino de montaña muy bonito. **7.** Voy a desayunar en
un bar.

5 — It's a good opportunity (occasion) for you to show me the refuge of (the one) which you have spoken to me.
6 — From what moment will you be free?
7 — From (the) Thursday (by the) afternoon to (the) Wednesday (by the) morning.
8 — Perfect. We can get the 10.00 pm train (the train of half past ten of the night)
9 and that way (thus) we will arrive at daybreak at the little village of (the one) which I have spoken to you.
10 We can [have] breakfast there and do the shopping for the five days.
11 — As the backpacks are big, there won't be [any] problem.
12 — (At) two kilometers from the village, the mountain path begins,
13 and as in this period there is a lot of snow, we can (we will be able to) take the skis.
14 — Don't forget that I have not done much cross-country skiing.

*****

NOTES
(3) Compare with : "the woman you told me about" : *la señora de la que me has hablado.*
(4) The verb *desayunar,* and the noun *desayuno :* "breakfast" are based on exactly the same logic as in English (and French). *Ayunar* is the verb "to fast", and *un ayuno* is "a fast". Logically, the opposite is *desayunar* and *desayuno.*

EXERCISE : 1. Next week there is a four-day break. – **2.** In an hour, I have an appointment. – **3.** I have come to an arrangement with my friends. – **4.** Will you introduce me to your family? – **5.** My backpack is very heavy. – **6.** I know a very nice mountain path. – **7.** I'm going to have breakfast in a bar.

EJERCICIO DE CONTROL
Ponga las palabras que faltan

1 *When will you be free?*

¿ . . . .

. . . . . ?

2 *Are you sure that there's a "bridge" next week?*

¿ . . . .

. . . . ?

****

LECCION CINCUENTA Y UNA

Un aspecto cultural

1 — Cuando fui a España hubo algo que me
sorprendió.
2 — ¿Qué es lo·que te sorprendió?
3 — No vi casi ningún perro, ni gato, ni pájaro,
en fin, todo ese tipo de animales
4 que suele haber en las casas, en las familias
en las que estuve. **(1)**
5 — Eres observador. En efecto, tienes razón.
6 En ese aspecto, España es muy diferente de
Francia.
7 — Yo pensaba que era todo lo contrario.
8 — ¿Y a qué crees que es debido?

3 *We will take the 7.00 am train.*

. . . .

. . . .

4 *My breakfast is cold.*

. . . .

5 *There is a lot of snow in those mountains.*

. . . .

THE MISSING WORDS : 1 dentro de cuánto tiempo estarás libre. **2** estás seguro de que hay un puente la semana que viene. **3** cogeremos el tren de las siete de la mañana. **4** mi desayuno está frío. **5** hay mucha nieve en esas montañas.

Segunda ola: 1ª lección.

****

LESSON FIFTY-ONE

A cultural aspect

1 — When I went to Spain there was something that surprised me.
2 — What (is that which) surprised you?
3 — I hardly saw a single (I didn't see almost no) dog, nor cat, nor bird, at least, all that type of animal(s),
4 that there usually are in the houses, in the families where (in those which) I was.
5 — You are observant (observer). In fact you're right.
6 In that aspect, Spain is very different from France.
7 — I thought it was quite (all) the opposite.
8 — And to what do you think it is due?

NOTES
(1) The verb *soler* expresses "to usually" + infinitive, or "to often" + infinitive. *Suele llover en marzo :* "it usually rains in March". See also paragraph 4 in Lesson 56.

Lección 51

9 — No lo sé. Quizás como es un país más cálido
    y la gente vive más fuera de casa, **(2)**
10   no necesita tanto introducir en su casa ese
    aspecto de la naturaleza. **(3)**
11 — Esa puede ser una razón, pero también hay
    otras.
12 — ¿Cuáles por ejemplo? **(4)**
13 — El ritmo de vida...
14 — ¿Tú crees?   (Continuará)

EJERCICIO: 1. Su interés me ha sorprendido. 2. Suele
venir todos los domingos. 3. Los países del sur de
Europa son más cálidos que los del norte. 4. Eso puede
ser una razón. 5. ¿Cuál es tu sitio? 6. No conocía este
aspecto de la cuestión. 7. El lunes la gente no está tan
animada.

EJERCICIO DE CONTROL
Ponga las palabras que faltan

1 *I liked what I saw.*

. . . .

2 *In Andalucia the people usually go to bed later.*

. . . .

acostarse . . . .

3 *I don't need [it] as much as you.*

. . . .

4 *What is your address?*

¿ . . . . ?

5 *Do you think he will come?*

¿ . . . . ?

9 — I don't know (it). Perhaps, as it is a hotte᷆
    and the people live more outside [the] hous᷆
10 — they don't need so much to introduce in their
    that aspect of (the) nature.
11 — That can be one reason, but there are also oth᷆
12 — What (Which), for example?
13 — The rhythm of life...
14 — Do you think [so]?

NOTES
(2) *Quizá* or *quizás* : "perhaps" or "maybe". *Quizás iré* : "I may go".
La gente is singular. *Las gentes* also exists. Note the
pronunciation of the *g* before an *e* : guttural, like the *jota* sound
(pron. **H**ente).
(3) *Tanto* : "as much" or "so much". Like *mucho* and *poco, tanto*
agrees with the noun it qualifies (e.g., *tanta gente* : "so many
people").
(4) *¿Cuál?* : "Which?". Masculine and feminine forms are
identical. The plural is *¿Cuáles?* The English "What?" is
translated by *¿Cuál?* in certain instances. We'll come back to
this.

EXERCISE : 1. His interest surprised me. – **2.** He usually comes
every Sunday. – **3.** The countries in the south of Europe are hotter
than those in the north. – **4.** That can be one reason.– **5.** Which is
your place? – **6.** I didn't know this aspect of the question. – **7.** On
Monday the people are not so lively.

THE MISSING WORDS :   **1** lo que he visto me ha gustado. **2** en
Andalucía la gente suele - más tarde. **3** no tengo tanta necesidad como
tú. **4** cuál es tu dirección. **5** crees que vendrá.

Segunda ola: 2ª lección.

LECCION CINCUENTA Y DOS

Un aspecto cultural (continuación y fin)

1 — Sí. El nivel de vida es menos alto en España que en Francia. (1)
2 Sobre todo en las ciudades, y un animal necesita estar bien cuidado.
3 — Sí, es posible que tengas razón.
4 ¿Crees que hay todavía otros motivos?
5 — Me parece que otro factor importante, y más aún en las ciudades, es éste: (2)
6 Tengo la impresión de que en Francia la gente vive más aislada, más sola.
7 En España se vive más con los otros, se está más acompañado, (3)
8 y quizá, no se busca tanto la compañía de un perro o un gato.
9 Este conjunto de razones y otras de diversa índole pueden servirte
10 para que te hagas una idea de ese detalle que te sorprendió en España.

11 — ¿Qué árbol da las aceitunas?
12 — Ninguno.
13 — Sí, hombre, el olivo.
14 — No señor, no las da, se las quitan. (4)

LESSON FIFTY-TWO

A cultural aspect (continuation and end)

1 — Yes. The standard of living (of life) is less high in Spain than in France.
2 Especially (Above all) in the cities, and an animal needs to be well cared [for].
3 — Yes, you may be right.
4 Do you think that there are still other reasons (motives)?
5 — It seems to me that [an]other important factors and even more in (the) towns, is this [one] :
6 I have the impression of (of) that in France the people live more isolated, more alone.
7 In Spain one lives more with the others, one is more accompanied,
8 and perhaps one does not seek so much the company of a dog or a cat.
9 This set (assembly) of reasons and others of [a] different kind may help you (serve you)
10 to (so that you might) make (yourself) an idea about (of) that detail that surprised you in Spain.

11 — Which tree gives olives?
12 — There isn't one (None).
13 — Yes, there is! The olive tree.
14 — No sir, it doesn't give them, one takes them away.

* * * * *

NOTES
(1) In the last lesson we saw *ritmo de vida* : "lifestyle". Here we have *nivel de vida* : "standard of living".
(2) *Aun* means "even" ; *aún* means the same as *todavía* : "still" or "yet". *Aun los que tienen dinero* : "even people with money" ; *aún* (with an accent) *está aquí* : "he's still here".
(3) *Se vive* : "one lives". Refer back to Lesson 42, paragraph 2, if you don't remember this construction.
(4) *Quitar* : "to take off" or "to remove". *Quítese el abrigo* : "take off your (pol.) coat" ; *este asunto me quita el sueño* : "this subject makes me lose sleep (removes the sleep to me)".

EJERCICIO: 1. Mi nivel de vida no es muy alto. **2.** Los niños necesitan cuidados particulares. **3.** No ha venido aún. **4.** En las ciudades, hay mucha gente que vive aislada. **5.** ¿Vienes sola o acompañada? **6.** Me gustó sobre todo el gesto que tuvo con los niños. **7.** ¡Sírvete!

EJERCICIO DE CONTROL
Ponga las palabras que faltan

1 *What is your profession?*

¿ . . . . ?

2 *Life is more expensive in cities than in villages.*

. .   . .

. . .   .

****

LECCION CINCUENTA Y TRES

En la carretera

1 — Venimos de Poitiers y vamos a Jaén, una de las capitales de provincia de Andalucía. **(1)**

2   Tenemos intención de pararnos a pasar la noche cerca de la frontera.

3 — Empiezo a estar un poco cansada de conducir.

EXERCISE : **1.** My standard of living is not very high. – **2.** Children need special care. – **3.** He hasn't come yet. – **4.** In cities there are lots of people who live isolated. – **5.** Are you (fem.) coming alone or accompanied? – **6.** I especially liked the gesture that he had with the children. – **7.** Help yourself!

3 *You seem very alone.*

. . . .

4 *I have the impression you worry too much.*

. . . .

. . . .

4 *He was right.*

. . . .

THE MISSING WORDS : **1** cuál es su profesión. **2** la vida es más cara en las ciudades que en los pueblos. **3** me parece que estás muy solo. **4** tengo la impresión de que te preocupas demasiado. **5** tenía razón.

Segunda ola: 3ª lección.

* *

LESSON FIFTY-THREE

On the road

1 — We are coming from Poitiers and we are going to Jaén, one of the provincial capitals of Andalucia.
2 We intend to stop (ourselves) to spend the night near (of) the border.
3 — I'm starting to be a bit tired of driving (to drive).

Lección 53

4   Se está haciendo de noche y hay que pensar en buscar un hotel o un lugar para poder acampar y dormir esta noche. **(1)**

5 — Y si, además, tú estás cansada, hay que pararse cuanto antes. **(2)**

6 — Mañana, en la frontera, preguntaremos cuál es el camino más corto para llegar a Jaén.

7   Al día siguiente, después de haber pasado la frontera: **(3)**

8 — Buenos días, señora. Vamos a Jaén ¿qué carretera nos aconseja tomar?

9 — Es muy sencillo. Yo les aconsejo lo siguiente:

10   De aquí a Madrid, pueden coger la autopista: **(4)**

11   la entrada está a un kilómetro de aquí, a mano derecha. **(5)**

12   Una vez en Madrid, pueden seguir todavía por la autopista

13   y dejarla un poco más tarde para coger las carreteras nacionales

14   y, así, tendrán la ocasión de visitar las tierras del Quijote.

15 — Muchas gracias. Adiós.

EJERCICIO: 1. ¿Tienes intención de pararte para comer? **2.** En invierno, se hace de noche más pronto. **3.** ¿Qué me aconseja usted? **4.** La entrada de la autopista no está lejos. **5.** La carretera nacional es más bonita. **6.** Una vez en la ciudad, es muy sencillo encontrar un hotel. **7.** Dímelo cuanto antes.

EJERCICIO DE CONTROL
Ponga las palabras que faltan

1 *What do you intend to do?*

¿ . . . . ?

4   It's starting to get dark and we must think of looking
        (in to look) for a hotel or a place to (be able to) camp
        and sleep tonight (this night).
5 — And if, moreover, you are tired, we must stop as
        soon as possible.
6 — Tomorrow, at the border, we will ask which is the
        shortest way to get to Jaén.
7   The next day, after having passed the border :
8 — Good day, Madam. We are going to Jaén. What
        road do you advise us to take?
9 — It's very simple. I advise you the following (thing) :
10   From here to Madrid, you can take the motorway :
11   the entrance is (at) one kilometer from here, on the
        right (at right hand).
12   Once at Madrid, you can continue (follow) still on
        the motorway
13   and leave it a bit later (for) to take the A roads
        (national highways)
14   and, that way (thus) you will have the opportunity
        (occasion) to visit Don Quixote country (the lands of
        the Quixote).
14 — Thank you very much. Goodbye.

NOTES
(1) *Se está haciendo de noche* : lit. "it is making itself of night".
Hay que : "it is necessary to". This impersonal construction is
often used instead of *tener que* + infinitive.
(2) *Cuanto antes* : "as soon as possible". This expression is also
used in *cuanto antes vengas más contentos estaremos* : "the
sooner you come the happier we will be". We'll come back to
this.
(3) *Mañana* : "tomorrow" ; *el día siguiente* : "the day after". *Al día
siguiente* : "on the next day".
(4) On Spanish motorways, you will have to pay at *el peaje* (pron.
pé**a**Hé) : "the toll".
(5) *A mano derecha* : "on the right hand" ; *a mano izquierda* : "on
the left hand" or "on the left".

EXERCISE : 1. Do you intend to stop to eat? – **2.** In winter it gets
dark earlier. – **3.** What do you advise me? – **4.** The motorway
entrance is not far. – **5.** The national highway is prettier. – **6.** Once
in the city, it's very simple to find a hotel. – **7.** Tell me as soon as
possible.

2 *I'm looking for a hotel in the centre of town.*

. . . .

. . . . . .

3 *Within an hour, we'll be at the border.*

. . . .

. . . .

4 *The following day he was ill.*

. .   . .

5 *I want to read "Don Quixote".*

. . . .

****

LECCION CINCUENTA Y CUATRO

Una costumbre

1   Las calles se animan.
2 — Me parece que ahora hay más gente por la
       calle.
3 — ¡Claro! Los comercios cierran y la gente sale
       del trabajo. **(1)**
4   Es la hora de volver a casa o de ir a tomar
       unos vinos.
5 — ¿Qué quieres decir? **(2)**
6 — Perdona, no te lo he explicado. Es casi un
       rito en España.

THE MISSING WORDS : 1 qué tienes intención de hacer. 2 busco un hotel en el centro de la ciudad. 3 dentro de una hora, estaremos en la frontera. 4 al día siguiente, estaba enfermo. 5 quiero leer el Quijote.

Segunda ola: 4ª lección.

****

LESSON FIFTY-FOUR

A custom

1 The streets are getting busy (are animating themselves).
2 — I think that now there are more people in the street.
3 — Of course! The shops are closing and (the) people are leaving (coming out of) work.
4 It's (the) time to return home or to go to drink a few wines.
5 — What do you mean?
6 — Excuse me, I haven't explained to you. It's almost a rite in Spain.

NOTES
(1) *Un comercio :* "a business". The man in the street would be more likely to talk of *las tiendas :* "the shops".
(2) *¿Qué quieres decir? :* "What do you mean?" (lit. "What do you want to say") ; *¿Qué quiere decir esta palabra? :* "What does this word mean?"

Lección 54

7   "Ir de vinos" quiere decir ir con algunos amigos a tomar algo a un bar o a una cafetería. **(3)**

8   En España es algo muy corriente, sobre todo el viernes por la tarde, el sábado y el domingo.

9   Se entra en un bar, se bebe un vaso,

10 y, si es mediodía, se toma, además, una tapa; **(4)**

11 luego se va a otro bar y se hace lo mismo.

12 Cada una de las personas paga una ronda.

13 — ¿Y no terminan borrachos?

14 — No más que en otros lugares. Cada país regula sus costumbres. **(5)**

EJERCICIO: 1. ¿A qué hora cierran los comercios? **2.** ¿Vienes a tomar unos vinos? **3.** ¡Vamos a beber un vaso! **4.** ¿Cierran ustedes a mediodía? **5.** Yo hago lo mismo que tú. **6.** Esta ronda la pago yo. **7.** Se ha ido a "dormir la mona".

EJERCICIO DE CONTROL
Ponga las palabras que faltan

1 *In my neighbourhood there are a lot of businesses.*

. . . .

7   *Ir de vinos* means to go with some friends to take something in (to) a bar or in (to) a café.
8   In Spain it's (something) very common, especially on Friday evening[s], on Saturday and Sunday.
9   One enters (in) a bar, one drinks a glass
10   and, if it's midday, one takes, moreover, a snack ;
11   then one goes to [an]other bar and one does the same [thing].
12   Each (one of the) person(s) pays a round.
13 — And doesn't one end [up] drunk?
14 — No more than in other places. Each country controls (regulates) its customs.

NOTES
(3) *Ir de vinos* is a familiar expression that is difficult to translate literally (lit. "to go of wines"). Each country has its own customs, and the evening "bar crawl" is one of Spain's. Rarely do the Spanish stay for more than one drink in each bar... but there are plenty of bars to visit!
(4) *Tapas* are the little dishes that you can choose in bars to go with your *aperitivo*. In some parts of Spain they are called *pinchos*.
(5) *Costumbre* : "custom" or "habit". *Tengo costumbre de... :* "I usually...".

EXERCISE : 1. At what time do the shops shut? – **2.** Are you coming for a few drinks? – **3.** Let's go and have a drink! – **4.** Do you close at midday? – **5.** I do the same as you. – **6.** This is my round. – **7.** He has gone to sleep it off.

2 *It's getting late.*

. .   . .

3 *It's time to go home.*

. .   . .

4 *This round is not paid [for] yet.*

. . . .   pagada   . . . .

5 *Each country has its customs.*

. . . .

****

LECCION CINCUENTA Y CINCO

Medios de transporte

1 — ¿Qué hay allí? Parece que hay mucha gente. **(1)**

2 — No ha pasado nada, es la parada del autobús y la gente está en la cola.

3 — Creí que era un accidente.

4 — A las horas punta, es siempre igual. **(2)**

5 La gente utiliza cada vez más los transportes colectivos. **(3)**

6 — Eso está bien, así habrá menos polución, menos tráfico y menos ruido.

7 — Actualmente, los ayuntamientos de las ciudades más importantes

8 se preocupan bastante por crear zonas peatonales,

9 sobre todo en los barrios viejos y alrededor de los monumentos artísticos.

10 — Me parece una excelente idea.

11 — Los habitantes de las ciudades exigen de las autoridades un sistema de vida más agradable.

THE MISSING WORDS : 1 en mi barrio, hay muchos comercios. 2 se hace tarde. 3 es la hora de volver. 4 esta ronda no está - todavía. 5 cada país tiene sus costumbres.

* * * * *

Segunda ola: 5ª lección.

* *

LESSON FIFTY-FIVE

Means of transport

1 — What is that (there) over there? There seem to be a lot of people.
2 — Nothing has happened. It's the bus-stop and the people are in the queue.
3 — I thought that it was an accident.
4 — At peak hours it's always the same.
5 — People use more and more (the) public transport (collective transports).
6 — That's good. That way there will be less pollution, less traffic and less noise.
7 — At present, the councils of the most important cities
8   are quite involved in creating (worry themselves enough to create) pedestrian zones
9   especially in the old neighbourhoods and around the artistic monuments.
10 — I think it's an excellent idea.
11 — The inhabitants of the cities demand from the authorities a more pleasant lifestyle (life system).

NOTES
(1) *Me parece :* lit. "it seems to me". The nearest equivalent in English is in fact "I think" (see note to Lesson 23).
Parece que : lit. "it seems that...".
(2) *A las horas punta* or *a las horas de punta* means "at rush hours". *Una punta* is "a sharp point" or "a tip".
(3) *Cada vez más :* (lit. "each time more") means "more and more".

Lección 55

Al pie de la letra

12 — No me ha tocado nada en la lotería. **(4)**
13 — ¿También jugabas?
14 — No, pero como dicen que es cuestión de
suerte...

EJERCICIO: 1. Parece que ha habido un accidente. **2.** La
parada del autobús está en esta misma calle. **3.** A las
horas punta, hay mucho tráfico. **4.** Llueve cada vez más.
5. Voy a visitar los barrios viejos. **6.** Me han tocado
novecientas cincuenta y ocho pesetas con setenta y
cinco céntimos en la lotería. **7.** Es excelente.

*****

EJERCICIO DE CONTROL
Ponga las palabras que faltan

1 *At the entrance to (of) the cinema, there was a big queue.*

. . . .

. . . .

2 *I'll wait for you near the bus-stop.*

. . . .

. . . .

3 *Public transport is more and more pleasant.*

. . . .

. . . .

Taking things literally (At the foot of the letter)

12 — I have won nothing (nothing has touched me) in the lottery.
13 — Did you play too?
14 — No, but as they say that it's a question of luck...

NOTES
(4) Here we have another meaning for the verb *tocar* (see Lessons 18 and 24). Compare *me toca a mi :* "it's my turn". *Me ha tocado una bici en la tómbola :* "I have won a bike in the tombola".

EXERCISE : 1. There seems to have been an accident. – **2.** The bus-stop is in this very (same) street. – **3.** At rush hour there is a lot of traffic. – **4.** It's raining more and more. – **5.** I'm going to visit the old neighbourhoods. – **6.** I have won 958.75 pesetas in the lottery. – **7.** It's excellent.

4 *The artistic monuments are often in the old neighbourhoods of towns.*

. . . .

. . . . , ... , ...

. . . .

THE MISSING WORDS :   1 a la entrada del cine, había una gran cola. 2 te esperaré cerca de la parada del autobús. 3 los transportes colectivos son cada vez más agradables. 4 los monumentos artísticos se encuentran, a menudo, en los barrios viejos de las ciudades.

Segunda ola: 6ª lección.

LECCION CINCUENTA Y SEIS

LESSON FIFTY-SIX

Revisión y notas

1. **Pronunciación.** As we are no longer going to give you detailed pronunciation notes, here are some general comments to take stock of what you already know, and to give you a point of reference if you come across any pronunciation difficulties in the future.

2. **The alphabet.** Here are the 28 letters in the Spanish alphabet, with the pronunciation of their names :

a, a - *b*, bé - *c*, cé (or thé) - *ch*, ché - *d*, dé - *e*, é - *f*, éfé - *g*, Hé - *h*, atché - *i*, i - *j*, Hota - *k*, ka - *l*, élé - *ll*, éllé (between éyé and elyé) - *m*, émé - *n*, éné - *ñ*, enyé - *o*, o - *p*, pé - *q*, kou - *r*, érré - *s*, ésé - *t*, té - *u*, ou - *v*, ouvé - *x*, ékiss - *y*, i griega [Greek i] - *z*, céta (or théta).

All the letters are feminine : *una a, una j, una z.* When you use a dictionary, remember that *ch* and *ll* are dealt with separately. This custom is changing in newer dictionaries, however.

3. **Spelling.** You will have noticed that Spanish spelling is very simple. It is completely phonetic, and, as we have said earlier, each letter has a face value that never changes.

There are a certain number of places where confusion can arise, notably with the letters *b* and *v*, which are pronounced the same way. As an illustration, look at this (but don't remember it!) : a hand-written sign announcing "nice cold drinks" (in Latin America) once read *AGUAS VIEN FRILLAS* instead of *AGUAS BIEN FRIAS.*) If you think about it, you can avoid making mistakes like this.

There can also be some confusion between the letters *g* and *j* in words like *mujer :* "woman", *región :* "region", *dirigir :* "to direct", since a *g* is pronunced guturally when it comes before an *e* or an *i*. Similarly, *c* and *z* are both pronounced like the unvoiced English "th" in words like *cero :* "zero", *zapata :* "shoe", *acción :* "action" (i.e., when the *c* comes before an *e* or an *i)*. In Southern Spain and Latin America, the "th" sound is a simple "s" sound.

The *s* and the *m* in Spanish are never doubled : *inmediato :* "immediate", *posible :* "possible", *impresión :* "impression". On the other hand, the *n* and the *c* sometimes appear as double letters, but should be pronounced as if they were separate :
Innumerable, innovación, acción, lección, etc.
The syllable ends between the two consonants. Remember that the real double consonants in Spanish *(ll, rr)* should never be split (at the end of a line, for instance).

4. **Soler** (see note 1 to Lesson 51). This verb is one of the many ways to express "often" or "usually". *Suele llover en primavera :* "it often rains in spring" ; *suelo tomar algo antes de cenar :* "I usually have a drink before dining".

Lección 56

5. **¿Cuál?** (see note to Lesson 51) : "Which?" or "What?".
When there is a noun involved, *¿Cuál?* becomes *Qué* : *¿Qué libro es el tuyo?* : "Which book is yours? ; *¿Qué carretera tomó usted?* : "Which road did you take?". But, when the noun does not figure immediately after the "Which...", we use *¿Cuál...* Thus, *¿Cuál es tu nombre?* : "What is your name?" *¿Cuál es tu dirección?* : "What is your address"? The difference seems minor in English, because we use the word "What?" in both senses. If you asked a Spanish person *¿Qué es tu dirección?*, he would explain that his address was the number and the name of the street where he lived.
Remember : *¿Qué es...?* demands an explanation, while *¿Cuál es...?* demands a description.

6. **Writing in Spanish**

1   In a month I will be in Rome.
2   What did you like so much about them? - Their friendliness.
3   I usually go to bed early.
4   I have given a lot of reasons. - Which ones?

****

LECCION CINCUENTA Y SIETE

Antes de las vacaciones

1 — He telefoneado a la estación y he reservado tres literas.
2 — Menos mal que no te has olvidado, creía que no íbamos a poder irnos. (1)
3   En Navidad, todo el mundo quiere coger el tren los mismos días.
4 — ¿Podrás pasar por la estación para coger los billetes y las reservas?
5 — Esta tarde tengo que arreglar unos asuntos pero tendré tiempo de ir.
6 — ¿Quieres que te haga un cheque?
7 — Sí, prefiero. Así, no tendré que ir al banco.
8 — Como ninguna de las tres fumamos, he pedido un compartimento (2)

5   We intend (have the intention) to take the motorway
        to (until) the border.
6   You seem more and more tired.

7. Translation

1   Dentro de un mes, estaré en Roma.
2   ¿Qué es lo que te ha gustado tanto? - Su simpatía.
3   Suelo acostarme pronto.
4   He dado muchas razones. - ¿Cuáles?
5   Tenemos intención de coger la autopista hasta la
     frontera.
6   Parece que estás cada vez más cansado.

*****

Segunda ola: 7ª lección (revisión).

****

LESSON FIFTY-SEVEN

Before the holidays

1 — I have phoned (to) the station and have reserved
       three sleepers.
2 — Luckily (Less badly) (that) you didn't forget
       (yourself), I thought that we weren't going to be able
       to go.
3   At (In) Christmas, everybody (all the world) wants to
       catch the train [on] the same days.
4 — Will you be able to call at (pass by) the station to
       take the tickets and the reservations?
5 — This afternoon I have to arrange some matters but I
       will have the time to go.
6 — Do you want me to write you (make you) a cheque?
7 — Yes. I [would] prefer [you to]. That way I won't have
       to go to the bank.
8 — As none of the three [of us] (we) smoke, I have
       asked for a compartment

NOTES
(1) *Menos mal :* lit. "less badly". The nearest equivalent in English
    would be "just as well".

9 en el que esté prohibido fumar.
10 — ¿Tenemos que hacer transbordo?
11 — A lo sumo una vez, en la frontera. Pero se me ha olvidado preguntarlo. **(2)**
12 — Me informaré esta tarde.
13 — Pregunta también si tenemos derecho a algún descuento. **(3)**
14 — No creo. A no ser que nos dejen viajar gratis por ser simpáticas. **(4)**

EJERCICIO: **1.** Quiero reservar una litera. **2.** Menos mal que has venido. **3.** Ya he comprado los billetes. **4.** Tengo un asunto importante entre manos. **5.** Este cheque no está firmado. **6.** Tenemos que hacer dos transbordos. **7.** Nos han hecho una reducción importante.

EJERCICIO DE CONTROL
Ponga las palabras que faltan

1 *I wasn't able to get sleepers.*

. . . .

2 *We will go sitting down.*

. . . .

3 *We have the reduction for large families.*

. . . .

. . . .

9   where it is prohibited to smoke.
10 —   Do we have to change (make transhipment)?
11 —   Once at the most, at the border. But I forgot to ask (to ask it has forgotten itself to me).
12 —   I will find out (inform myself) this afternoon.
13 —   Ask also if we are allowed (have right) (to) any reduction.
14 —   I don't think so. Unless (if not that) they let us travel free for being nice.

NOTES
(2) *A lo sumo* : "at the most".
(3) *Descuento* : "discount". The word *reducción* also exists, but is less common. You will find this word in the exercises.
(4) *A no ser que* : an idiomatic construction meaning "unless".

EXERCISE : 1. I want to reserve a sleeper. **– 2.** It's just as well you have come. **– 3.** I have already bought the tickets. **– 4.** I have an important matter on my hands. **– 5.** This cheque is not signed. **– 6.** We have to change twice. **– 7.** We have got a big reduction.

4 *I am going to find out at the station.*

. . .   .

5 *Smoking is prohibited here.*

. . . . , ...

THE MISSING WORDS :   **1** no he podido coger literas; **2** iremos sentados. **3** tenemos el descuento de familia numerosa. **4** voy a informarme en la estación. **5** aquí está prohibido fumar.

REMEMBER
– *Turn back if you come across a difficulty with the pronunciation.*
– *Carry on making references about recurring difficulties.*
– *From now on, pay close attention to idiomatic phrases and sentences that do not have a direct equivalent in English. Many of these idioms are very common in Spanish. See Notes 1, 2 and 4 of this lesson.*

Segunda ola: 8ª lección.

LECCION CINCUENTA Y OCHO

Bromeando

1 — Me estoy lavando la cabeza. Luego, si tienes tiempo, me cortarás el pelo. **(1)**

2 — Bien. ¿Vas a tardar mucho?

3 — No, enseguida termino. ¿Puedes traerme una toalla limpia?

4 — Toma. Voy a coger el peine y las tijeras.

5 — No me hagas una escabechina ¡eh!

6 — Con tal de que no te deje calvo, ya valdrá. **(2)**

7 — ¡Cuidado! Hazlo despacito y no me cortes una oreja. **(3)**

8 — Eres un miedoso.

9 — Y tus comentarios me dan buenas razones.

10 — ¡Ya está! Ya puedes ir a ver si te aceptan para hacer el servicio militar.

11 — ¡A sus órdenes, mi sargento! Voy a mirarme en el espejo.

12 — Por haber tenido miedo, usted se pondrá el uniforme de faena

13 y me pelará tres toneladas de patatas de aquí a mediodía.

LESSON FIFTY-EIGHT

Joking

1 — I am washing my hair (my head). Then, if I have time, you will cut my hair (cut me the hair).
2 — Right. Will you be long? (Are you going to delay much?)
3 — No, I am finishing straight away. Can you bring me a clean towel?
4 — Here. I am going to get the comb and the scissors.
5 — Don't make a mess of me!
6 — Provided I don't leave you bald, everything will be OK (already it will be worthwhile).
7 — [Be] careful! Do it slowly and don't cut (me) an ear.
8 — You're a scaredy-cat (a fearful one).
9 — And your comments give me good reason(s) [to be].
10 — That's it! Now (Already) you can go to see if they accept you to do military service.
11 — At your orders, sergeant! I'm going to look at myself in the mirror.
12 — For having been afraid (had fear), you'll put on the uniform to do the household chores
13 and you will peel me three tons of potatoes by midday (from now until midday).

NOTES
(1) *Lavarse :* "to have a wash" is a reflexive verb.
Lavarse los manos : "to wash one's hands", or, literally, "to wash the hands to oneself". Similarly, *pelo :* "a hair" ; *cortarse el pelo* (sing.) : "to cut one's hair" **or** "to get one's hair cut".
(2) *Con tal de que* or *con tal que :* "provided that". Takes the subjunctive.
(3) *Despacio :* "slowly" ; the diminutive *despacito* means "nice and slowly".

14 — Con gusto. ¡Siempre listo para servir!

EJERCICIO: 1. Mañana, quiero cortarme el pelo. **2.** Me voy a lavar. **3.** Coge la toalla de baño. **4.** Vete despacio. **5.** El niño se mira en el espejo. **6.** Tiene un uniforme de enfermera. **7.** Voy a pelar dos melocotones.

EJERCICIO DE CONTROL
Ponga las palabras que faltan

1 *I'm going to have a wash.*

. . . .

2 *Here, take this comb.*

. . . . , ...

3 *I have cut myself with the scissors.*

. . . .

****

LECCION CINCUENTA Y NUEVE

Un nuevo programa de radio

1 — Niños, señoritas, señoras, señores, buenas tardes.
2 He aquí nuestro nuevo programa: "¡Basta de hechos, pasemos a las palabras!" **(1) (2)**
3 En nuestra primera emisión, tenemos el honor de presentarles a
4 Pedrito Martínez, "el Terrible". Seis años y medio de edad y 875 presidente **(3)**

14 — With pleasure (taste). Always ready to serve!

EXERCISE : 1. Tomorrow, I want to get my hair cut. – **2.** I'm going to have a wash. – **3.** Get the bathtowel. – **4.** Go slowly. – **5.** The child is looking at himself in the mirror. – **6.** She has a nurse's uniform. – **7.** I'm going to peel two peaches.

***** *****

4 *The mirror is broken.*

. . . .

5 *Will you peel the potatoes?*

¿ . . . . ?

THE MISSING WORDS : **1** voy a lavarme. **2** toma, coge este peine. **3** me he cortado con las tijeras. **4** el espejo está roto. **5** quieres pelar las patatas.

Segunda ola: 9ª lección.

****

LESSON FIFTY-NINE

A new radio programme

1 — Children, ladies [and] gentlemen, good evening.
2 Here is our new programme, "Enough of action (deeds), let's move on to (the) words".
3 In our first broadcast, we have the honour of presenting (to present) [to] you (to)
4 Pedrito Martinez "the Terrible". Six years and [a] half of age and 875th president.

NOTES
(1) *He aquí :* "here is". This expression is less common in everyday speech than *aquí está.*
(2) *¡Basta!* is part of the verb *bastar :* "to suffice". Remember also *bastante :* "enough" or "quite".
(3) Many diminutives can be made with the suffix *-ito.* Here we have "little Pedro" : *Pedrito,* used, as are many diminutives, to express familiarity, pity, etc.

5   de la República de los niños que, como ya
     saben ustedes,

6   tiene como divisa "La cosa tiene que dar
     vueltas".

7 — Buenas tardes, señor Presidente.

8 — Menos protocolo y al ajo, que no tengo
     tiempo que perder. **(4)**

9 — Perdone. Nuestra primera pregunta le será
     formulada por el enviado especial de la
     revista: "Esto no marcha".

10 — Señor Presidente: ¿Cuáles son sus proyec-
     tos immediatos?

11 — Tengo el proyecto de reciclarme. Nuestros
     expertos han constatado que si no se
     cambia se hace siempre lo mismo. **(5)**

12   Por mi parte, quisiera reciclarme como
      parado.

13   He constatado que cuando como bien y
      bebo bien, resisto mucho tiempo sin
      trabajar. **(6)**

14 — Muchas gracias, señor Presidente.

EJERCICIO: 1. He aquí mi tío. **2.** Quiero hablar con él
cara a cara. **3.** Iré incluso si él no está allí. **4.** Como ya
sabes... **5.** No quiero perder el tiempo. **6.** Pienso cambiar
de trabajo. **7.** Nos pidieron nuestra opinión.

5   of the Republic of (the) children, that, as you know
        (already)
6   has as [its] motto "Things must work" ("The thing
        has to make turns").
7   —   Good evening, Mr President.
8   —   Less protocol and [let's get] straight to the kernel (to
        the garlic), (that) I haven't [any] time to lose.
9   —   Excuse me. Our first question will be made up
        (formulated) by the special correspondent of the
        magazine "This isn't working".
10 —   Mr President : What (Which) are your immediate
        plans (projects)?
11 —   I plan to retrain (I have the project to recycle
        myself). Our experts have stated that if one doesn't
        change, one does always the same [thing].
12   As far as I'm concerned (For my part) I would like to
        retrain (myself) as an unemployed person.
13   I have noticed that when I eat and drink well, I can
        go (withstand) a long time without working (to
        work).
14 —   Thank you very much, Mr President.

NOTES
(4) *Vamos al ajo :* "Let's get straight to the point" (literally : "let's
go to the garlic"). The *que* links the two phrases together in a
causal relationship (i.e., it could be replaced by *porque*).
(5) *Si no se cambia, se hace siempre lo mismo :* the reflexive
formula can sometimes be translated by the impersonal "one".
(6) *Resistir :* "to resist" or "to withstand". Often translated by the
English verb "to go", with a sense of endurance, e.g., *resisto
mucho tiempo bajo el agua.*

* * * * *

EXERCISE : 1. Here is my uncle. – **2.** I want to speak with him face
to face. – **3.** I will go even if he isn't there. – **4.** As you already
know... – **5.** I don't want to waste my time. – **6.** I am thinking of
changing jobs. – **7.** They asked for our opinion.

EJERCICIO DE CONTROL
Ponga las palabras que faltan

1 *There is a new television programme.*

. . . .

2 *It's the first number of the new magazine which I told you about.*

. . . . la . . . . .

. . . . de la que . . . .

3 *He always does the same thing.*

. . . .

****

LECCION SESENTA.

La calefacción

1 — El invierno se acerca y comienza a hacer frío.

2 — Ya va siendo hora de que nos decidamos a comprar algo para calentarnos. **(1)**

3 — El problema son los precios, están por las nubes.

4 — Ayer eché una ojeada a algunos escaparates y todo me pareció carísimo. **(2)**

5 — Los aparatos de gas son más caros que los eléctricos.

6 — ¡Claro! Pero una factura de electricidad es más elevada que una de gas.

4 *Have you changed address?*

¿ · ·   · · · · · · · · · · ·   · ·   · · · · · · · · · ?

5 *A lot of unemployed people retrain themselves.*

· · · · · ·   · · · · · · · · ·   · · · · · · · ·

*****

THE MISSING WORDS :   **1** hay un nuevo programa de televisión. **2** es el primer número de - nueva revista - te he hablado. **3** hace siempre lo mismo. **4** ha cambiado de domicilio. **5** muchos parados se reciclan.

Segunda ola: Lección 10ª

****

LESSON SIXTY

(The) heating

1 — Winter is approaching (itself) and it's starting to get (to make) cold.
2 — We're going to have to (Already it goes being time of that we) buy something to heat ourselves.
3 — The problem is (they are) the prices, they are sky-high (in the clouds).
4 — Yesterday I had a look at some shop-fronts and everything seemed (to me) extremely expensive.
5 — Gas units are more expensive than electric ones.
6 — Of course! But an electricity bill (bill of electricity) is higher than a gas bill (than one of gas).

NOTES
(1) *Ya va siendo hora* : "it is getting to be time". *Los precios van aumentando* : "prices are increasing" provides another example of the verb *ir* with a gerund, to express a continuous progression in time.
(2) *Escaparate* is akin to the English "escapement" (cliff, promontory) and has retained a meaning of "front" or façade. *Ir de escaparates* : "to go window shopping".

7 — Exactamente. Lo que quiere decir que, a largo plazo, el gas es más rentable.

8 — Por el momento, lo que podemos hacer es abrigarnos un poco más en casa; **(3)**

9 — y, mientras tanto, mirar a ver si alguno de nuestros amigos

10 puede proporcionarnos un aparato de segunda mano o conoce un lugar en el que ese tipo de cosas sea más barato.

11 — Ángela es fontanera, quizá ella sepa algo. Voy a llamarla para decirle que venga a cenar y así podremos charlar. **(4)**

¡Viva el desarrollo científico!

1 Comentario oído en un congreso internacional:

2 "Yo he aprendido la lectura rápida: leí "La Biblia" en veintitrés minutos y medio; trata de Dios".

EJERCICIO: 1. Ya va siendo hora de que nos vayamos. **2.** Las patatas están por las nubes. **3.** Voy a calentarme un poco. **4.** La factura era muy elevada. **5.** Hace frío, hay que abrigarse. **6.** A largo plazo es rentable. **7.** Llama al fontanero.

7 — Exactly. Which means that, in the long term, gas is
more economical (profitable).
8 — For the moment what we are going to do is to keep
ourselves warm (shelter ourselves) a bit more at
home ;
9 — and, meanwhile, to look to see if any of our friends
10 can procure us a second hand unit or knows a place
where (in which) that type of thing(s) is cheaper.
11 — Angela is a plumber. Perhaps she knows
something. I'm going to call her to tell her to come
(that she come) to (have) dinner, and that way we
can chat.

Long live scientific development!

1 Comment heard at an international congress :
2 "I have learnt speed-reading : I read the Bible in
twenty-three and a half minutes (23 minutes and
half) ; it's about God."

NOTES
(1) *Abrigo :* "overcoat" ; *abrigarse,* as we saw in Lesson 39,
means to "cover up" or "to take shelter".
(4) *Charlar :* "to chat". The English "charlatan" has the same root.
Indeed, the Spanish *charlatán* can mean "charlatan" or
"chatterbox" depending on the context.

*A preliminary word should be given about the subjunctive.
You will have noticed forms of the present subjunctive turning
up in recent lessons, sometimes when the verb appears after
a particular construction, but in general terms, when there is
a sense of **hypothesis** in the sentence. The subjunctive
exists in English, but has largely fallen into disuse in familiar
speech. When the statement relies on something other than
proven fact, the subjunctive comes into its own in Spanish,
and it is important to recognize the sense (and added
subtlety) of this mood of the verb. For the time being, try to
identify the uses.
We'll come to the form later.*

EXERCISE : 1. It's time we were leaving. – **2.** The potatoes are
terribly expensive. – **3.** I'm going to warm myself up a bit. – **4.** The
bill was very high. – **5.** It's cold, we must dress up well. – **6.** It's
profitable in the long term. – **7.** Call the plumber.

EJERCICIO DE CONTROL
Ponga las palabras que faltan

1 *The summer is coming to its end.*

. . . . a . . . .

2 *Gas units are terribly expensive.*

. . . .

. . . . .

3 *In winter the people dress up well.*

. . . . a . . . .

* *

LECCION SESENTA Y UNA

Una sorpresa

1 Anoche, estaba tan cansado que me acosté nada más cenar. **(1) (2)**
2 He dormido bien; me he despertado a las ocho.
3 Como no tenía que ir a trabajar, me he dado una vuelta en la cama
4 con la intención de dormirme otra vez.
5 ¡Imposible! Ayer no bajé las persianas y la claridad me ha impedido dormirme.
6 Me he levantado, he encendido el tocadiscos, he puesto un disco **(3)**

* * * * *

4 *Meanwhile I have started to read.*

. . . .   puse   . . . . .

5 *The plumber won't be able to come this week.*

. . . .

. . . . . .

* * * * *

THE MISSING WORDS :   **1** el verano se acerca - su fin. **2** los aparatos de gas están por las nubes. **3** en invierno la gente se abriga. **4** mientras tanto me - a leer. **5** el fontanero no podrá venir esta semana.

Segunda ola: lección 11.

****

LESSON SIXTY-ONE

A surprise

1   Last night, I was so tired that I went to bed straight after dining (nothing more to dine).
2   I slept well. I woke up at eight o'clock.
3   As I didn't have to go to work, I stayed for a while in bed
4   meaning to (with the intention of) go(ing) [back] to sleep again.
5   Impossible! Yesterday I didn't pull down the blinds and the light (clarity) stopped (impeded) me [from] sleeping.
6   I got up, I turned on the record player [and] put on a record.

NOTES
(1) *Anoche* or *ayer por la noche :* "last night". *Anochecer :* "to start to get dark" ; *al anochecer :* "at dusk" ; *al amanecer :* "at dawn".
(2) *Nada más* here means "as soon as" or "straight after".
(3) *Encender :* "to light" or "to turn on". Similarly, *apagar :* "to put out" or "to turn off", applies to fires as well as to electrical goods. Remember the meaning of *tocar :* "to play (music)". (See note 3 to lesson 18).

7   y he ido al cuarto de baño a ducharme.
8   Luego, me he vestido mientras mi desayuno se calentaba.
9   A eso de las nueve, han llamado a la puerta y han gritado: **(4)**
10 — ¿Se puede?
11 — ¡Adelante! He respondido;
12   y, de pronto, he visto aparecer en el umbral de la puerta cinco personas gritando: **(5)**
13 — ¡Felicidades! **(6)**
14 — Yo, ni me acordaba de que era mi cumpleaños.

EJERCICIO: 1. Anoche, fuimos a cenar al restaurante. 2. Me lo he imaginado nada más verte. 3. La claridad y el ruido me impiden dormir. 4. Tenemos un tocadiscos nuevo. 5. Me ducho cuando me levanto. 6. Te veré a eso de las once y media. 7. Mi cumpleaños es el quince de enero.

EJERCICIO DE CONTROL
Ponga las palabras que faltan

1 *Did you sleep well?*

¿ . . .   . ?

2 *We went to bed as soon as you went away.*

. . .   .

. . . .

3 *Your room is lighter than mine.*

. .   . .

4 *I'm going to put on a record that you will like.*

. . .   .

5 *I take a shower with hot water.*

. . .   .

7	and I went to the bathroom to take a shower (to shower myself).
8	Then, I got dressed (dressed myself) while my breakfast was warming (itself) [up].
9	Around nine o'clock, the dooorbell rang and somebody shouted (they called at the door and shouted) :
10	— Can we come in (May one)?
11	— "Come in!" I replied ;
12	— and, suddenly, I saw five people (persons) appearing in the doorway shouting :
13	— Congratulations!
14	— I didn't even remember (Nor did I remember) (of that) it was my birthday.

NOTES
(4) *A eso de las nueve* : "around nine o'clock".
(5) *De pronto* : "suddenly" ; *pronto* : "early" or "quickly".
(6) *Felicidad* : "happiness". In the plural, it means "best wishes" or "congratulations" on any happy occasion.

EXERCISE : 1. Last night we ate at the restaurant. – **2.** I thought so as soon as I saw you. – **3.** The light and the noise stop me from sleeping. – **4.** We have a new record player. – **5.** I take a shower when I get up. – **6.** I'll see you around eleven-thirty. – **7.** My birthday is [on] the fifteenth of January.

THE MISSING WORDS : **1** has dormido bien. **2** nos acostamos nada más que os fuisteis. **3** tu habitación es más clara que la mía. **4** voy a poner un disco que te gustará. **5** me ducho con agua caliente.

Segunda ola: lección 12.

LECCION SESENTA Y DOS

Rubio y moreno

1 Estoy de paso en Cáceres y he alquilado una habitación en la ''Pensión franco-belga''.

2 Me hace gracia porque no tiene nada de francés ni de belga. Los dueños y los huéspedes son españoles; yo soy el único extranjero. (1)

3 Hay cuatro estudiantes, un abogado, un rentero y dos parejas que visitan Extremadura.

4 Aunque se come en mesas independientes, la conversación es, a menudo, general. La cena de anoche fue muy animada. (2)

5 Me colocaron en la misma mesa que al abogado, y enseguida nos pusimos a hablar.

6 Antes de acabar la cena, me dio su tarjeta: ''Emilio Rubio'', y yo le di la mía: ''Marc Lebrun''.

AQUÍ, LAS CENAS SON SIEMPRE ANIMADAS.

7 — Se me ha olvidado casi todo el francés que aprendí en el colegio, pero supongo que Marc en francés es lo mismo que Marcos en castellano.

8 — Sí, - contesté - es un nombre muy corriente en muchos países.

9 — ¿Su apellido tiene alguna significación particular? (3)

LESSON SIXTY-TWO

Blond and Brown

1   I am passing through Cáceres and have rented a room in the "Pension franco-belge".

2   I find it amusing (it makes me grace) because it has nothing (of) French (n)or (of) Belgian. The owners and the guests are Spanish ; I am the only foreigner.

3   There are four students, a lawyer, a tenant farmer and two couples (pairs) (who are) visiting Extremadura.

4   Although we are (one is) eating on separate (independant) tables, the conversation is often general. Last night's dinner was very lively (animated).

5   I was put (They put me) at the same table as the lawyer, and straight away we started to (we put ourselves to) talk.

6   Before finishing (to finish) dinner, he gave me his card : "Emilio Rubio", and I gave him mine : "Marc Lebrun".

7 —   I have forgotten (It has forgotten to me) almost all the French that I learnt at school (in the college), but I suppose that Marc in French is the same as Marcos in Spanish (Castilian).

8 —   "Yes", I answered, "it's a very common (current) name in many countries.

9 —   Does your surname have any particular meaning?

NOTES

(1) *Gracia :* "grace". *Me haces gracia :* "you amuse me" ; *eso no tiene gracia :* "there's nothing funny about that" : *tiene gracia :* "it's funny" ; *¡qué gracia! :* "how funny".

(2) *Aunque... :* "although" **or** "even if". This word illustrates the use of the subjunctive rather well (see note on page 202). When *aunque* is followed by the indicative, it means "although" (e.g., *aunque el libro es interesante :* although the book is interesting). When it is followed by the subjunctive, however, there is a sense of hypothesis : *aunque el libro sea interesante :* "even if the book was interesting" (which it implicitly isn't)... *Sea* is the present subjunctive of the verb *ser*.

(3) *Apellido :* surname. Not to be confused with *nombre :* "first name".

10 — Efectivamente, quiere decir "el moreno".

11 — ¡Qué curioso! Yo me llamo Rubio y soy moreno y usted se llama Moreno y es rubio.

12 — Tenemos que cambiar de apellido... o de pelo.

13 — Por mi parte no hay ningún problema, yo llevo peluca. Así que... cuando usted quiera.

14 — Per...done... no sabía... estaba bromeando.

EJERCICIO: 1. Estoy de paso. 2. A mi llegada a Bruselas, alquilaré un coche. 3. Tome mi tarjeta. 4. Escriba aquí su nombre y apellido. 5. Tienes que cambiar la rueda de la bicicleta. 6. Cuando usted quiera. 7. No sabía que me habías llamado.

EJERCICIO DE CONTROL
Ponga las palabras que faltan

1 *Are you passing through or are you going to stay for a few days?*

¿ . . . . te . . . .

unos . . . . ?

2 *My telephone number is on the card I have given you.*

. . . . en la

. . . . le he . . . .

****

LECCION SESENTA Y TRES
LESSON SIXTY-THREE
Revisión y notas

1. **Diminutives.** These are formed by adding a suffix *(-ito, -ita ; -illo, -illa ; -ecito, -ecita ; -ecillo, -ecilla)* to any word (frequently a noun). Thus *un momentito* is smaller than *un momento*, and *mi hermanita* is smaller than *mi hermana*. Smallness, however, is often accompanied with a sense of familiarity or endearment.

10 — Well yes, actually, (effectively) it means "brown-haired".

11 — How curious! My name is (I am called) Rubio and I have brown hair, and your name is (your are called) Moreno and you have blond hair.

12 — We have to change (of) name[s]... or (of) hair.

13 — As far as I am concerned there is(n't) no problem. I wear [a] wig. So (thus that)... when[ever] you want.

14 — I'm sorry... I didn't know... I was joking.

EXERCISE : 1. I am passing through. – **2.** On my arrival at Brussels, I will rent a car. – **3.** Take my card. – **4.** Write your full name (name and surname) here. – **5.** You have to change the wheel of the bicycle. – **6.** Whenever you want. – **7.** I didn't know that you had called me.

3 *I didn't learn Spanish at school.*

. . . . , ...

. . . . . .

4 *My first name is not common.*

. . . .

5 *Your hair is blond.*

. . . .

THE MISSING WORDS : **1** estás de paso o - vas a quedar - días. **2** mi número de teléfono está - tarjeta que - - dado. **3** no aprendí el castellano en el colegio. **4** mi nombre no es corriente. **5** tu pelo es rubio.

Segunda ola: lección 13.

* *

Augmentatives : These are formed by adding another type of suffix to the word *(-ón, -ona ; -azo, -aza ; -ote, -acho)*, and express bigness. Together with bigness, however, there is often a pejorative sense.

Lección 63

Certain diminutives and augmentatives have become words in their own right (e.g., *un sillón,* which is the augmentative of *una silla* : "a chair", means, specifically, "an armchair" ; and *una cerilla,* which is the diminutive of *cera* : "wax" means "a match" because Spanish matches are often made of waxed paper).

Diminutives and augmentatives are very common in Spanish (and even commoner in parts of Latin America), but you should use them with caution. Look at the examples given below, and try to remember them. Only when you have recognized the different forms and the subtle shades of meaning of each one will you be able to use them confidently in speech.

espere un momentito	"just wait a moment"
pequeñito	"tiny little"
animalito	"nice little animal"
pancillo	"bun" or "small loaf"
florecita	"little flower"
hombrón	"big man"
hombrote	"brute of a fellow"
mujerota	"big fat woman"
palabrota	"swear word"
animalejo	"nasty animal"

2. **Superlatives :** See also sentences 10, 11 and 12 in lesson 47. The comparative, as we saw in lessons 47 and 49, is formed with the word *más (más pequeño, más barato* : "smaller", "cheaper"). The superlative also needs the word *más,* but here we also use the definite article *el* or *la* : *el libro más pequeño, la casa más barata* : "the smallest book", "the cheapest house". (The distinction is not drawn, as it is in English, between "the smaller of two" and "the smallest of three").
Este es el más pequeño : "this is the smallest one", **but** *Este es más pequeño* : "this one is smaller".
La mujer más pobre del pueblo : "the poorest woman in the village",
La casa más bonita que he tenido jamás : "the nicest house I have ever had".

The irregular comparatives *mejor, peor, mayor, menor* (See note 1 to lesson 46) also become superlatives when preceded by the definite article, e.g., *es la peor de sus pinturas* : "it's his worst painting".

Superlatives are very often expressed by adding *-ísimo, -ísima* to the adjective. This suffix intensifies the adjective, and is equivalent to "very" or "extremely". Remember the accent on the first *i,* and the changes in spelling to retain the hard pronunciation of *c, z* or *g.* Examples : *caro, carísimo ; largo, larguísimo ; mucho, muchísimo.*

3. **Lo :** the "neuter article". There are no neuter nouns in Spanish, but the article *lo* can be used with adjectives or adverbs as follows : *lo difícil es hablar :* "the difficult thing is to speak" ; *lo importante es... :* "the important thing is..." (or "what's important is"...). *Lo* can thus best be translated as "that which is". *Lo mío :* "that which is mine" ; *lo dicho :* "that which is said" ; *lo siguiente :* "that which is following" or "the following". Similary with *lo más : lo más difícil de la vida :* "the most difficult thing in life" ; *lo más pronto posible :* "as soon as possible".

- The neuter article *lo* used with an adjective or an adverb expresses the indeterminate. *Lo de mi padre es también mío :* "that which (or "what") is my father's is also mine". When we are · talking about something determinate, however, we use the masculine and feminine articles. *La casa de mi padre es también la mía :* "my father's house is also mine" ; *el problema de la inflación y el del paro :* "the problem of inflation and that of unemployment" ; *La casa más bonita es la de mi hermana :* "the nicest house is my sister's (or "the one of my sister")".

- *Lo que :* "that which" or "what" used with verbs : *lo que me fastidia :* "what annoys me" ; *dime lo que quieres :* "tell me what you want" ; *lo que dices :* "what you say".

- Check back for the uses of *lo* we have already come across : lesson 36, N° 3 ; lesson 40, n° 5 ; lesson 44, n° 7 ; lesson 48, note 1 ; lesson 51, n°s 2 and 7 ; lesson 53, n° 9, lesson 60, n°s 7 and 8.

Lección 63

- Note also a number of idiomatic uses of *lo* :
  -*lo* + an adjective or adverb folled by *que* : *lo mal que trabajas* : "how badly you work" ; *no sabes lo cansada que estoy* : "you don't know how tired I am"

a lo más or *a lo sumo*	"at the most"
por lo menos	"at least"
a lo mejor	"at best"
a lo mejor	"maybe"
a lo más tarde	"at the latest"
en lo sucesivo	"in future"

4. **The subjunctive :** As we said on page 202, the subjunctive is used in subordinate clauses where the action of the verb is not presented as fact or reality, but as a theoretical or future possibility. We will go into fuller details in the next *revisión y notas* section, but for the time being contrast the following sentences :

No dudo que vendrá : "I do not doubt that he will come"
No creo que venga : "I do not think that he will come"

(*Vendrá* is subordinate to the certainty in the main verb ("there is no doubt"), while the action contained in *venga* is hypothetical, since its doubtful context is expressed in "I do not think".

5. **Writing in Spanish**

1 I will go with you unless I have to go to the station.
2 My grandfather walks really slowly.
3 As far as I am concerned, I'll go even if it rains. - It won't rain.
4 It's time to decide. - I'm going to put on my overcoat.
5 Last night I got home around three in the morning.
6 Although we talked a lot, we didn't say anything interesting.

6. **Translation**

1 Iré con vosotros a no ser que tenga que ir a la estación.
2 Mi abuelo anda despacito.
3 Por mi parte, iré incluso si llueve. - No lloverá.
4 Ya va siendo hora de decidirse. - Voy a ponerme el abrigo.
5 Anoche llegué a casa a eso de las tres de la mañana.
6 Aunque charlamos mucho, no dijimos nada interesante.

LECCION SESENTA Y CUATRO

Baldomero tiene problemas

1 Baldomero es un joven de unos cuarenta y tantos años, soltero, guapo y con dinero. **(1)**

2 Lleva un bigote gris, tiene las piernas cortas, el vientre abultado, botas de charol, chaleco blanco y una gorra con los colores del arco iris **(2)**

3 y manifiesta un altruismo exagerado hacia él mismo.

4 Sin embargo, no es eso lo que le preocupa aunque, por supuesto, es consciente de ser un "joven con problemas". En eso, está al día. **(3)**

5 Se considera "liberado" y le gusta decirse intelectual, a menudo dice: "Cuando era más joven, seguí cursos de Derecho durante dos años en la Universidad de Pamplona".

6 Pero volvamos a "sus problemas", de los que él dice, no sin orgullo: "son mi profesión". **(4)**

7 Baldomero tiene ratos de angustia horrorosos a los que él llama: "instantes depresivos, acompañados de extrema lucidez"

LESSON SIXTY-FOUR

Baldomero has problems

1 Baldomero is a young [man] of some forty or so (and so many) years, [a] bachelor, good-looking and rich (with money).

2 He has (He wears) a grey moustache, has (the) short legs, [a] pot-belly (the stomach swollen), (with) patent-leather boots, [a] white waistcoat and a cap with the colours of the rainbow

3 and he manifests [an] exaggerated altruism towards himself.

4 However, it is not this that (which) worries him, although, of course, he is aware (conscious) of be[ing] a "young man with problems". In this [respect], he is up-to-date.

5 He considers himself "liberated" and likes to call himself (say of himself) intellectual.' Often he says "When I was younger, I followed law classes (courses) for two years at Pamplona University".

6 But let's come back to "his problems", of (those) which he says, not without pride, "they are my profession".

7 Baldomero has periods of dreadful anxiety (to those) which he calls : "depressive instants accompanied with (of) extreme lucidity"

NOTES

(1) *Tanto* : "so much" or "as much". Like *mucho, poco,* etc. *tanto* is variable. Notice how *unos* and *tantos* are used here : *Tengo unas* (or *algunas) pesetas :* "I have a few pesetas". *Tengo unas veintitantas pesetas :* "I have twenty or so pesetas" (See sentence 1 in the exercise).

(2) *Abultado :* swollen. The word is often used merely to express "big" or "bulky" *(un paquete abultado :* "a fat parcel"). From *bulto :* "bulk".

(3) *Estar al día :* "to be in fashion, up-to-the-minute", but, depending on the context, the expression can also mean "to be up-to-date" in the sense of "well informed".

(4) *Volvamos a :* "let's come back to". The verb is *volver,* but we're using the imperative. And the imperative uses some of the same forms as the present subjunctive. More about this later!

8   y que, según él, se manifiestan — él prefiere decir: "son somatizados" — como atroces sudores fríos.

9   Pero Baldomero, a través del autoanálisis — pues claro, Baldomero se autoanaliza — cree haber descubierto la raíz de sus males.

10   En efecto, según lo que ha leído en un librito de psicología científica, que el hijo de la portera, un sordomudo muy simpático, le prestó hace cinco años,

11   Baldomero ha llegado a la conclusión siguiente: la causa de sus problemas no es otra que su extraordinaria facultad de aburrimiento.

12   Por supuesto, la conclusión de tan funesto diagnóstico **(6)**

13   postró a Baldomero en un estado de aguda crisis depresiva.

14   Menos mal que su nueva novia — él prefiere decir: "compañera" — Remedios, se ocupa un poco de él. Ella le anima mucho. Enormemente, incluso. **(7)**

EJERCICIO: 1. Es una señora de una treintena de años. **2.** ¿Qué es lo que te preocupa? **3.** He pasado un rato muy agradable con ellos. **4.** Según lo que ha dicho no creo que venga. **5.** Volvamos a nuestro trabajo. **6.** Por supuesto que yo te esperaré. **7.** Yo, prefiero ir a pie.

8	and which, according to him, manifest themselves – he prefers to say "are somatized" – as atrocious cold sweats.
9	But Baldomero, through self-analysis – well of course, Baldomero analyzes himself – thinks he has (thinks to have) discovered the root of his ills.
10	Indeed (In effect), according to what he read in a scientific psychology booklet, that the caretaker's son, a very friendly deaf-mute, lent him five years ago,
11	Baldomero has reached the following conclusion : the cause of his problems is nothing other than (is not other that) his extraordinary faculty for (of) boredom.
12	Of course, the conclusion of so ill-fated [a] diagnosis
13	plunged (to) Baldomero in a state of acute depression (depressive crisis).
14	Just as well his new girlfriend – he prefers to say "companion" – Remedios, looks after (occupies herself of) him a little. She encourages him a lot. Enormously even.

NOTES
(6) *Tan :* "such" or "so". *Es una casa tan bonita :* "it's such a nice house" – in English, we put in the indefinite article after "such". The Spanish construction is more like "so nice a house". *Tan lejos de todo :* "so far from everything". *Tan pequeño como el tuyo :* "as small as yours".

(7) *Novio, novia :* in Spain, these words are close in meaning to fiancé(e) in English. The name *Remedios,* without being common, is particular to the Catholic custom of naming children after saints. *Mercedes* and *Maria de la Asunción* are commoner examples of elaborate first names.

*****

EXERCISE : 1. She is a lady of about thirty. – **2.** What is worrying you? – **3.** I have spent a very pleasant time with them. – **4.** Judging by what he has said, I don't think he is coming. – **5.** Let's get back to our work. – **6.** Of course I'll wait for you. – **7.** I prefer to go on foot.

EJERCICIO DE CONTROL
Ponga las palabras que faltan

1 *María is a spinster of about fifty or so years.*

. . . .

. . . .

2 *However, she has got herself right up-to-date.*

. . . .

. . . . . .

3 *She has followed her brother to his room.*

. . . .

. . . .

4 *I haven't seen her for a while.*

. . . .

5 *Of course I'll take a taxi.*

. . . .

****

LECCION SESENTA Y CINCO

Volverán (1)

1   Volverán las oscuras golondrinas
en tu balcón sus nidos a colgar,
y otra vez con el ala en sus cristales,
jugando llamarán;

THE MISSING WORDS : 1 María es una soltera de unos cincuenta y tantos años. 2 sin embargo, se ha puesto enseguida al día. 3 ha seguido a su hermano hasta su habitación. 4 hace un rato que no la veo. 5 por supuesto que tomaré un taxi.

*****

Has Baldomero got to you? Are you, too, experiencing attacks of acute depression? *¡Por supuesto que no!* There was a lot of new, and new-sounding, vocabulary in this lesson, but there is nothing to worry about. The construction of the sentences is no more complicated than before, and you have come across all the small points and idioms in previous lessons. Here are some of them :

a menudo : lesson 56 sentence 4
lo que, a lo que : lesson 63, N° 3
aunque : lesson 62, note 2
decirse : lesson 21, N° 2

Read through the lesson again, and see if you can find other common expressions and constructions.

Segunda ola: lección 15.

****

LESSON SIXTY-FIVE

They will come back

1   The dark (obscure) swallows will again hang their nests on your balcony, and again, playing, will knock (call) with their wings (the wing) at your window panes ;

NOTES
(1) *Volverán :* "(they) will come back". *Volver a* is often used with a verb in the infinitive to express repetition. We will see this in greater detail in the next revision exercise.

2   pero aquéllas que el vuelo refrenaban
     tu hermosura y mi dicha al contemplar;
     aquéllas que aprendieron nuestros nombres,
          ésas... ¡no volverán!

3   Volverán las tupidas madreselvas
     de tu jardín las tapias a escalar, **(2)**
     y otra vez a la tarde, aún más hermosas,
          sus flores abrirán;

4   pero aquéllas cuajadas de rocío, **(3)**
     cuyas gotas mirábamos temblar **(4)**
     y caer, como lágrimas del día...,
          ésas..., ¡no volverán!

5   Volverán del amor en tus oídos
     las palabras ardientes a sonar;
     tu corazón, de su profundo sueño
          tal vez despertará;

6   pero mudo y absorto y de rodillas **(5)**
     como se adora a Dios ante su altar, **(6)**
     como yo te he querido..., desengáñate,
          ¡así no te querrán! **(7)**

                     Gustavo A. Bécquer : Rimas

EJERCICIO: 1. Volverán a venir mañana. **2.** Se lo he dicho otra vez. **3.** Aquéllas de las que te hablé. **4.** Abriré la puerta más tarde. **5.** Me gusta la música y tengo buen oído. **6.** Me despertaré a eso de las ocho. **7.** Querrán que vengas.

2   but those that were slowing down their flight in contemplating your beauty and my happiness, those that learnt our names, those... will not come back!

3   The dense honeysuckle will again scale the walls of your garden, and once again in (at) the afternoon, even more beautiful, its flowers will open ;

4   but those laden with dew, whose drops we were watching trembling and dropping, like tears of the day... those will not come back!

5   The ardent words of love will sound again in your ears ; your heart, from its profound sleep, perhaps will wake up ;

6   but silent (dumb) and in ecstasy (absorbed) and on [your] knees, as one adores (to) God before his altar, as I have loved you... disillusion yourself... they won't love you like that!

NOTES
(2) *Tapia* : "wall" (around a garden or a field) ; *una pared* : "wall" (of a house) ; *muro* : "wall" (around a castle, etc.) ; *muralla* : "wall" (as in the Great Wall of China). *Tapiar una puerta* : "to wall up a door".
(3) *Cuajadas en rocío* : "laden with dew". Literally, the word *cuajado* means "coagulated" or "clotted" when referring to milk, blood, etc. It can be used figuratively (as here) in expressions such as *un rosal cuajado de flores* : "a rose-bush laden down with blooms".
(4) *Cuyas* : "whose". *Cuyo* is variable, and agrees with the noun to which it refers ; otherwise it is used exactly like the English "whose" : *el hombre cuyos hijos son en mi clase* : "the man whose children are in my class".
(5) *De rodillas* : "on one's knees". *De puntillas* : "on tiptoe".
(6) *Ante* : "before" (place). The word is rather more poetic than *delante de*. Not to be confused with *antes de* : "before" (time). *Delante de la casa* : "in front of the house" ; *ante Dios* (without a preposition) : "before God" (i.e., "in the presence of God") ; *antes de venir* : "before coming".

EXERCISE : 1. They will come back tomorrow. – **2.** I have told him (it) again. – **3.** The ones I spoke to you about. – **4.** I will open the door later. – **5.** I like music and I have a good ear. – **6.** I'll wake up around eight o'clock. – **7.** They will want you to come.

EJERCICIO DE CONTROL
Ponga las palabras que faltan

1 *The swallows will announce the spring.*

. . . .

. . . .

2 *The rain on the window-panes will wake you up.*

. . . .

. . . .

3 *Will you come back tomorrow?*

¿ . . . . ?

4 *The children will cry if you don't come.*

. . . .

5 *The flight of those birds will please you.*

. . .   .

THE MISSING WORDS : **1** las golondrinas anunciarán la primavera.
2 la lluvia sobre los cristales te despertará. **3** volverás mañana. **4** los
niños llorarán si no vienes. **5** el vuelo de esos pájaros te gustará.

This lesson is based on the future tense, and certain other
aspects of Spanish, which we will have the opportunity to
review more closely in the next revision section. This lesson
is really intended as relaxation.

*It is not in the same vein as other lessons, so you should try
to look at it from a different angle : forget for a moment the
idea of "learning Spanish ", and...* **listen!** *Listen to the
sounds and the rythm of these few lines of Bécquer's poetry.
If you like, read to the end of next page before re-reading the
text of the lesson.*

You will have noticed that the Spanish sentence is far more flexible than the English sentence. The order of the different parts of speech (subject, verb, object, etc.) is not as rigid, and inversions — even in everyday language — are very common. Often we put the part of speech we want to emphasize in pride of place at the beginning of the sentence :
a esa mujer no la convencerá nadie : literally, "to that woman will not convince her nobody".

Not surprisingly, inversions are even more common in poetic language. Bécquer provides a striking example : his word order does not rely on mere caprice, but is calculated to produce a specific poetic effect. The auxiliary *volverán* placed at the beginning of each verse and mirrored by the verb *no volverán* "they will not return" ; the symmetry of each verse enhanced by the infinitives *(a colgar, a escalar, a sonar)* at the end of each second line, and by the identical future forms in the fourth and eighth lines.

Here is what the text would look like if there were fewer inversions :

Las oscuras golondrinas volverán a colgar sus nidos en tu balcón y otra vez jugando llamarán con el ala en sus cristales; pero aquéllas que refrenaban el vuelo al contemplar tu hermosura y mi dicha, aquéllas que aprendieron nuestros nombres, ésas no volverán.
Las tupidas madreselvas volverán a escalar las tapias de tu jardín y, otra vez, a la tarde, sus flores abrirán, aún más hermosas; pero aquéllas, cuajadas de rocío, de las que (cuyas) mirábamos las gotas temblar y caer como lágrimas del día, ésas no volverán.
Las palabras ardientes del amor volverán a sonar en tus oídos; tal vez tu corazón despertará de su profundo sueño, pero mudo, etc.

Segunda ola: lección 16.

LECCION SESENTA Y SEIS

En Correos

1 — ¡Qué barbaridad! Llevo más de tres cuartos de hora en esta cola y me parece que, a este paso, voy a pasar aquí la noche. **(1)**

2 — ¿Tres cuartos de hora solamente? ¡Vaya suerte! Yo llevo aquí más de hora y media y estoy pensando que lo mejor que puedo hacer

3 es enviar un telegrama a mi casa para que me traigan la fiambrera. **(2)**

4 — ¡Pues yo! He dejado los garbanzos en el fuego, pensando que no tardaría mucho.

5 — Perdone la indiscreción, señora; ¿Vive usted cerca de aquí?

¿QUIERE CAMBIAR? ESTOY SEGURO DE QUE ÉSTA NO ES LA BUENA

6 — Sí, ahí al lado. ¿Por qué me lo pregunta?

7 — No quiero asustarla pero acabo de oír pasar a los bomberos. De todas las formas, no se preocupe, están bien entrenados para apagar los fuegos.

8 — Bueno, ya me toca a mí. Buenos días, señor. Quisiera enviar esta carta certificada.

9 — Sí, pero no es aquí. Tiene que dirigirse a la ventanilla número nueve.

LESSON SIXTY-SIX

At the Post Office

1 — It's atrocious (What barbarity!) I've been in this queue for more than three-quarters of [an] hour, and it seems to me that at this rate (pace) I'm going to spend the night here.

2 — Three-quarters of an hour? You're in luck! I've been here more than an hour and [a] half and I am thinking that the best [thing] that I can do

3 is to send a telegram home (to my home) so that they can bring me something to eat (the lunch basket).

4 — What about me! I left the chick-peas on the fire, thinking I wouldn't be long.

5 — Excuse my (the) indiscretion, Madam, [but] do you live close to here?

6 — Yes. Just down the road (there at the side). Why do you ask (me it)?

7 — I don't want to scare you, but I have just heard (to) the firemen passing (to pass). Anyway, don't worry. They're well trained to put out fires.

8 — Good. It's my turn (already it touches me to me). Good morning, Sir. I would like to send this registered letter.

9 — Yes, but it isn't here. You have to go (direct yourself) to window N° 9.

NOTES
(1) *Llevar* translates various English words : "to wear", "to carry" and "to take". With time clauses, it is used to mean "to have spent" : *llevo tres meses en España* : "I have spent three months in Spain" or, more precisely, "I have been in Spain for three months".

(2) *Enviar :* "to send". *Poner un telegrama :* literally "to put (in) a telegram" is rather more common. See also *poner una conferencia :* "to put in a (phone) call", sentence 12.

*****

10 — ¡Es el colmo de los colmos! Una hora de espera para que no le atiendan a uno. Voy a escribir una carta al ministro para quejarme. (3)

11 — Dése prisa, señor, a partir de mañana estamos en huelga. El siguiente, por favor.

12 — Soy yo, quisiera poner una conferencia a cobro revertido con Australia.

13 — Ventanilla número seis, señorita. Aquí no se sirven más que los sellos. Y dése prisa porque va a ser la hora del bocadillo. El siguiente, por favor. (4)

14 — ¿Tiene cinco duros en monedas para telefonear desde una cabina? (5)

15 — No, pero justo detrás de usted hay una máquina donde puede cambiar. (6)

EJERCICIO: 1. Llevo más de dos meses en Tarragona. 2. Lo mejor que puedes hacer es telefonear. 3. Ha ido a poner un telegrama a su familia. 4. Los bomberos han apagado el incendio. 5. La ventanilla cerrará a las siete. 6. He recibido una carta certificada. 7. Voy a darme prisa.

EJERCICIO DE CONTROL
Ponga las palabras que faltan :

1 *We have to queue.*

. . . .

10 — It's the last straw (It's the height of the heights)! An hour of wait[ing] so that they don't attend to one. I'm going to write a letter to the Minister to complain.

11 — Hurry up, Sir. As from tomorrow, we're on strike. Next, please.

12 — It's me (I am me), I would like to put in a reverse charge call to (with) Australia.

13 — Window number six, Miss. Here only stamps are served. And hurry up because it's going to be time for our break (the hour of the sandwich). Next, please.

14 — Do you have 5 five-peseta pieces in coins (for) to phone from a box?

15 — No, but just behind you there is a machine where you can [get] change.

EXERCISE : 1. I have been in Tarragona for more than two months. – **2.** The best thing you can do is to phone. – **3.** He has gone to send a telegram to his family. – **4.** The firemen have put out the fire. – **5.** The window will close at seven o'clock. – **6.** I have received a registered letter. – **7.** I am going to hurry.

NOTES

(3) *Para que no atiendan a uno :* "so that you don't get served". *Atiendan* (from *atender*) is in the "they" form referring to the impersonal "them". *Uno :* "one" is also impersonal. In current English, we would use "you".

(4) *No más que* (literally "no more than") means "only". *No quedó más que una hora :* "he only stayed an hour". *Bocadillo* is connected with *boca :* "mouth", and means a small snack, often a sandwich.

(5) *Una moneda de cinco duros :* "a twenty-five peseta coin" ; *un duro :* "a five-peseta piece".

(6) *Cambiar :* "to change" ; *suelto :* "change" in the sense of small change. *No hay suelto :* "There is no change".

* * * * *

2 *I am thinking that I have forgotten to put out the fire.*

. . . . me . . olvidado . .

. . . .

Lección 66

3 *I would like to send him a telegram.*

. . . .

4 *If you want to arrive in time you will have to hurry.*

. .   . .   tienes   . . .

. . . .

****

LECCION SESENTA Y SIETE

Presente de subjuntivo

1 Todos deseamos que apruebes el examen.
2 Más vale que se lo digas antes de que se ponga a comer.
3 Hagamos lo que hagamos, intentaremos hacerlo bien.
4 Lo mejor es que nos enviéis una muestra.
5 Es muy importante que lleguen a la hora.
6 Ven cuando puedas.
7 ¿Vienes para que te diga lo que ha pasado?
8 Come lo que te guste.
9 Lo queramos o no, es así.
10 Es posible que no vengan.
11 No creo que estén en casa.
12 Espero que seáis bien recibidos.

Ternura

Por teléfono:
1 — Sí, dígame... ¡Ah, eres tú, amor mío! ¿Qué pasa?
2 — Mamá acaba de morir en la bañera, ¿qué hago?
3 — Telefonea a la funeraria y exige que la entierren boca abajo.
4 — Tienes razón... nunca se sabe...

5 *Stamps are bought at window five.*

. . . . compran . . . .

. . . .

THE MISSING WORDS : **1** hay que hacer la cola. **2** estoy pensando que - he - de apagar el fuego. **3** quisiera enviarle un telegrama. **4** si quieres llegar a tiempo - que darte prisa. **5** los sellos se - en la ventanilla número cinco.

Segunda ola: lección 17.

****

LESSON SIXTY-SEVEN

Present subjunctive

1. We all hope that you pass ´(approve) the examination.
2. You had better (It is worth more that you) tell him before he starts to eat.
3. Whatever we do (Let us do that which we may do) we will try to do it well.
4. The best [thing] is that you send us a sample.
5. It is very important that they arrive in time.
6. Come when you can.
7. Are you coming for me to tell (so that I tell) you what has happened?
8. Eat what[ever] you like.
9. Whether we want it or not, it is like that.
10. They may not come (It is possible that they do not come).
11. I don't think that they are at home.
12. I hope that you are well received.

Tenderness

On the (by) telephone :
1. — Yes, hello (tell me)... Oh! it's you, my sweetheart (love). What's up?
2. — Mother has just died in the bathtub. What do I do?
3. — Phone (to) the undertaker's and demand that they bury her face down (the mouth down).
4. — You're right... one never knows.

EJERCICIO: **1**. Más vale que no vayas. **2**. Digas lo que digas, ese libro es caro. **3**. Lo mejor es que vengáis hacia las siete. **4**. Quieras o no, tienes que hacerlo. **5**. Espero que las manzanas no estén demasiado verdes. **6**. Deseo que llegues a tiempo. **7**. No creo que pueda terminar antes del sábado.

EJERCICIO DE CONTROL
Ponga las palabras que faltan

1 *Whatever you give, let it be willingly.*

Des . . . ., . . . sea . . . .

2 *I wish you to tell him before he leaves.*

. . . . de . . .

. . . . . .

3 *Phone me when you can.*

. . . .

4 *You (fam. pl.) had better send a telegram.*

. . . .

5 *Demand that it be done like that.*

. . . .

THE MISSING WORDS : **1** - lo que des, que - de buen corazón. **2** deseo que se lo digas antes - que se vaya. **3** telefonéame cuando puedas. **4** más vale que enviéis un telegrama. **5** exige que se haga así.

EXERCISE : 1. You had better not go. – **2.** Whatever you say, this book is expensive. – **3.** The best thing to do is to come around seven. – **4.** Whether you want to or not, you have to do it. – **5.** I hope that the apples are not too green. – **6.** I want you to arrive in time. – **7.** I don't think I can finish before Saturday.

There are no notes to this lesson.

All the new grammar involves the present subjunctive. Here are the endings for regular verbs :

Verbs in -*ar* : stem + e, es, e, emos, éis, en

Verbs in -*er* :

        stem + a, as, a amos, áis, an

Verbs in -*ir* :

In other words, you just need to switch the endings of the present indicative from one group of verbs to the other, remembering that -*er* verbs have the same endings as -*ir* verbs.

Segunda ola: lección 18.

Lección 67

LECCION SESENTA Y OCHO

Ferias y fiestas

1 A la entrada de la ciudad multitud de carteles anuncian el acontecimiento; se respira alegría y movimiento.

2 El vino, la cerveza y los refrescos corren con fruición. Las calles están engalanadas desde hace unos días.

3 Guirlandas, globos, luces, trajes regionales, pasacalles, risas por todos lados: son las fiestas de la ciudad.

CUANDO SEA MAYOR SERÉ DOMADOR

4 Helados, niños de vacaciones, bares llenos a reventar, mercados con productos de cada pueblo, música... algarabía alegre.

5 En una gran explanada que se encuentra cerca del Paseo de los Artistas,y que todos los años, por la misma época, es destinada al mismo efecto

6 se encuentran las barracas: casetas de tiro, autos de choque, tiovivos, norias, tómbolas, etc. y las clásicas churrerías y puestos ambulantes de algodones rosas y blancos bien azucarados. (1)

7 Un poco más allá, bajo una carpa inmensa el ayuntamiento ha hecho instalar el circo: enorme caja de resonancia de sueños infantiles de pequeños y grandes. (2)

LESSON SIXTY-EIGHT

Fairs and festivals

1   At the entrance to the town, [a] multitude of posters announce the event ; one breathes happiness and movement.

2   The wine, (the) beer and (the) refreshments are flowing freely (running with fruition). The streets have been (are) decorated for (it makes) several days.

3   Garlands, balloons, lights, regional costumes, slow dances ["passacaglie"], laughs from (by) all sides : it is (they are) the town festival(s).

4   Ice-creams, children on (of) holiday(s), bars fit (full) to burst, markets with products from each village, music... happy bustle and noise.

5   On a big esplanade that is (finds itself) near the Paseo de los Artistas, and that every year, at (by) the same period, is used for the same purpose (destined to the same effect)

6   are (found) the [fairground] stalls : shooting galleries, bumper cars, roundabouts, big-wheels, tombolas, etc., and the classic "churrerías" and mobile stands (posts) of pink and white and well-sugared candy-floss (cottons).

7   A short distance away (more over there), under an immense marquee, the town council has had the circus installed : an enormous echo-chamber (resonance box) of childhood dreams of young and old (little and big).

NOTES
(1) *Churrerías* are generally stands selling *churros* (See sentence 13). We have not translated these words, as they are particularly Spanish. *Churros* are like stick-shaped doughnuts (and are delicious with hot chocolate!).
(2) *Un poco más allá :* "just over there" (literally : "a little further over there").

8　Mal que bien, consigo abrirme paso hasta las vallas desde las que una multitud de niños observa a los animales diciendo a sus acompañantes: "Cuando sea mayor, seré domador". (3) (4)

9　Al otro lado del río, están instaladas las diversas ferias de ganado.

10　Entre los mugidos de las vacas y los olores de paja húmeda, oigo a dos tratantes concluir un contrato.

11　Luego sigo de lejos, durante más de un cuarto de hora, a un grupo folklórico gallego que anima con sus gaitas y sus danzas las calles por las que pasa.

12　Decido ir a dar una vuelta por los barrios viejos. Sé que allí encontraré caras conocidas.

13　Sí. Allí están. Son mis amigos. Compramos churros y nos sentamos en un banco a contemplar el vaivén que nos rodea.

EJERCICIO: **1**. He visto los carteles que anunciaban la película. **2**. Es un gran acontecimiento. **3**. El circo estaba lleno a reventar. **4**. Todos los domingos a la misma hora vamos a pasearnos. **5**. Mal que bien, he conseguido terminar. **6**. Al otro lado del paseo está mi casa. **7**. Voy a presentarte a mis amigos.

EJERCICIO DE CONTROL
Ponga las palabras que faltan

1 *At the entrance to the town there is a petrol pump.*

. . . .

. . . .

2 *It's hot, I'm going to have a cold drink.*

. . . .

8   As best I can, I manage to get through (I succeed to open me [a] passage) to the fence(s) from where (from those which) a multitude of children are observing (to) the animals, saying to their companions "When I'm bigger, I'll be [animal] a tamer".

9   On (At) the other side of the river, the various cattle fairs are installed.

10 Between the mooing(s) of the cows and the smell of wet straw, I hear (to) two dealers concluding (conclude) a contract.

11 Then I follow from afar, for (during) more than a quarter of [an] hour, (to) a Galician folk group that is animating with its bagpipes and its dances the streets through (those) which it passes.

12 I decide to go for (to give) a walk through the old neighbourhoods. I know that there I will meet familiar (known) faces.

13 Yes. They are there. They are my friends. We buy *churros* and sit (ourselves) down on a bench to contemplate the comings-and-goings that surround us.

NOTES
(3) *Mal que bien* : "as best one can".
(4) *Cuando sea mayor, seré domador* : note the use of the subjunctive in the clause that depends on a main verb in the future. This is an example of the hypothetical sense of the subjunctive.

EXERCISE : 1. I have seen the posters announcing the film. – **2.** It is a great event. – **3.** The circus was full to overflowing. – **4.** We go for a walk every Sunday at the same time. – **5.** Come what may, I have managed to finish. – **6.** My house is on the other side of the promenade. – **7.** I am going to introduce you to my friends.

*****

A "passacaglia" is a slow dance originating in Spain and Italy.

3 *Children often dream of living in a circus one day.*

. . . . con . . . . .

. . . .

4 *It is difficult to get through with this queue.*

. . . .

****

LECCION SESENTA Y NUEVE

"Falsos amigos" (1)

1 Su habitación era larga y oscura.
2 Cuando vayas a Turquía, cómprame un sable y un jarrón orientales.
3 Esta mesa es muy práctica y aquella silla muy cómoda.
4 Le contesté que aquel día subí a su casa varias veces para enseñarle el mapa.
5 El padre de mis amigos, un oficial retirado, compró un pastel y lo partió en cuatro para que nos lo comiéramos, luego nos dio caramelos.
6 Estuvimos largas horas en las salas del museo, contemplando algunos de los cuadros más célebres del mundo y sobre todo los de Goya.
7 Ana, que es enfermera, exprime un limón para dárselo al enfermo.
8 A lo lejos, se divisa la montaña por la que tendremos que subir.

5 *Are you (fam. pl.) going to go for a walk to see the town festival?*

¿ . . . .

. . . . ?

THE MISSING WORDS :   **1** a la entrada de la ciudad hay una gasolinera. **2** hace calor, voy a tomar un refresco. **3** a menudo los niños sueñan - vivir un día en un circo. **4** es difícil abrirse paso con esta cola. **5** vais a dar una vuelta para ver la ciudad en fiestas.

Segunda ola: lección 18.

****

LESSON SIXTY-NINE

"False friends„

1 His room was long and dark.
2 When you go to Turkey, buy me an oriental sabre and an oriental vase.
3 This table is very useful (practical) and that chair [is] very comfortable.
4 I answered him that that day I went (up) to his house several (various) times to show him the map.
5 My friends' father, a retired officer, bought a cake and shared it in four so that we might eat it, then gave us [some] sweets.
6 We spent (were) long hours in the rooms of the museum, contemplating some the most famous pictures in (of) the world, and above all those of Goya.
7 Ana, who is [a] nurse, squeezes (expresses) a lemon to give it (to him) to the sick man.
8 In the distance, we (one) make(s) out the mountain by which we will have to go up.

NOTES
(1) The lesson has no new points of grammar, and, although there is some new vocabulary, it should not pose any particular problems.

*****

9   Corría tan de prisa que parecía volar; tocó el poste el primero.
10 Las esposas hicieron una herida al prisionero en las muñecas.
11 Voy a salir para echar un par de cartas.
12 Es preciso que vengas a arreglar la avería del coche.
13 Los labradores viven del cultivo de los campos.
14 Tomás tiene una gran cultura musical.

EJERCICIO: 1. La calle era muy ancha y muy larga. **2.** Los niños jugaban en la playa con la arena. **3.** El enfermo escribe una carta. **4.** Cuando iba a correos vio caer el poste. **5.** Mi esposa ha comprado un par de pasteles. **6.** Voy a salir para comprar una mesa. **7.** Me gusta el jarrón y el vaso que me has regalado.

*****

NOTES (continued)

The main point of the lesson is to introduce the idea of *falsos amigos*. These are words that look the same in two languages, but that have taken on different meanings. They can thus be misleading, and you should be on the lookout. *Largo,* for example, does not mean "large", but "long". *Exprimir* comes from the same root as "to express", but has retained only the physical meaning of "to squeeze". *Expresar* is the word for "to express". And *embarazada* does not mean "embarrassed", but "pregnant" so be careful what you say!

There are many other examples. But don't worry : the mistakes you may make are not disastrous, and, in any case, making mistakes is a healthy and necessary step in the learning process.

9   He was running so fast that he seemed to fly ; he touched the post (the) first.
10 The handcuffs made a wound on the prisoner's wrists.
11 I am going to go to put a couple of letters [in the post].
12 It is necessary that you come to fix the breakdown of the car.
13 The workers live from the cultivation of the fields.
14 Tomás has a great musical culture.

* * * * *

EXERCISE : 1. The street was very narrow and very long. – **2.** The children were playing on the beach with the sand. – **3.** The sick man is writing a letter. – **4.** When I was going to the post office I saw the post fall. – **5.** My wife has bought a couple of cakes. – **6.** I am going to go out to buy a table. – **7.** I like the vase and the glass that you have given me.

EJERCICIO DE CONTROL
Ponga las palabras que faltan

1 *I like your house, it's very comfortable, although a little dark.*

. . . . aunque

. . . .

2 *He has sent me the map of Canada by mail.*

. . . . de Canadá . . .

. . . . . .

****

LECCION SESENTA

LESSON SEVENTY

Revisión y notas

1. **Volver** (See note N° 5, lesson 23 ; note N° 6, lesson 45 ; note N° 4, lesson 64 ; note N° 1, lesson 65).
The idea of repetition that is so often expressed by the prefix "re-" in English is rendered in Spanish using the verb *volver* + *a* + an infinitive. We can also express the idea of repetition by using *de nuevo* or *otra vez*. The verb *volver* used alone means "to come back" or "to return" : *volver a casa :* "to go home" or "to come home".

Volverse (the reflexive form) means "to become" : *se ha vuelto loco :* "he has gone mad" ; *se ha vuelto agradable :* "he has become friendly".

3 *Get into the train : it's going to leave.*

. . . . al . . . . . , ...

4 *My little brother says that he would like to fly like the birds.*

. . . . le gustaría

. . . .

5 *Squeeze me an orange.*

. . . .

THE MISSING WORDS : **1** me gusta tu casa, es muy cómoda - un poco oscura. **2** me ha enviado el mapa - por correo. **3** sube - tren, va a salir. **4** mi hermano pequeño dice que - volar como los pájaros. **5** exprímeme una naranja.

Segunda ola: lección 20.

* *

2. Correct usage of Spanish relative pronouns and adjectives is easy if you recognize the different categories in English. Remember that in English, we can omit the relative pronoun when it refers to the object of the relative clause e.g., "There is the car we saw yesterday", or "That is the man we spoke to yesterday". None of this is possible in Spanish.
A relative clause can be "restrictive" or "non-restrictive". Compare : "The man who speaks Spanish is going to Spain" (restrictive) with "The man speaks Spanish, is going to Spain" (non-restrictive).
In the "restrictive" example, the Spanish relative would be *que*. In the "non-restrictive" relative clause, however, we have to say *el cual* (or *la cual, los cuales, las cuales*) when referring to feminine nouns or plurals. *El cual*, etc. can be replaced by *quien* when referring to persons.
Lo cual is used to express "which" in sentences such as "He gave me a book, which surprised me" : *Me dio un regalo, lo cual me extrañó* (It is the "giving" that surprised me, and not "the book" ; if "the book" had "surprised me", we would say *Me dio un libro que me extrañó*).

Cuyo, a, os, as : "whose". This a relative adjective, and agrees in number and gender with the thing that is possessed. Thus, in *el hombre cuyos niños están en mi clase, cuyos* agrees with *niños*. When the main role of the relative clause is to indicate the ownership of something, the use of *cuyo* is replaced by the verb *pertenecer a :* "to belong to". *Conozco al hombre a quien pertenece este coche :* "I know the man whose car this is". Similarly, remember that in "Whose is this book?", "whose" is grammatically different (interrogative adjective). In this case "whose" must be expressed by *¿a quién...?*

3. **Present subjunctive** (see lesson 67, note 4 ; lesson 68, sentences 2 and 12 ; lesson 69).
In general, the subjunctive is used to express future possibilities or hypotheses.

- It is also used after expressions of wanting, requesting, permitting, forbidding, causing, necessity, etc. *(Es preciso que vengas :* literally "it is necessary that you come").

- It is used with verbs of ordering, permitting, and preventing. *(Dile que venga :* "tell him to come").

- It is used when the statement in the subordinate clause is contrary to fact. *(Dudo que venga :* "I doubt that he will come" **but** *No dudo que vendrás).*

- *It is used after expressions of possibility or probability. (Es probable que venga :* "it is probable that he will come").

- It is used after conjunctions introducing future or hypothetical actions. *(Te llamaré en cuanto venga :* "I will call you as soon as he comes" ; *Trabajo para que podamos ir de vacaciones :* "I am working in order that we can go on holiday").

- It is used after relative pronouns when the antecedent is indeterminate. *(No tengo nadie quien me escriba :* "Nobody writes to me" ; *Estoy buscando a alguien que me arregle mi coche :* "I'm looking for someone to fix my car.".

4. Writing in Spanish

1   Speak to me again about what you spoke to me about this morning.
2   The birds whose nests are in those trees are coming back.
3   I only have two five-peseta pieces.
4   Tell me what you want.
5   Just over there there was an officer's sabre.
6   We waited for long days before being able to see him.

5. **Translation**

1 Vuelve a hablarme de lo que me has hablado esta mañana.
2 Los pájaros cuyos nidos están en esos árboles volverán.

****

LECCION SETENTA Y UNA

Baldomero va al psicoanalista

1 A pesar de los esfuerzos de Remedios, Baldomero no consigue levantar el ánimo y se debate en su lecho como un animal enjaulado. **(1)**
2 En el fondo, lucha contra sí mismo, contra lo que él llama "la tragedia de mi vida"; contra ·el destino oscuro que le persigue desde su más tierna infancia.
3 Remedios no puede más y, a escondidas, una noche estrellada de luna llena ha ido a tirarse al río. **(2)**
4 Un acreedor que se inquieta mucho por la salud de Baldomero — menos mal que siempre hay buenos amigos — vino a verle al día siguiente.
5 Después de largas horas de discusión, Baldomero quedó convencido de la necesidad de ir a ver a un médico. **(3)**

3   No tengo más que dos monedas de cinco duros.
4   Dime lo que quieras.
5   Un poco más allá había un sable de oficial.
6   Esperamos largos días antes de poder verlo.

Segunda ola: lección 21 (revisión).

****

LESSON SEVENTY-ONE

Baldomero goes to the psychoanalyst

1   In spite of the efforts of Remedios, Baldomero does not manage to raise his spirits (the spirit) and fights (himself) on his bed like a caged animal.
2   Basically he is fighting against himself, against what he calls "the tragedy of my life" ; against the dark destiny that has been (is) pursuing him since his most tender childhood.
3   Remedios cannot [take] any more, and sneaked off one starry full-mooned night and threw herself in the river.
4   A creditor who is worrying a lot about (for) Baldomero's health – just as well there are always good friends – came to see him the next day.
5   After long hours of discussion, Baldomero was (remained) convinced of the necessity to go to see (to) a doctor.

NOTES
(1) *Levantar el ánimo* could be translated as "to get over it". Literally, it means "to raise one's spirit". *¡Ánimo! :* "cheer up!" ; *estar animado :* "to be in high spirits".
(2) *A escondidas :* "on the quiet". *Esconder* is the verb "to hide" ; *escondido :* "hidden". Compare with *a puntillas :* "on tiptoes".
(3) *Doctor* also exists in Spanish, to refer either to a "doctor of medecine" or to a "doctor of letters", for example : *doctor en letras*.

6   Pero como es vegetariano y tiene ideas muy fijas sobre los diferentes métodos de cura, no ha elegido cualquier médico.

7   Ha elegido, ni más ni menos, un psiquiatra que no es muy conocido pero del que le han hablado muy bien.

8   Dos días más tarde, Baldomero llama a la puerta. Un ama de llaves tuerta abre, saluda a Baldomero efusivamente y le hace pasar al despacho.

9   — Buenos días doctor, no puedo más, tengo ganas de llorar, no sé que hacer, necesito su ayuda, ¡ah...! ya empiezo a llorar... pero... ¡por el amor del cielo, dígame algo!

10 — Vamos... Vamos... no se abandone así... ¿Sabe? Comportándose así usted da una muy lamentable impresión. ¡Animo! ¡La vida es bella!

11 — Tiene usted razón doctor, sus palabras son un rayo de luz en la noche de mi corazón herido. De ahora en adelante, pensaré a menudo en ellas.

12 — Bueno, hemos sobrepasado el tiempo que nos habíamos fijado. Me debe cinco mil pesetas. Sí, sí, puede hacerme un cheque. Nos veremos la semana que viene a la misma hora.

13 — ¡Ah... doctor! ¿Qué voy a hacer sin usted durante una semana? Pero comprendo... La vida es, a veces, cruel y sin piedad. Adiós, doctor.

EJERCICIO: 1. A pesar de que pensábamos que no vendrías te esperamos. **2.** En el fondo es muy simpático. **3.** No puede más, está muy cansada. **4.** A escondidas se comía los caramelos. **5.** No elijas cualquier película. **6.** Hágale pasar a la sala de espera. **7.** No sé qué hacer.

6 But as he is a vegetarian and has very fixed ideas about (on) the different methods of treatment (cure), he didn't choose (elect) just any doctor.

7 He chose, neither more nor less, a psychiatrist who is not very [well] known but who is very well spoken of (of whom they have spoken to him very well).

8 Two days later, Baldomero knocks (calls) at the door. A one-eyed housekeeper (mistress of keys) opens [the door], greets (salutes to) Baldomero effusively and makes him go through into (pass to) the study.

9 — Good morning, Doctor, I can't [take it] any more, I feel like crying, I don't know what to do, I need your help. Oh!... I'm already starting to cry... but for the love of God (Heaven), say something to me!

10 — Come along, come along... don't let yourself go (Don't abandon yourself) like this. Do you know [that] behaving like this gives a very pathetic impression? Cheer up! Life is beautiful!

11 — You are right, Doctor, your words are a ray of light in the night of my wounded heart. From now on, I will often think about (in) them.

12 — Right. We have overrun the time that we had fixed. You owe me five thousand pesetas. Yes, yes, you can write me (make me) a cheque. We'll see each other next week at the same time.

13 — Oh Doctor! What am I going to do without you for a week? But I understand... (The) life is, at times, cruel and without pity. Goodbye, Doctor.

* * * * *

EXERCISE : 1. Although we thought that you would not come, we waited for you. – **2.** He is very nice at heart. – **3.** She can't take it any more, she is very tired. – **4.** He secretly ate the sweets. – **5.** Don't choose just any film. – **6.** Have him go into the waiting room. – **7.** I don't know what to do.

EJERCICIO DE CONTROL
Ponga las palabras que faltan

1 *Although I hurried, I didn't arrive in time.*

. . .   .

. . .   .

2 *Neither more nor less.*

. . .   .

3 *Tell me what you think of it.*

. . . .

4 *From now on I will go often.*

. . .   .

5 *They have overrun the time they had given themselves.*

. . .   .

. . . .

THE MISSING WORDS :   **1** a pesar de haberme dado prisa no he llegado a tiempo. **2** ni más ni menos. **3** dígame lo que piensa de ello. **4** de ahora en adelante iré a menudo. **5** han sobrepasado el tiempo que se habían fijado.

*****

Comments :
1. You will notice that the sentences have become longer in this lesson. Your knowledge of Spanish is getting better and better, and now you can tackle denser texts. But even if the sentences are longer, and the vocabulary is new, the grammatical construction of the lessons is developing only very gradually, because we don't want to saturate you. The main aim is to increase your vocabulary, and that is why you may detect a certain Gothic aspect to the continuing saga of our friend Baldomero.

2. You will have noticed also that the tenses do not always correspond in the English translation. The present tense is often used in Spanish narratives, where English would use the simple past. Further, the Spanish perfect (e.g., *ha dicho*) occasionally does not correspond to the English perfect in narratives. The Spanish perfect can be used when the action is recent, but there is not always (as this is in English) a sense of continuity into (or up to) the present time. The preterite (simple past) is used much more frequently than the perfect in certain parts of the Spanish-speaking world.

3. From now on, we suggest that you refer to the grammatical appendix at the back of this book, so that you can check up on irregular verb-forms. When you see a verb-form that you do not recognize, check which tense (and/or which verb) it is. There will be notes, of course, as we go along, and the lessons will bring in plenty of examples so that you can pick up more and more Spanish **gradually** without having to learn anything off by heart.

Segunda ola: lección 22

LECCION SETENTA Y DOS

¿Suicidio? ¿Asesinato?
O, las palabras, esos monstruos

1 El célebre escritor R.I.P. ha sido encontrado muerto

2 en su residencia veraniega de "Los crisantemos". **(1)**

3 Según fuentes bien informadas, ayer noche, **(2)**

4 el escritor se retiró a su despacho con objeto de redactar **(3)**

5 las últimas páginas de sus memorias.

6 Al parecer, en un momento de inadvertencia, **(4)**

7 al inclinarse sobre el diccionario, en persecución de un término, el infortunado cayó en él.

8 Un número indeterminado de palabras que se encontraban agazapadas

9 en dicho diccionario, saltaron a la garganta del desgraciado

10 ahogándole instantáneamente.

11 La familia se ha negado a hacer cualquier tipo de comentario, **(5)**

12 así como a responder a las preguntas que llegan de todas las partes del mundo.

13 La ciudad entera ha quedado muda de estupefacción.

14 Algunos se aventuran a decir que hay silencios que hablan. **(6)**

EJERCICIO: 1. Cervantes es célebre en el mundo entero. **2.** Maite y Antonio pasan unos días en su residencia de verano. **3.** Estaré a las ocho en el despacho. **4.** Me han regalado un nuevo diccionario. **5.** Le duele la garganta. **6.** ¿Te han hecho preguntas? **7.** Me gusta escuchar al silencio.

LESSON SEVENTY-TWO

Suicide? Murder? or "Those monsters (the) words"

1 The famous writer, RIP, has been found dead
2 in his summer residence of "The Chrysanthemums".
3 According to well informed sources, last (yesterday) night
4 the writer retired (himself) to his study intending (with [the] object of) [to] write
5 the last pages of his memoirs.
6 Apparently, in a moment of inadvertance
7 while leaning over the dictionary, in the pursuit of a term, the unfortunate [one] fell on it.
8 An indeterminate number of words that were (found themselves) lurking
9 in [the] said dictionary jumped at the throat of the unfortunate [one]
10 suffocating him instant(aneous)ly.
11 The family has refused (denied itself) to make any type of comment,
12 or (as well as) to answer (to) the questions that arrive from all (the) parts of the world.
13 The entire town has remained dumb with (of) stupefaction.
14 Some venture (themselves) to say that there are silences that talk.

EXERCISE : 1. Cervantes is famous all over the world. – **2.** Maite and Antonio are spending a few days in their summer residence. – **3.** I will be at the office at eight o'clock. – **4.** I have been given a new dictionary. – **5.** He has a sore throat. – **6.** Were you asked any questions? – **7.** I like to listen to the silence.

NOTES
(1) *Veraniega :* (adjective) "summer" ; *los veraneantes :* "(summer) holidaymakers" ; *ir de veraneo :* "to go on (summer) holiday".
(2) *Ayer noche, ayer por la noche* or *anoche* all mean the same thing : "last night".
(3) *Despacho :* "office" or "study", but also "despatch" in the sense of "diplomatic" or "military despatches".
(4) *Al parecer :* "apparently". Remember also the construction *a salir :* "on leaving" (see *al inclinarse,* sentence 7).
(5) *Cualquiera :* "anybody" or "whichever" ; the word apocopates into *cualquier* when it comes before a masculine noun : *cualquier libro :* "any book [you like]".
(6) *Algunos :* "some people" or "certain people". Compare with *el infortunado* (sentence 7) : "the unfortunate [one]".

EJERCICIO DE CONTROL
Ponga las palabras que faltan

1 *They have found a small beach a little further on.*

. . . .

. . . .

2 *He is sleeping.*

. . . .

3 *Where did you come from?*

¿ . . . . ?

4 *The comments were favourable.*

. . . .

5 *He didn't know what to say.*

. . . .

****

LECCION SETENTA Y TRES

¿Qué nos aconseja?

1 Luis y Mari-Angeles van a casarse pronto y, de común acuerdo, han decidido comprar algo que tenga techo. **(1)**

2 No tienen dinero pero juegan mucho a la lotería y son de los que creen que la esperanza es lo último que se pierde.

3 En este mismo momento se dirigen en un taxi a la agencia inmobiliaria en la que tienen cita con el director.

THE MISSING WORDS : 1 han encontrado una playa pequeña un poco más lejos. 2 está durmiendo. 3 de dónde sales. 4 los comentarios fueron favorables. 5 no supo qué decir.

Segunda ola: lección 23

****
LESSON SEVENTY-THREE
What do you advise us?

1   Luis and Mari-Angeles are going to get married (marry themselves) soon and, by common agreement, have decided to buy something with a roof (that has a roof).

2   They don't have [any] money, but they play a lot at the lottery and they are of those who believe that hope is the last thing to lose.

3   At this moment they are going in a taxi to the estate agent where (in which) they have an appointment with the director.

NOTES
(1) *Algo que tenga techo :* "something with a roof". Note the present subjunctive of *tener,* used with the hypothetical *algo. Busco a alguien que pueda ayudarme :* "I am looking for somebody who might be able to help me" (Cf. *He encontrado a alguien que puede ayudarme,* where *alguien* is an actual person, and not somebody fictitious).

Lección 73

4 — Yo diría que no es por aquí, aunque no he venido nunca, mi intuición femenina me dice que éste no es el camino.

5 — ¿Cómo puedes poner en duda la honradez profesional de un taxista? Aunque... Señor, ¿está seguro de que es por aquí?

6 — Si no están contentos no tienen más que bajarse ¡pues no faltaba más! Y el taxista piensa y se dice: — ¡Qué clientes! Y en alta voz: — Es aquí. (2)

7 — El taxímetro marca cuatrocientas cincuenta pesetas; tome quinientas y quédese con la vuelta. (3)

8 — Mientras pagas voy a llamar el ascensor, así no tendremos que esperar.

9   El director, que cree tener buen olfato para los negocios, ha mandado servir en su despacho café para tres personas.

10   Una vez hechas las presentaciones, Luis comienza la conversación: — Mi futura esposa y yo quisiéramos comprar una casa.

11 — No, una casa no, un piso. Una casa da mucho trabajo y, además, no tenemos dinero. Un pisito con tres o cuatro habitaciones nos basta.

4 — I would say that it isn't this way (by here), even if I have never come, my female intuition tells me that this is not the way.

5 — How can you put into doubt the professional integrity (honesty) of a taxi-driver. Although... Sir, are you sure that it is this way?

6 — If you aren't happy, all you need to do is to get out (get down). That's all we need! And the taxi-driver thinks and says to himself "What clients!" And [then says] out loud "Here it is".

7 — The meter says (marks) four hundred and fifty pesetas. Here's (Take) five hundred and keep (stay behind with) the change.

8 — While you pay I'm going to call the lift. That way we won't have to wait.

9 The director, who thinks he has (to have) a good nose (sense of smell) for business, has ordered coffee for three to be served in his office.

10 Once the introductions (presentations) [are] made, Luis begins the conversation : – My future wife and I would like to buy a house.

11 — No, not a house, a flat. A house makes (gives) a lot of work and, moreover, we don't have [any] money. A little flat with three or four rooms is enough for us.

NOTES
(2) *¡Pues no faltaba más!* : literally "Well, there was nothing else missing" (*que eso* : "than that"). In English, we would say "that's all we needed".
(3) *Quédese con la vuelta* : "keep the change". *La vuelta* (connected with the verb *volver*) : literally, "what comes back".
(4) *Un piso* : "a flat". The word *apartamento* also exists for "small apartment". *Piso* also means "storey", so *una casa de tres pisos* is "a three-storey house".

12 — ¿No tienen dinero? ¿Y qué hacen ustedes aquí? Me hacen perder el tiempo y desperdiciar mi café.

13 — No se enfade, nuestro problema es que mi futura esposa y yo no estamos a menudo de acuerdo y... ¿quién mejor que usted puede aconsejarnos?

14 — ¿Aconsejarles? ¡Enseguida! Tienen dos posibilidades: la más razonable es que no se casen y si se casan, entonces, les aconsejo que tomen cada uno un abogado.

EJERCICIO: 1. En este mismo momento estaba pensando en ti. 2. No creo que ésta sea su casa. 3. ¿Estás seguro de que no es por aquí? 4. Puedes bajarte de ahí, ya he terminado. 5. No faltabas más que tú. 6. Quédate con la vuelta. 7. ¿Sabes si hay ascensor en su casa?

EJERCICIO DE CONTROL
Ponga las palabras que faltan

1 *I have ordered breakfast in bed.*

. . . . que . . . .

en la . . . .

2 *We would like to go and see you next week.*

. . . .

. . . .

3 *That's all I need, wiih a little milk.*

. . . .

4 *It isn't worth getting angry.*

. . . .

12 — You don't have [any] money? And what are you doing here? You are making me waste (lose) my time and waste my coffee.
13 — Don't get angry. Our problem is that my future wife and I do not often agree and... who better than you can advise us?
14 — Advise you? Straight away! You have two possibilities : the more reasonable [one] is that you don't marry, and if you do marry, well then, I advise you each to take (that you take each one) a lawyer.

EXERCISE : 1. At this very moment I was thinking of you. – **2.** I do not think that this is your house. – **3.** Are you sure that it isn't this way? – **4.** You can get down from there, I have finished. – **5.** You were all we needed. – **6.** Keep the change. – **7.** Do you know if there is [a] lift in his house?

5 *What do you advise us?*

¿ . . .   . ?

THE MISSING WORDS :   **1** he dicho - me sirvan el desayuno - cama. **2** quisiéramos ir a veros la semana próxima. **3** me basta con un poco de leche. **4** no vale la pena que te enfades. **5** qué es lo que nos aconsejas.

There are some conditional tenses in this lesson. Look at some of the endings for regular verbs : *me gustaría ir :* "I would like to go". *Ahora beberíamos algo fresco :* "now we would [like to] drink something cool". *¿Irías ahora? :* "Would you go now?"

Direct translation of the Spanish constructions is becoming more and more difficult. The Spanish expressions are nevertheless very common, and you should try to put yourself in the context before you can imagine what an English speaker would say in a similar situation. Here are a few examples that you already know : *en el fondo :* "at the heart of the matter" or "basically" ; *a pesar de* "in spite of" ; *darse prisa :* "to hurry" ; *en seguida :* "straight away".

Segunda ola: lección 24

LECCION SETENTA Y CUATRO

Los Reyes Magos (1)

1   Nochebuena, Navidad, nochevieja, año nuevo, aunque recientes, les parecen lejanas a los niños la noche del cinco de enero.

2   Para ellos, el día cinco es un día de febril espera, de sueño permanente, de inquietud alegre: el día seis son los Reyes Magos.

3   Los adultos se ven desbordados por oleadas de preguntas que no son siempre fáciles de responder.

4 — Hoy, hay que irse muy pronto a la cama para que cuando vengan los Reyes estemos dormidos. (2)

ESTE AÑO LOS REYES LES DEJARÁN COMO REGALO UNA BUENA SORPRESA

5 — ¡Claro que sí! Y tendrás que dejar tus zapatos bien limpios en la ventana para que los Reyes los vean cuando lleguen y te dejen lo que les has pedido. (3)

6 — Espero que ya habrán recibido mi carta y que me traigan todo lo que les he pedido:

7   un juego de construcción de madera, discos y libros de cuentos, una pelota y muchas cosas y he pedido también juguetes para todos mis amigos,

LESSON SEVENTY-FOUR

The Three Wise Men / The Magi

1   Christmas Eve, Christmas Day, New Year's Eve, New Year's Day, although recent, (to them) seem far away to the children the night of the fifth of January.

2   For them, the fifth is a day of feverish waiting, of permanent dream[ing], of happy worry : the sixth is (they are) the Magi.

3   The adults are (see themselves) swamped (overflowed) with waves of questions that are not always easy to answer.

4 — Today, we must (it is necessary to) go to bed very early so that we'll be asleep when the Kings arrive.

5 — Of course! And you will have to leave your shoes nice and clean in the window so that the Kings see them when they arrive and leave you what you asked for.

6 — I hope that they will have received my letter and that they bring me everything (that which) I asked them for :

7   a wooden construction kit (toy), records and story-books, a ball and lots of things, and I have also asked for toys for all my friends,

NOTES
(1) In Spain (and many other countries), Father Christmas doesn't come to deliver presents to children on Christmas Eve. The traditional mythical present-giving is performed by the Three Wise Men (or Magi) who visit on January 6th. However, there is an increasing tendency to give Christmas presents on Christmas Eve.
(2) The conversation is between an adult and a child. The tone is thus rather different... but notice that the subjunctive is no obstacle even for the child!
(3) *Pedir :* "to ask for" ; *preguntar :* "to ask".

8   y también he pedido flores para ti y colonia para la abuela. Al final de la carta he puesto "y lo que sus majestades quieran". **(4)**

9 — No sé si van a poder traerte tantas cosas porque tienen que pasar por todas las casas. Mañana veremos todo.

10 — ¿Vamos a ir a ver la cabalgata? Yo quiero ver a Baltasar porque es mi rey y quiero recordarle donde vivimos.

11 — Sí, vístete porque vamos a salir dentro de un rato. Luego volveremos y te tendrás que ir pronto a la cama. **(5)**

12 — Eso es lo que menos me gusta del día de los reyes.

13   Al año que viene les voy a escribir para decirles que vengan a nuestra casa al final, así podré irme a la cama más tarde.

EJERCICIO: 1. Pasamos la nochevieja entre amigos. **2.** Dentro de dos días será Navidad. **3.** Tendrás que decirles que vengan más pronto. **4.** Cuando vienen suelen traernos flores. **5.** ¿Qué te ha pedido? **6.** A los niños les gustan los juguetes. **7.** Traed lo que queráis.

EJERCICIO DE CONTROL
Ponga las palabras que faltan

1 *I hope that they will have seen the note I left them.*

. . . .   nota

. . . .

2 *Where is the eau de Cologne that you bought me?*

¿ . . . .

. . . . ?

3 *I do not know if they are going to be able to come.*

. . . .

8 and I have also asked for flowers for you and eau de Cologne for (the) grandmother. At the end of the letter I (have) put "and whatever Your Majesties wish".

9 — I don't know if they are going to be able to bring you so many things because they have to visit (pass by) all the houses. Tomorrow we'll see everything.

10 — Are we going (to go) to see the procession? I want to see (to) Balthazar because he is my king and I want to remind him where we live.

11 — Yes, get dressed because we are going to go out in (within) a while. Then we will come back and you will have to go [off] to bed early.

12 — That is what I like least about the day of the Magi.

13 Next year I'm going to write to them to tell them to come (that they come) to our house at the end. That way I will be able to go to bed later.

NOTES
(4) *Y lo que sus majestades quieran* : "and that which Your Majesties wish". Note that the verb is in the subjunctive (because the subject *lo que* is the indeterminate "whatever").
(5) *Te tendrás que ir* : the verb is the reflexive *irse* : "to go" or "to go away", and its reflexive pronoun *te* can go either before the auxiliary (as here) or be attached to the infinitive *(tendrás que irte)*.

*****

EXERCISE : 1. We spent New Year's Eve among friends. – **2.** In two days it will be Christmas. – **3.** You will have to tell them to come earlier. – **4.** When they come they usually bring us flowers. – **5.** What has he asked you for? – **6.** Children like toys. – **7.** Bring (fam. pl.) what you want.

4 *That is what I like most.*

. . . .

5 *I arrived last.*

.. . .

****

LECCION SETENTA Y CINCO

Favores entre amigos

1 — Susana me ha propuesto que vaya a pasar la tarde a su casa para ayudarle a revelar las fotos que hicimos el último día que fuimos de excursión.

2 — ¡Estupendo! Tengo muchísimas ganas de verlas. Ya ni me acuerdo si eran fotos en blanco y negro o en color. **(1) (2)**

3 — Son en color, fui yo misma la que compró el carrete. De las mejores, haremos diapositivas. ¡Al final, podrás estrenar tu proyector! **(3)**

4 — Estaba pensando que no sería una mala idea que te lleves unas cuantas cintas para grabarlas en su casa. **(4)**

5 — ¡Es verdad! El nuevo equipo estereofónico que le han regalado tiene un sonido maravilloso.

6 — Haz una selección de los mejores discos que tenga. ¡Ah! y, sobre todo, no olvides ese disco de música irlandesa que me gusta tanto.

7 — No te preocupes, ya conozco tus gustos. Yo pienso grabar para mí un poco de música oriental, otro poco de música clásica y algo de Graeme Allwright.

THE MISSING WORDS :   1 espero que habrán visto la - que les he
dejado. 2 dónde está la colonia que me has comprado. 3 no sé si van a
poder venir. 4 eso es lo que más me gusta. 5 he llegado el último.

The expressions we saw in earlier lessons are coming back
more and more : *soler :* "to be in the habit of..." ; *¡Claro que
sí! :* "Of course!", etc.

****

LESSON SEVENTY-FIVE

Favours among friends

1 — Susana has proposed to me to go (that I go) to
spend the evening at her house [in order] to help
her develop (reveal) the photographs that we took
(we made) the last day that we were on [an]
excursion.

2 — Great! I really feel like seeing them. I don't even
remember if they were black and white or colour
photographs.

3 — They're in colour. I bought the film myself (It was me
myself the one that bought the roll). Of the best
ones, we will make slides. You will finally be able to
try out your projector!

4 — I was thinking that it would not be a bad idea that
you take (yourself) a few tapes to record (them) at
her house.

5 — That's true! The new stereo (equipment) that she's
been given (they have given her) has a marvellous
sound.

6 — Make a selection of the best records she has. Oh,
and above all, don't forget that record of Irish music
that I like so much.

7 — Don't worry, I already know your tastes. I am
thinking of recording (I think to record) for me a bit
of oriental music, another bit of classical and
something by (of) Graeme Allwright.

NOTES
(1) *Estupendo :* "great" or "fantastic".
(2) *Tengo muchísimas ganas de :* the superlative of *tengo ganas
de :* "I want to".
(3) *Estrenar :* "to use *or* to wear for the first time". In cinema or
theatre, *estrenar* means "to release" or "to make a première".
Un estreno : "a debut".
(4) *Grabar :* "to record (tapes and records)" has the same root as
the English "engrave".

8 — Si necesitas cintas vírgenes, coge las que hay encima de la biblioteca, las acabo de comprar.

9   ¡Vaya chollo que vamos a tener! Con el nuevo aparato de Susana, podremos escuchar música de buena calidad.

10 — Me parece que, de ahora en adelante, va a ser más difícil hacerte salir de casa.

11 — No, no te preocupes, lo uno no quita lo otro. Es verdad que escucharé con mucho más gusto la música. **(5)**

12   Pero eso no me impedirá salir.

Horror al desperdicio

A cualquiera que le diga que hace un mes que le ponía arsénico en el café y que tontamente ha sido atropellado por un autobús... ¡Es increíble! **(6)**

EJERCICIO: **1.** Esta tarde estoy ocupada, me han propuesto un nuevo trabajo. **2.** ¿Has visto las fotos que hicimos el año pasado? **3.** No sería mala idea ir de campo. **4.** Tengo un nuevo equipo. **5.** Me he olvidado de seleccionarte los libros que querías. **6.** Juan conoce bien mis gustos. **7.** Acabo de comprar cintas nuevas.

8 — If you need blank (virgin) tapes, take the ones that (there) are on top of the bookcase : I have just bought them.

9 We're going to have such a great time! With Susana's new machine (apparatus) we will be able to listen to good quality music.

10 — I think (It seems to me that) from now on, it's going to be more difficult to make you go out (of the house).

11 — No, don't worry. (The) one doesn't stop (remove) the other. It's true that I will enjoy listening to music more (I will listen to the music with more taste).

12 But that won't stop me going out (to go out).

What a waste! (Horror of waste)

To think (To whomever that I may tell him) that I have been putting arsenic in his coffee for a month (it makes a month that I put), and that stupidly he has been knocked over by a bus... It's incredible!

NOTES
(5) *Quitar :* "to take off" or "to remove". *Quitar una mancha :* "to remove a stain" ; *quitar la tapa :* "to take off the lid". *Lo uno quita lo otro* is a set expression with an idiomatic use of *quitar.*
(6) *Cualquiera :* see note 5 to lesson 72. *Cualquiera* can be an adjective or a pronoun. When used as a pronoun ("anybody") it is invariable, but as an adjective ("any" or "whichever") it loses its final -*a* in front of the masculine noun it qualifies : *cualquier pueblo :* "any village" or "whichever village". (With feminine nouns, this apocopation is not obligatory).

EXERCISE : 1. This afternoon I am busy, I have been offered a new job. – **2.** Have you seen the photos we took last year? – **3.** It wouldn't be a bad idea to go to the countryside. – **4.** I have a new stereo. – **5.** I have forgotten to choose you the books you wanted. – **6.** Juan knows my tastes well. – **7.** I have just bought some new tapes.

EJERCICIO DE CONTROL
Ponga las palabras que faltan

1 *Bring me three tapes and five records.*

. . . .

2 *In this shop we only sell good quality things.*

. . . .   nada más   . . .

. . . .

3 *From now on you can come and see me often.*

. . . .

. . . .

****

LECCION SESENTA Y SEIS

El participio (1)

1 Después de haberme fumado un puro, me he tomado un café, no me ha gustado, estaba muy amargo.
2 Para engañar el hambre, me he comido un bocadillo de tortilla de patata y he bebido una cerveza. (2)
3 La semana pasada encontré en el jardín un pequeño pájaro herido, lo he curado durante unos días y ha sobrevivido.
4 He visto lo que has hecho con las pinturas de colores que te he regalado, me ha gustado mucho.

4 *I hope your work doesn't stop you coming.*

. . . .

. . . . .

5 *What he has told me is incredible.*

. . . .

THE MISSING WORDS :   1 tráeme tres cintas y cinco discos. 2 en esta tienda no vendemos - que cosas de buena calidad. 3 de ahora en adelante podrás venir a verme a menudo. 4 espero que tu trabajo no te impida venir. 5 es increíble lo que me ha dicho.

Segunda ola: lección 26

* *

LESSON SEVENTY-SIX

The participle

1   After smoking (having smoked myself) a cigar, I had (have taken) a coffee ; I didn't like (haven't liked) it, it was very bitter.
2   To stave off (to deceive) the hunger, I have eaten a potato-omelette sandwich and have drunk a beer.
3   Last week I found in the garden a little injured bird ; I have treated it for a few days, and it has survived.
4   I have seen what you have done with the colour paints that I gave you ; I liked it a lot.

NOTES
(1) This lesson presents some of the more common past participles. You already know many of them, and you can revise them in this lesson. Note also the use of the perfect tense. For recent actions, or actions leading up to the present time, we use the Spanish perfect tense. The Spanish preterite refers more specifically to finished actions in a more distant past (see sentence 3).
(2) *Engañar :* "to deceive". *Engañar el hambre* or *engañar el estómago :* lit. "to deceive the hunger or to deceive the stomach". We would say "to stave off the hunger".

5 He puesto la mesa en el sitio en el que me has dicho. Ahora, la habitación es más espaciosa. **(3)**

6 ¡Entra! Estoy despierto, me he despertado hace una hora y me he puesto a leer en la cama. **(4)**

7 Esta mañana he escrito una postal a mis vecinos para desearles un feliz año nuevo. Me llevo muy bien con ellos.

8 Ha venido a vernos, y se ha llevado los discos y los libros que nos había prestado, los necesitaba.

9 Han ido a dar un paseo y a sacar los billetes a la estación. No creo que tarden mucho en volver.

10 He vuelto a ver a los amigos de José que conocimos el día de su cumpleaños en su casa.

11 Tengo ya escritas cinco cartas pero todavía no he terminado. **(5)**

INTENTA ENGAÑAR EL HAMBRE

76

Sentido de la propiedad

— ¿Sabes? Voy a dedicarme al teatro, me han ofrecido un papel como coprotagonista en una obra muy importante y tomaré un seudónimo. El novio celoso: — ¡Pues os mataré a los tres!

5   I have put the table where (in the place in that which) you (have) told me. Now the room is more spacious.

6   Come in! I am awake. I woke up an hour ago and started to read in (the) bed.

7   This morning I wrote a postcard to my neighbours to wish them a happy New Year. I get on (I carry myself) very well with them.

8   He has come to see us, and has taken (himself) the records and the books that he had lent us ; he needed them.

9   They have gone for a walk and to get (take out) the tickets at the station. I don't think they'll be long in coming back.

10 I have again seen (to) the friends of José whom we met (knew) the day of his birthday at this house.

11 I've already written five letters (I have already five written letters) but I still haven't finished.

Sense of ownership

—   Did (Do) you know? I am going to devote myself to the theatre ; I have been offered a role as co-star in a very important play (work) and I will take a pseudonym.
     The jealous fiancé : I will kill all three of you, then.

NOTES

(3) *Puesto* and *dicho* are past participles of *poner* and *decir*. In sentence 4, *hecho* (from *hacer*) and *visto* (from *ver*) are further examples of irregular past participles.

(4) *Estoy despierto* : "I am awake" ; *me he despertado* : "I have woken up". Certain verbs have two past participles : one regular and one irregular. The regular one is used to make up the perfect tense (with *haber*), while the irregular one behaves as an adjective.

(5) *Tengo ya escritas* : here, the past participle is used as an adjective, and it thus agrees with the noun it qualifies. Here, the sense is "I possess the letters in a written state" rather than "I have written them". With the straightforward perfect tense, the past participle is invariable and so does not agree with anything.

Lección 76

EJERCICIO: **1.** ¿Has visto cómo estaba vestido? **2.** He enviado una carta certificada. **3.** Nos hemos dormido y no hemos oído el despertador. **4.** Habéis tenido que volver. **5.** Se ha paseado durante toda la tarde. **6.** Han comido un poco para engañar el hambre. **7.** No echaron la carta que me habían escrito.

EJERCICIO DE CONTROL
Ponga las palabras que faltan

1 *I have done what you told me.*

. . . .

2 *We are going to eat a little to stave off the hunger.*

. . . .

. . . .

3 *On my birthday they gave me a camera.*

. . . .

. . . . máquina . . . .

****

LECCION SETENTA Y SIETE

LESSON SEVENTY-SEVEN

Revisión y notas

1. **Verb conjugations :** For the last fifteen to twenty lessons we have been gradually introducing the present subjunctive, and you now have enough knowledge of this type of construction to make wide use of it. What is most important now is to build on that knowledge, and to practise until the "subjunctive feeling" becomes a reflex.

As for the indicative, you will probably have very few problems now. Naturally, the irregular verbs may cause some problems : this is to be expected. But do not despair! We have already used many of the more common irregular

EXERCISE : 1. Have you seen how he was dressed? – **2.** I have sent a registered letter. – **3.** We fell asleep and didn't hear the alarm clock. – **4.** You have had to come back. – **5.** He has walked around all evening. – **6.** They have eaten a little to stave off the hunger.– **7.** They didn't post the letter they had written me.

4 *My neighbours have still not come back from holiday.*

. . . .

. . . .

5 *I have been awake since five in the morning.*

. . . .

. . . .

THE MISSING WORDS :   **1** he hecho lo que me habías dicho. **2** vamos a comer un poco para engañar el estómago. **3** el día de mi cumpleaños me regalaron una - de fotos. **4** mis vecinos no han vuelto todavía de vacaciones. **5** estoy despierto desde las cinco de la mañana.

Segunda ola: lección 27

* *

verbs, and you will recognize the forms. Don't forget what we said in Lesson 71 : start to leaf through the grammatical appendix at the end of the book. Even if you glance at the verb lists, get into the habit of looking for the verb-forms you cannot place. It will take you quite a long time to become fully proficient in all verbs, but if you develop the reflex of "looking them up in the back", you will find they come more and more easily.

The past participle : we have seen how the past participle is formed, and the basic ways to use it.

In the last few lessons, we have also come across the **conditional** tense (the English "would"). Here are the endings :

all verbs : infinitive + -*ía, ías, ía, íamos, íais, ían*

Examples : *yo fumar-ía* : "I would smoke" ; *tú comerías* : "you would eat" ; *él escribir-ía* : "he would write" ; *nosotros cantar-íamos* : "we would sing" ; *vosotros beber-íais* : "you would drink" ; *ellos vivir-ían* : "they would live".
We will look at conditional sentences in more detail very soon.

2. The English "than" is usually *que* in Spanish. Thus, *más vale tarde que nunca* : "better late than never".
With "more than" and "less than", however, we use *más de* and *menos de*. Compare *No más de quince minutos* : "no more than fifteen minutes" with *no más que quince minutos* : "only fifteen minutes". *No he cerrado más que una ventana* : "I have only closed one window". These are called quantitative restrictions.
With qualitative restrictions, we use the word *sino* : *no hubo sino una equivocación* : "there was only a misunderstanding". *Sino* also replaces "pero" when there is a sense of contradiction. *No es francés sino inglés* : "he is not French but English". *Sino que* is used to introduce contradictory clauses.

Another common negative form, "no longer" or "not... any more" is expressed in Spanish by *no... ya* or *ya no* (*ya no* goes before the verb) : *ya no volverán* : "they won't come back any more" ; *ya no tenemos ganas de ir* : "we no longer feel like going".

3. **Piso** : see note n° 4 lesson 73.
We have seen that *un piso* can mean both "a flat" and "a storey". It can also mean "a floor" : *un piso de madera* : "a wooden floor" : *Piso principal* : "first storey" ; *piso bajo* : "ground floor".

Pisar means "to tread" or "to tread on someone's foot", and there are various idiomatic uses of this verb, such as *no dejarse pisar* : "not to let oneself be walked over" ; *pisar el acelerador* : "step on the accelerator" ; *se oían sus pisadas* : "his footsteps could be heard" ; *seguir las pisadas de alguien* : "to follow someone's tracks".

MIRA, ALGUIEN QUE NO QUERÍA QUE LE VIERAN EN EL ASCENSOR

4. Writing in Spanish

1   He sneaked out of the house ; nobody saw him.
2   They both went for a swim in the sea.
3   The flat I have bought is sufficient for me.
4   I will record you a tape of the music you like so much.
5   This eau de Cologne you have brought me is fantastic.
6   I no longer remember what you told me.

5. Traducción

1   Ha salido de casa a escondidas, nadie lo ha visto.
2   Ambos han ido a bañarse al mar.
3   Me basta con el piso que me he comprado.
4   Te grabaré una cinta con la música que tanto te gusta.
5   Esta colonia que me has traído es estupenda.
6   Ya no me acuerdo de lo que me has dicho.

Segunda ola: lección 28 (révision)

LECCION SETENTA Y OCHO

Quien manda, manda **(1)**

1 Bajo este título vamos a introducir el imperativo.
2 Para poder reinar sin que la gente
3 se ría delante de sus narices **(2)**
4 hoy ya no hace falta que usted se disfrace de Nerón. **(3)**
5 Dominar es algo fácil. He aquí algunos ejemplos
6 que podrán serle útiles para llevar a cabo,
7 de una manera satisfactoria, su aprendizaje
8 — del castellano, por supuesto —:
9 Alejandro, deja de fumar y friega, **(4) (5)**
10 o, ven aquí y ponte de rodillas.
11 También: — mamá, vete a dar una vuelta
12 o, ''déjame en paz amor tirano'' **(6)**
13 E incluso: Tío lávate las manos antes de hacer la comida.
14 El tono y la actitud determinan el sentido que toma el imperativo.

EJERCICIO: 1. Compra el periódico cuando vengas. 2. Lleva a cabo lo que te has propuesto. 3. Pon la mesa. 4. Ven aquí. 5. Déjame un bolígrafo. 6. Come algo. 7. Si te duele la cabeza quédate en casa.

LESSON SEVENTY-EIGHT

Orders are orders (He who orders, orders)

1 Under this title we are going to introduce the imperative.
2 To be able to reign without (that) the people
3 laugh[ing] in your face (in front of your nostrils)
4 you no longer need to disguise yourself as Nero.
5 To dominate is something easy. Here are a few examples
6 that could be useful to follow through to the end (bring to the end)
7 in a satisfactory manner your apprenticeship
8 – in Spanish, of course – :
9 Alejandro ; stop smoking and do the washing up,
10 or, come here and kneel down (put yourself on your knees).
11 Also : Mummy, go and have a walk
12 or, "leave me in peace, tyrant love"
13 And even : Here, pal (Uncle), wash your hands before you make the meal.
14 The tone and the attitude determine the meaning that the imperative takes [on].

NOTES
(1) *Quien manda, manda* : literally "who orders, orders". This sentence is often repeated in Spain, and takes on different meanings according to the way it is said (humour, resignation, authority, etc.).
Remember that *mandar* also means "to send" : *mandar una carta* "to send a letter".
(2) *Nariz* : "nose" or "nostril".
(3) *Ya no hace falta que usted* : "you no longer need to" (literally "it is already not necessary that you...") For a further note on *hace falta,* see note 3b in lesson 84.
(4) *Dejar de* : "stop... ing". *Deja de hacer ruido* : "stop making a noise".
(5) *Fregar* or *fregar los platos* : "to wash the dishes".
(6) The order given in quotation marks is a famous saying by Luis de Góngora.

EXERCISE : 1. Buy the newspaper when you come. – **2.** Follow what you proposed to the end. – **3.** Lay the table. – **4.** Come here. – **5.** Leave me a biro. – **6.** Eat something. – **7.** Stay at home if you have a headache.

EJERCICIO DE CONTROL
Longa las palabras que faltan

1 *Before you go, phone him.*

. . . .

2 *Don't come if you are tired.*

. . . .

3 *Write to us when you arrive.*

. . . .

****

LECCION SETENTA Y NUEVE

No molesten (1)

1 El imperativo es utilizado en España tanto por
2 el honrado padre de familia
3 como por la abnegada ama de casa,
4 el sereno ejecutivo, el tierno niño e incluso por
el melenudo "progre". (2)

4 *If you can, buy me some flowers.*

. .   . .

5 *Here, it's a present for you.*

. . . , ...

THE MISSING WORDS : 1 antes de ir telefonéale. 2 no vengas si estás cansado. 3 escríbenos cuando llegues. 4 si puedes cómprame flores. 5 ten, es un regalo para ti.

Segunda ola: lección 29

* *

LESSON SEVENTY-NINE

Do not disturb

1 The imperative is used in Spain as much by
2 the honest father (of [the] family)
3 as by the devoted (self-denying) housewife,
4 the serene executive, the tender child, and even by
the long-haired "progre".

NOTES
(1) The imperative will be examined in detail in the next revision exercise (lesson 84). For the time being, remember that certain imperatives (first person plural, third person singular and plural) use the present subjunctive form.
(2) *Un progre* (derived from *progresista*) is a popular word applying mainly to young people with progressive and/or revolutionary ideas (Cf. *reaccionario*).

5   No sería justo olvidar el imperativo
6   administrativo: "entre sin llamar" o "no haga ruido",
7   "absténganse de hacer cheques sin fondos", etc.
8   Un agradable paseo en una bella tarde de sol
9   puede facilitarle la ocasión de familiarizarse
10   con lo que podríamos llamar:
11   "el caluroso imperativo civilizado":
12   empuje, tire, no fume, pasen, esperen, corran, etc.
13   Incluso cuando se está enamorado el imperativo puede ser útil;
14   he aquí un ejemplo: "abrázame, amor mío, que tengo frío" **(3)**

EJERCICIO: 1. Sírvase, yo no tengo apetito. 2. Niños, jugad en vuestra habitación. 3. Cierren la puerta al salir. 4. Pon el disco que me gusta. 5. Peatones pasen. 6. Venid a vernos la semana que viene. 7. Id con ellos al cine.

EJERCICIO DE CONTROL
Ponga las palabras que faltan

1 *Take and drink, this is a good wine.*

. . . .

2 *Tell me who you are going with and I'll tell you who you are.*

. . . . andas . . . .

. . . .

3 *Say what you want.*

. . . . queráis.

4 *Here, and keep the change.*

. . . .

5 It would not be fair (just) to forget the
6 administrative imperative : "enter without knocking" or "make no noise",
7 "do not write (abstain from making) cheques that "bounce" (cheques without funds)", etc.
8 A pleasant walk on a beautiful sunny evening
9 can facilitate [for] you the opportunity to familiarize yourself
10 with what we could call :
11 "the warm, civilized imperative" :
12 push, pull, do not smoke, cross, wait, run, etc.
13 Even when one is in love, the imperative can be useful ;
14 Here is an example : "Hug me, my love, (that) I'm cold".

EXERCISE : 1. Help yourself ; I have no appetite. — 2. Children, play in your room. — 3. Close the door on the way out. — 4. Put on the record I like. — 5. Pedestrians cross. — 6. Come to see us next week. — 7. Go with them to the cinema.

NOTES
(3) *Abrázame :* hug me. Personal object pronouns join onto the end of the imperative in the same way as they do to infinitives and gerunds. Similarly with reflexive pronouns : *lávate :* "have a wash".

5 *Don't forget that tomorrow is Sunday and we close.*

. . . .

. . . .

THE MISSING WORDS : 1 tomad y bebed, éste es un buen vino. 2 dime con quien - y te diré quien eres. 3 decid lo que - . 4 tenga y quédese con la vuelta. 5 no olviden que mañana es domingo y cerramos.

There are a number of irregular imperatives in the familiar singular for. : *di* (from *decir*) ; *dime :* "tell me" ; *haz* (from *hacer*) ; *oye :* (from *oír* "to listen") ; *pon* (from *poner*) ; *sal* (from *salir* ("to go out") ; *sé* (from *ser*) ; *ve* (from *ir*) ; *vete* ("go away" ; *ven aquí* (from *venir*) : "come here".

Segunda ola: lección 30

LECCION OCHENTA

¡Dulce pereza!

1 — Esta mañana nos hemos levantado temprano y hemos ido al monte a coger setas. **(1) (2)**

2 — A mí, también me hubiera gustado ir pero...
3   se está tan bien en la cama que...

4 — Me apuesto lo que quieras que, para comer, no tendrás pereza. **(3)**

5 — Te prometo hacer un esfuerzo.

6 — Bueno, voy a encender el horno y a lavar las setas.

7   Yo, voy a poner la mesa.

8   Y si tú bajaras a comprar pan y vino podríamos comer enseguida.

9 — Imposible, tengo unas agujetas horribles
10   y, además, tengo las manos llenas de ampollas.

11 — ¡No digas bobadas! Has estado durmiendo todo el fin de semana.

12 — No me entendéis. ¡Si supierais! **(4)**
13   Me he pasado el sábado y el domingo
14   soñando que trabajaba en una mina.

EJERCICIO: 1. ¿Te vas a levantar temprano mañana? **2.** Si vinieras a verlo le gustaría. **3.** Te apuesto lo que quieras. **4.** Haré un esfuerzo. **5.** Si hubiera sabido que ibas a venir no habría salido. **6.** Me voy a lavar las manos. **7.** ¡Si supieras!

LESSON EIGHTY

Sweet laziness !

1 — This morning we got up early and went to the mountain to pick (to take) mushrooms.
2 — I, too, would have liked to have gone (to go) but...
3 one is so well [off] in bed that...
4 — I bet (myself) what you want that, to eat, you will not be lazy (will not have laziness).
5 — I promise you I will make (to make) an effort.
6 — Good. I'm going to light the oven and wash the mushrooms.
7 I'm going to lay the table.
8 And if you go down and (to) buy bread and wine, we could eat straight away.
9 — [That's] Impossible. I'm terribly stiff (I have some horrible stiffnesses)
10 and besides, (I have) my hands [are] full of blisters.
11 — Don't talk nonsense (Don't tell silly things)! You have been sleeping all (the) weekend.
12 — You don't understand (me). If only you knew!
13 I have spent (the) Saturday and (the) Sunday
14 dreaming that I was working in a mine.

NOTES
(1) *Temprano* : "early". This adverb can be used with *levantarse* as an alternative to *madrugar* : "to get up early".
(2) *Seta* : "mushroom". The word *champiñon* also exists.
(3) *Me apuesto lo que quieras* : "I bet you anything you want".
(4) *Si supieras* : imperfect subjunctive. We will come back to this construction later, but for the time being check out the other uses in this lesson : sentence 8 ; exercise : sentences 2,5 and 7 ; *ejercicio de control* : sentence 4.

EXERCISE : 1. Are you going to get up early tomorrow? – **2.** He would be pleased if you came to see him. – **3.** I bet you what you want. – **4.** I will make an effort. – **5.** I wouldn't have gone out if I'd known you were going to come. – **6.** I'm going to wash my hands. – **7.** If only you knew!

EJERCICIO DE CONTROL
Ponga las palabras que faltan

1 *Tomorrow we will go to pick mushrooms.*

. . . .

2 *I am tired : I am stiff.*

. . . . : . . . . . , ...

3 *Have you got a light, please? I have lost the matches.*

¿ . . . . ? . . . .

. . . .

****

LECCION OCHENTA Y UNA.

Por amor al arte

1 — Me gustaría ir a escuchar un concierto.
2 — Si lo hubiera sabido, habría reservado unas
   entradas para la semana que viene.
3   El domingo se inaugura la temporada.
4 — He oído decir que hay un programa muy
   bueno.
5 — Quizás se pueda arreglar todavía.
6   A menudo hay gente que ha reservado por
   teléfono
7   y a última hora no va.
8 — Sí, pero para eso hay que ir unas horas antes
   a hacer cola. **(1)**
9 — ¡Ya sé lo que vamos a hacer! **(2)**
10 Enviaremos a la criada con tres horas de
   antelación

4 *If she had a little time, she would have gone.*

. .   . .

. . . .

5 *Tell me what time you arrive.*

. . . .

THE MISSING WORDS :   1 mañana iremos a coger setas. **2** estoy cansado, tengo agujetas. **3** ¿tiene fuego, por favor? he perdido las cerillas. **4** si hubiera tenido un poco de tiempo hubiera ido. **5** dime a qué hora llegarás.

Segunda ola: lección 31

****

LESSON EIGHTY-ONE

For the love of (to the) art

1 — I would like to go to listen to a concert.
2 — If I had known, I would have reserved some tickets (entrances) for next week.
3 The season opens (inaugurates itself) on Sunday.
4 — I have heard (heard said) that there is a very good programme.
5 — Maybe it can still be arranged.
6 Often there are people who have reserved by phone
7 and at [the] last minute (hour) don't go.
8 — Yes, but for that you have to go a few hours before and (make) queue.
9 — I know what we are going to do!
10 We will send (to) the maid (with) three hours in (of) advance

NOTES
(1) *Hay que ir :* literally "it is necessary to go". The *hay que* construction is widely used to replace *tener que :* with *hay que,* and with *hace falta que* (see note 3 to lesson 78), the construction is impersonal.
(2) *Ya* is often untranslatable in English, but adds a sense of affirmation to the Spanish sentence. (Cf. note 2 in revision lesson N° 77).

11   para que saque las entradas. ¿Qué te parece? **(3)**

12 — Perfecto. Dile que saque seis entradas. Invitaremos a los Carrillo y a los González.

Si Mozart levantara la cabeza... **(4)**

13 — La semana pasada fuimos a las "Bodas de Figaro"

14 — Nosotros estábamos invitados pero no pudimos ir. Enviamos flores.

EJERCICIO: 1. Hemos reservado tres entradas para el próximo concierto. **2.** Ven con nosotros. **3.** A última hora no pudo venir. **4.** Había mucha gente haciendo cola. **5.** Saca tres mil pesetas del banco. **6.** Nos ha invitado a su cumpleaños. **7.** Cinco días antes ya no había entradas.

EJERCICIO DE CONTROL
Ponga las palabras que faltan

1 *If it was sunny we would go for a walk.*

. . . .

2 *We heard that he had come to Granada.*

. . . .

Granada.

11   so that she [can] buy (take out) the tickets. What do you think?
12 — Perfect. Tell her to get six tickets. We will invite the Carrillo and the Gonzalez.

        If Mozart raised his head...

13 — Last week we went to the "Marriage of Figaro".
14 — We were invited but we couldn't go. We sent flowers.

NOTES
(3) *Sacar :* "to take out". In Spanish, one "takes out" tickets to a show. *Sacar las maletas del maletero :* "to take the cases out of the boot".
(4) "If Mozart raised..." : *Si Mozart levantara.* We mentioned this construction in note 4 in the last lesson. See also sentence 2 in the present lesson, and sentence 1 in the *ejercicio de control.* If you want to know more about the construction, turn to the next revision lesson.

EXERCISE : 1. We have reserved two tickets for the next concert. – **2.** Come with us. – **3.** At the last minute, he couldn't come. – **4.** There were a lot of people queuing. – **5.** Take three thousand pesetas out of the bank. – **6.** He has invited us to his birthday party. – **7.** Five days before, there were no more tickets.

* * * * *

3 *On Saturday the new market is being opened.*

   . .   . .

   . . . . . .

4 *He says he knows what he is going to do.*

   . . . .

5 *What do you think?*

¿ . . .   . ?

****

LECCION OCHENTA Y DOS

Una cierta cultura (continuación de la lección 81)

1 El domingo, un cuarto de hora antes del concierto,
2 nuestros simpáticos amigos buscan a su criada entre la multitud.
3 — ¡Uf! Está usted aquí...
4 Ya creíamos que no íbamos a encontrarla.
5 ¡Esto es una locura! ¡Hay muchísima gente!
6 — No me hablen, me he mareado, me han empujado, me han robado el bolso
7 y con los empujones he perdido un zapato,
8 pero... ¡tengo las entradas!
9 — ¡Sensacional! ¡Vamos! ¡Empujad! ¡Hay que entrar cueste lo que cueste!
10 Un poco más tarde, en la sala, la gente se sienta cómodamente,
11 dignamente, da un último toque a la corbata
12 o al broche del vestido, susurra un comentario irónico
13 sobre la ausencia de los Suárez o de los Iribarne
14 y se dispone a aplaudir la entrada del director de orquesta.

EJERCICIO: 1. Necesito salir porque me mareo. **2.** Había sitio para todos. **3.** Siéntate aquí. **4.** ¿Puedes planchar mi corbata? **5.** Carmen no pudo ir porque estaba de viaje. **6.** Vendrá un poco más tarde. **7.** El tenor fue muy aplaudido.

THE MISSING WORDS : **1** si hiciera sol iríamos a pasearnos. **2** hemos oído decir que había venido a -. **3** el sábado se inaugura el nuevo mercado. **4** dice que sabe lo que va a hacer. **5** que os (or : le) parece.

Segunda ola: lección 32

* *

LESSON EIGHTY-TWO

A certain culture (continued from lesson 81)

1	On Sunday, a quarter of [an] hour before the concert,
2	our nice friends are looking for their maid in (among) the crowd.
3	— Phew ! You're here...
4	We were starting to think we weren't going to find you.
5	It's crazy (This is a madness) ! There are an awful lot of people!
6	— You don't say. I feel sick. I've been pushed [around] and my bag has been stolen
7	and with [all] the pushing(s) I have lost a shoe,
8	but... I have the tickets!
9	— Tremendous! Come on! Push! We've got to get in at all costs (let it cost what it may cost).
10	A little later, in the hall, the people sit down comfortably,
11	dignified, give(s) a finishing touch to their (the) tie[s]
12	or to the brooch on their (of the) dress[es], whisper[ing] an ironical comment
13	on the absence of the Suárez or of the Iribarne
14	and get ready (dispose themselves) to applaud the entrance of the conductor.

EXERCISE : **1.** I need to go out because I feel sick. – **2.** There was room for everyone. – **3.** Sit down here. – **4.** Can you iron my tie? – **5.** Carmen could not go because she was away on a trip. – **6.** He will come a little later. – **7.** The tenor was much applauded.

EJERCICIO DE CONTROL
Ponga las palabras que faltan

1 *We will go an hour before.*

. . . .

2 *We thought it was going to rain.*

. . . .

3 *If we don't hurry, we'll arrive late.*

. . . .

. . .   .

4 *Those chairs are very comfortable.*

. . . .

5 *He is not here now ; he will be back soon.*

. . . . , ...

. . . . . .

****

LECCION OCHENTA Y TRES

Cría cuervos... (1)

1 En casa de amigos:
   — Tiene usted un hijo muy simpático.
     ¿Cómo te llamas, pequeño?
   — ¡Curiosa!

THE MISSING WORDS : **1** iremos una hora antes. **2** creíamos que iba a llover. **3** si no nos damos prisa llegaremos con retraso. **4** esas sillas son muy cómodas. **5** ahora está ausente, no tardará en volver.

* * * * *

There is nothing new in this lesson, but refresh your memory (if need be) on the following points :

Sentence 4 – *Ya :* see note 2, lesson 81
Sentence 6 – *Me he mareado :* see note 3, lesson 47
Sentence 6 – avoiding the passive : note 2, lesson 42
Sentence 9 – *Cueste lo que cueste :* lesson 67.

Segunda ola: lección 33

* *

LESSON EIGHTY-THREE

Raise ravens...

1   At the house of friends :
— You have a very nice son.
What's your name, sonny (little one)?
— Nosy!

NOTES
(1) *Cría cuervos...* was the title of a famous film by Carlos Saura. It comes from the proverb *Cría cuervos y te sacarán los ojos :* "raise ravens and they'll tear your eyes out". *Criar :* "to raise (animals or children)".

2 En la panadería:
— ¿Es su hija?
— No, es mi sobrina Maribel.
— Toma, te regalo un pastel.
— ¡Vamos! ¿Qué se dice Maribel? **(2)**
— ¡Tacaña!

3 En el colegio:
— Sí, señor, su hijo podría trabajar más.
— ¡Chivata !

4 En la tienda:
— ¿Quieres mucho a tu mamá, Julito?
— Sí señor, ¿y usted quiere a su mujer?
— ¡Julito! no seas mal educado.
— Pero mamá... es él el que ha empezado a hablar de deberes morales.

5 El niño precoz:
— Dentro de unos meses vas a tener un hermanito.
— Decidme la verdad. ¿Tenéis conocimientos de economía?
— No, pero... ¿Qué quieres decir, hijo mío?
— No estoy seguro de que la ampliación de nuestra empresa de amor, en esta época de crisis, no nos conduzca a la quiebra.

EJERCICIO: 1. Tenemos tres hijos, dos chicos y una chica. **2.** Mi hermana tiene dos hijas, son mis sobrinas. **3.** Si su hijo jugara más en casa, trabajaría más en el colegio. **4.** He visto un vestido muy bonito para ti. **5.** Dentro de unos meses estaré de vacaciones. **6.** Dime lo que piensas de esa máquina de fotos. **7.** Conduce con precaución.

EJERCICIO DE CONTROL
Ponga las palabras que faltan

1 *You are very pretty with this dress [on].*

. . . .

2   At the baker's :
     — Is this your daughter?
     — No, it's my niece, Maribel.
     — Here, Have (I give you) a cake.
     — Come along! What do you (does one) say, Maribel?
     — Stingy old woman!

3   At school :
     — Yes, sir, your son could work more.
     — Snitch!

4   In the shop :
     — Do you love (to) your Mummy a lot, Julito?
     — Yes, sir. Do you love (to) your wife?
     — Julito! Don't be rude (badly educated)!
     — But, Mummy... It was *he* who started talking about moral duties.

5   The precocious child :
     — In a few months, you're going to have a little brother.
     — Tell me the truth. Do you know anything about (have knowledge of) economics?
     — No, but... What do you mean, my son?
     — I am not sure that the expansion of our company of love, in this time of crisis, will not lead us to bankruptcy.

NOTES
(2) *Vamos* : "come on" or "come along" or "let's go". This is the only exception to the rule we spoke about in note N° 1 to lesson 79 : the first person plural imperative uses the present subjunctive form, but *vamos* is in the indicative. You will find more details of this in paragraph 1 of the next lesson.

EXERCISE : 1. We have three children : two boys and a girl. — **2.** My sister has two daughters ; they are my nieces. — **3.** If your son played more at home, he would work more at school. — **4.** I have seen a very nice dress for you. — **5.** I'll be on holiday in a few months. — **6.** Tell me what you think of this camera. — **7.** Drive carefully.

2 *She is a very cultured woman.*

. . . . culta.

3 *What did he mean?*

¿ . . .   . ?

4 *I am sure that he will come.*

. . . .   de   . . .   .

5 *Their company is in bankruptcy.*

. .   . .

THE MISSING WORDS : **1** estás muy guapa con este vestido. **2** es una mujer muy -. **3** qué ha querido decir. **4** estoy seguro - que vendrá. **5** su empresa está en quiebra.

****

LECCION OCHENTA Y CUATRO

LESSON EIGHTY-FOUR

Revisión y notas

1. **The imperative :** see lessons 78 and 79, note 1, and lesson 83, note 2.

In the familiar form, the imperative is very simple : for *-ar* verbs, the ending is *-a :* for *-er* and *-ir* verbs, the ending is *-e :* *habla :* "speak" ; *bebe :* "drink!" ; *abre la puerta :* "open the door!". There are a certain number of irregular imperatives, some of which you have already seen at the end of lesson 79.

In the familiar plural form (informally addressing more than one person), the imperative is similarly simple : take the infinitive and change the final *r* into *d : hablad más alto :* "speak louder" ; *leed este libro :* "read this book" ; *escribid a vuestro amigo :* "write to your friend". There are no exceptions to this.

¡ CURIOSA !

Segunda ola: lección 34

* *

In polite imperative forms (third person singular *usted* and plural *ustedes),* we use the corresponding forms of the present subjunctive. Thus, the polite imperative (singular) of *decir* is *diga :* "tell me" (as on the telephone), of *venir : venga,* of *ser : sea,* of *hacer : haga,* and so on. The first person imperative "let us..." is also formed with the subjunctive, except for the word *vamos :* "let's go" as we saw in the last lesson.

In negative imperatives, we use the present subjunctive throughout. Thus, "do not say that" : *no digas eso* (fam. sing.) ; *no digáis eso* (fam pl.), *no diga eso* (pol. sing.), *no digan eso* (pol. pl.).

The subjunctive of regular verbs, as we have seen, is formed by adding *-er* endings to the stem of *-ar* verbs, and *-ar* endings to the stem of *-er* and *-ir* verbs. For irregular verbs, the same endings are added to the stem of the **first person singular,** provided this ends in an *-o* (i.e., excluding *dar, estar, haber, ser, saber* and *ir*). Thus, the subjunctive of *poner* is *ponga,* since "I put" is *pongo.*

Lección 84

2. The use of the subjunctive was explained in some detail in lesson 70. Refer back to that lesson, and check that the basics are clear. The key to the subjunctive is that the action is **hypothetical.** It is thus logical that the imperative is often in the subjunctive of the two moods : *Compramos una casa, en Marruecos :* "let's buy a house in Morocco" ; *Que vivan' muchos años :* "May they live many years ; *Que le vaya bien :* "all the best!".

3. The imperfect subjunctive is used in certain conditional sentences, where the possibility is felt to be rather distant, or even fictitious. Compare the following ;

a) If I work, I can eat : *Si trabajo, puedo comer.*

b) If I worked, I could eat : *Si trabajaba, podía comer.*

c) If I worked, I could eat : *Si trabajara, podría comer.*

The first sentence is not complicated : it is a straightforward condition. The second and third sentences, however, need some clarification. Sentence (b) is in the imperfect tense, and the meaning must thus be : "If I was working, I was able to eat". In sentence (c), the use of the word "could" is ambiguous.
Not so in Spanish! *Si trabajara* is the imperfect subjunctive, which suggests therefore that the "working" is fictitious ; and the confirmation comes in the conditional tense of *podría :* "I would be able to". *Si trabajara* is a remote conditional, that is contrary to established fact... and therefore in the subjunctive.

Here are some other examples of the use of the imperfect subjunctive in conditional sentences : *Si vinieras, iríamos juntos :* "If you came, we would go together" ; *Si pudiera lo haría :* I would do it if I could" ; *Si todos supiéramos hablar dos o tres lenguas extranjeras, borraríamos otras tantas fronteras :* "If we all could (knew how to) speak two or three foreign languages, we would get rid of just as many borders".

The forms of the imperfect subjunctive are as follow :

Verbs in *-ar* (cantar)	Verbs in *-er* or *-ir* (comer - vivir)	
cant ara	com - viv.	iera
cant aras	com - viv	ieras
cant ara	com - viv	iera
cant áramos	com - viv	iéramos
cant arais	com - viv	ierais
cant aran	com - viv	ieran

You will notice that, with *-ar* verbs, the endings for the three persons singular and the third person plural are identical to the future endings. The difference is in the accent : when there is no written accent, as you know, the stress falls on the next-to-last syllable (e.g., *cantara*) : in the future, there is a written accent on the last syllable *(cantará)*.

The alternative forms of the imperfect subjunctive are as follows :

Verbs in *-ar* (cantar)	Verbs in *-er* or *-ir* (comer - vivir)	
cant ase	com - viv	iese
cant ases	com - viv	ieses
cant ase	com - viv	iese
cant ásemos	com - viv	iésemos
cant aseis	com - viv	ieseis
cant asen	com - viv	iesen

In fact, there are two forms of the imperfect subjunctive in Spanish. There is no semantic difference whatever, and the choice is up to you. Phonetically, one form can be preferable to the other in certain sentences, or with certain verbs. The most important thing to do is to be aware that the two forms exist, so that you will recognize them in speech. From now on, we will be mixing the two forms in the lessons and exercise, so you'll have plenty of practice in recognizing them!

SÍ HICIERA BUENO IRÍAMOS A BAÑARNOS

****

LECCION OCHENTA Y CINCO

Novedad

1 Los verbos irregulares son considerados, a menudo,
2 como la dificultad mayor de la lengua caste-llana.
3 A partir de ahora, los estudiaremos
4 de una manera más detallada.

Al despertar

5 Fuera nieva. La claridad que atraviesa las cortinas me despierta.

4. Writing in Spanish

1   Bring me a litre of milk when you come back.
2   Telephone (pol. sing) him before eight o'clock.
3   Hurry up (fam. pl.), we are going to arrive too late.
4   If it were hotter, we would go for a swim.
5   If you read more you would know more.
6   The shopping will have to be done for tonight.

5. Translation

1   Tráeme un litro de leche cuando vuelvas.
2   Llámelo por teléfono antes de las ocho.
3   Daos prisa, vamos a llegar demasiado tarde.
4   Si hiciera (or hiciese) más calor iríamos a bañarnos.
5   Si leyeras (or leyeses) más sabrías más.
6   Habrá que hacer las compras para esta noche.

Segunda ola: lección 35

****

LESSON EIGHTY-FIVE

Something new (Newness)

1   (The) irregular verbs are often considered
2   as the major difficulty of the Spanish (Castilian)
     language.
3   From now on, we will study them
4   in a more detailed manner.

On waking up

5   Outside it is snowing. The light (clarity) that crosses
     the curtains wakes me up.

6   El frío no me alienta a levantarme.
7   Cómplice de mi deseo, cierro de nuevo los ojos.
8   Pero no acierto a negar la evidencia.
9   Me confieso vencido y me siento en la cama,
10 tiemblo, aprieto los dientes y no pierdo más tiempo.
11 Una vez en la cocina enciendo el fuego,
12 caliento un poco de leche y preparo el café.
13 Mientras espero, abro la ventana y digo:
14 ¡Bienvenido!

BUENOS DÍAS

EJERCICIO: 1. Los verbos son difíciles, hay que estudiarlos. 2. Ayer nevó e hizo mucho frío. 3. Todos los días no me levanto temprano. 4. No niego que tengas razón. 5. La leche ya está caliente. 6. Voy a encender el fuego. 7. Abre la ventana, hace calor.

EJERCICIO DE CONTROL
Ponga las palabras que faltan

1 *I confess that I don't know what to say.*

. . . .   sé   . . .   .

2 *Close your eyes, I have a surprise for you.*

. . . .   sorpresa

. . . .   . .

6	The cold does not encourage me to get up.
7	Accomplice of my desire, I close again my (the) eyes.
8	But I cannot (manage to) deny the evidence.
9	I admit defeat (I admit myself defeated) and sit down on the bed,
10	I tremble, grit my teeth and waste no (do not waste) more time.
11	Once in the kitchen, I light the fire,
12	warm a little milk and prepare the coffee.
13	While I am waiting, I open the window and say :
14	Welcome! [masc.]

EXERCISE : 1. Verbs are difficult, they must be studied. − **2.** Yesterday it snowed and was very cold. − **3.** I don't get up early every day. − **4.** I do not deny that you are right. − **5.** The milk is hot already. − **6.** I am going to light the fire. − **7.** Open the window, it is hot.

*****

Here we are going to start looking systematically at irregular verbs.
You have seen a number of new verbs, or new verb forms that are far enough removed from their infinitives as to be barely recognizable.
This is because the **stem** of many verbs change vowels in the three persons singular and the third person plural, in the present tenses. For example, "I think" is not "penso" but *pienso. Nevar :* "to snow" becomes (as we saw in the lesson) *nieva* in the third person singular : "It is snowing". The pure vowel sound strengthens or becomes a diphthong when the stress falls on it. Thus, *pensamos :* "we think", and *piensan :* "they think". Look out for the tonic accent : stressed vowels are **in boldface.**
(The major changes are : *e* changes to *ie* (first group) ; *o* changes to *ue* (second group) ; *e* changes to *i* (third group). See information on page 91 sqq. − "radical-changing verbs").

*****

3 *Have you lit the oven?*

¿ . . . . ?

4 *I'm trembling because I'm cold.*

. . . .

5 *Welcome (fem.) to our house*

¡ . . . . nuestra . . . . !

****

LECCION OCHENTA Y SEIS

La sopa de ajo

1 He aquí una receta típicamente castellana: **(1)**
2 Se hace hervir agua con sal en una cazuela
3 y se echan rebanadas de pan, que han sido fritas previamente **(2)**
4 con el fin de dorarlas. Se echan también dos pizcas de pimentón. **(3)**
5 En una sartén, con aceite muy caliente,
6 se hace un refrito de ajos; luego se retiran éstos
7 y se vierte el aceite en la cazuela **(4)**
8 dejando que la sopa hierva lentamente.
9 Un poco antes de servirla,
10 se echa un huevo para cada persona; se espera que las claras cuajen

SE ESTÁ CALENTANDO EL AMBIENTE

THE MISSING WORDS : 1 confieso que no - que decir. 2 cierra los ojos tengo una - para ti. 3 has encendido el horno. 4 tiemblo porque tengo frío. 5 bienvenida a - casa.

Segunda ola: lección 36

****

LESSON EIGHTY-SIX

Garlic soup

1 Here is a typically Castilian recipe :
2 You boil (One boils) salted water (water with salt) in a pan
3 and put (puts) in slices of bread that have previously been fried
4 in order to turn them golden. You also put in two pinches of hot pepper.
5 In a frying pan, with very hot oil,
6 you fry up some garlic(s), then take these out
7 and pour the oil in the pan
8 and leave (leaving) the soup to simmer (boil slowly).
9 A little [while] before serving it,
10 you put in an egg for each person, wait for the whites to cook (coagulate)

NOTES
(1) *Receta :* "recipe" or "prescription". "A receipt" is *un recibo*.
(2) *Se echan :* the verbs in this lesson are in the reflexive. Here, "the slices of bread" actually "put themselves (in the pan)". *Echar* is a much used verb : *echar sal :* "to salt" ; *echar la siesta :* "to have a siesta" ; *no me eche agua en el vaso :* "don't put water in my glass".
(3) *Dorar :* "to gild" or "to brown (as in cooking)" ; *dorado :* "golden".
(4) *Vertir :* "to pour" is another example of the behaviour of a "radical-changing verb" – a verb whose stem changes its vowel when the tonic accent falls on it (see note on page 300).

11 y se sirve caliente enseguida.
12 En Castilla, suele tomarse esta sopa en recipientes — especie de tazas —
13 de barro consagrados a este uso,
14 pero en un plato también está muy buena.
15 ¡Buen provecho! **(5)**

EJERCICIO: **1**. Alberto nos ha regalado un libro de cocina. **2**. El agua está hirviendo. **3**. Necesito otra cazuela. **4**. Hoy comeremos patatas fritas. **5**. Echa un poco de sal. **6**. Los ajos son caros. **7**. La sopa está buena.

EJERCICIO DE CONTROL
Ponga las palabras que faltan

1 *There is very little oil in the pan.*

. . . .

2 *I don't much like eating cold.*

. . . .

3 *I've bought some eggs for dinner.*

. . . .

****

LECCION OCHENTA Y SIETE

Advertencia por adelantado o "La letra mata, el espíritu vivifica" **(1)**

1 Incluso cuando se escribe en la lengua materna

11 and serve it hot straight away.
12 In Castile, it is usually eaten (taken) in recipients –
kind of cups –
13 [made] of earth meant for (consacrated to) this use,
14 but in a dish it's also very good.
15 Enjoy your meal!

EXERCISE : **1.** Alberto has given us a cookery book. – **2.** The water is boiling. – **3.** I need another pan. – **4.** Today we will eat fried potatoes. – **5.** Put in a bit of salt. – **6.** The garlic is expensive. – **7.** The soup is good.

NOTES
(5) *¡Buen provecho!* or *¡que aproveche!* is Spanish for "bon appetit!". *¡Que aproveche!* comes from the verb *aprovechar* : "to take advantage" or *"to profit"*. Logically, one should say *¡que aprovechen!* when addressing more than one person.

4 *The meal is ready.*

. . . .

5 *We usually eat in these dishes.*

. . . .

THE MISSING WORDS :   **1** hay muy poco aceite en la sartén. **2** no me gusta mucho comer frío. **3** he comprado huevos para cenar. **4** la comida está lista. **5** solemos comer en estos platos.

Segunda ola: lección 37

****

LESSON EIGHTY-SEVEN

Advanced warning, or "The letter kills, the spirit brings to life"

1 Even when one writes in one's mother language

NOTES
(1) *Adelantado* : "advanced" ; *por adelantado* : "in advance" ; *mi reloj adelanta 5 minutos* : "my watch is 5 minutes fast". Remember also *de aquí en adelante* : "from now on".

2 — quizás con la excepción de una carta dirigida a amigos o personas próximas —

3 escribir bien una carta puede ser considerado

4 como una auténtica proeza.

5 La Administración, un hospital, una escuela, una empresa, una agencia, etc.,

6 aunque ''seres abstractos'' son enormemente exigentes.

7 Se debe saber comenzar una carta y terminarla.

8 En medio se debe saber, ya se trate de alabar **(2)**

9 manifestar, hacer discernir, mentar, defender, sosegar, pedir, etc. **(3)**

10 decir con formulas hechas que, en general, no quieren decir nada,

11 aquello que se quiere decir.

12 Y... ¡atención a las faltas de ortografía!

13 Se conocen muchos casos en los que el autor de una falta **(4)**

14 ha sido llevado a la silla eléctrica.

EJERCICIO: 1. Hablo inglés pero mi lengua materna es el italiano. **2.** Escribir bien una carta es difícil. **3.** Hemos escrito al hospital pero no nos han contestado. **4.** Julia está aprendiendo a escribir. **5.** No te pongas en medio. **6.** Eso no me concierne. **7.** Las faltas de ortografía se pueden evitar.

2	– perhaps with the exception of a letter (directed) to friends or somebody (persons) close –
3	to write a letter can be considered
4	as a real (authentic) prowess.
5	The Administration, a hospital, a school, a company, an agency, etc.,
6	although "abstract beings", are extremely demanding.
7	One must know [how] to begin a letter and finish it.
8	In the middle, one must know, whether it is about praising,
9	manifesting, making the distinction, mentioning, defending, reassuring, requesting, etc.,
10	[how] to say with [ready-]made formulas that, in general, mean nothing,
11	what (that which) one wants to say.
12	And... watch out for spelling mistakes!
13	Many cases have been known in which the author of a mistake
14	has been taken to the electric chair.

NOTES
(2) *Ya se trate de :* "whether it's about...". Compare with *ya sea esto o aquello, me es igual :* "whether it's this or that, I don't mind". Notice the use of the subjunctive again.
(3) Remember that the verbs with the tonic accent in boldface are radical-changing verbs (see page 300). In the infinitive, of course, the tonic accent falls at the end, so the stem is unaffected.
(4) Notice the two verbs "to know" : *saber :* "to know (facts)" or "to know how to" ; *conocer :* "to know (people)" or "to know of" or (when used in past tenses) "to meet".

* * * * *

EXERCISE : 1. I speak English, but my mother tongue is Italian. – **2.** It is difficult to write a letter well. – **3.** We have written to the hospital, but they have not replied. – **4.** Julia is learning to write. – **5.** Don't get in the way. – **6.** That doesn't concern me. – **7.** Spelling mistakes can be avoided.

EJERCICIO DE CONTROL
Ponga las palabras que faltan

1 *This letter is addressed to you.*

. . . . a ti.

2 *He started to manifest himself at the end.*

. . . . al final.

3 *What do you mean?*

¿ . . . . ?

4 *Do you make many mistakes when you write?*

¿ . . . .

. . . . ?

5 *Many cases are known of where this illness has been able to be cured.*

. . . .

. . . . curada.

****

LECCION OCHENTA Y OCHO

Baldomero pide disculpas por carta

1 Estimado Doctor: (1)
2 Le ruego tenga la extrema amabilidad (2)

*****

THE MISSING WORDS : : 1 esta carta está dirigida --. 2 comenzó a manifestarse --. 3 qué quieres decir. 4 haces muchas faltas cuando escribes. 5. se conocen muchos casos en los que esta enfermedad ha podido ser -.

Comment :

It is true that letter-writing can be a stumbling block. We might have a good command of a language – when speaking, understanding, and reading – but when it comes to composing a formal letter, a number of set expressions and seemingly over-polite formulas must be used.

In the next lesson, Baldomero will be using his inimitable style to write a letter of apology to his psychoanalyst. Remember one basic rule : it's not what you say that counts, it's the way you say it!

Segunda ola: lección 38

* *

LESSON EIGHTY-EIGHT

Baldomero apologizes by letter

1 Dear Doctor :
2 Please have the extreme kindness

NOTES
(1) *Estimado* replaces the more informal *querido*.
(2) *Le ruego tenga :* literally "I ask you to have". The verb *rogar* is a radical-changing verb. The full form of this expression would be *le ruego que tenga*, but the *que* has been dropped through long usage.

3   de disculpar mi no asistencia a nuestra cita de la semana pasada.

4   En efecto, su actitud comprensiva hacia mí

5   ha cambiado de arriba a abajo mi concepción de la vida.

6   La euforia me hizo olvidar que le había conocido,

7   impidiéndome así el personarme en sus oficinas a la hora prevista.

8   Como usted sabe, soy un hijo de la beneficencia pública

9   — la desgracia se abatió muy pronto sobre mí —,

10 luego tuve dificultades de crecimiento y el servicio militar no hizo de mí un hombre, etc.

11 Le ruego pues me comprenda y me disculpe.

12 Dándole las gracias anticipadas y quedando a su entera disposición, **(3)**

13 le saluda atentamente — Baldomero Soltero Guapo y con Dinero. **(4)**

14 P.D. Le quiero. **(5)**

EJERCICIO: 1. Le ruego me perdone. **2.** No asistiremos a la próxima sesión. **3.** Tenemos el honor de anunciarle... **4.** Según lo que me han dicho las vacaciones comienzan el lunes. **5.** Si sabes algo, comunícamelo. **6.** Disponemos de mucha información. **7.** Gracias anticipadas.

3	to excuse my absence (non-presence) at our appointment (of) last week.
4	In fact (In effect), your understanding attitude towards me
5	has completely changed (from top to bottom) my conception of life.
6	Euphoria made me forget that I had known you,
7	and thus prevented me (preventing me thus) [from] (the) coming to your offices at the planned time.
8	As you know, I am a child of (the) public welfare (charity)
9	– misfortune fell very early on me –
10	later I had growth difficulties and military service did not make a man of me, etc.
11	I ask you therefore [to] understand me and excuse me.
12	With (Giving you) thanks in advance (anticipated) I remain (and remaining) at your full disposal
13	Yours sincerely – Baldomero Bachelor Handsome and with Money.
14	P.S. I love you.

NOTES
(3) *Dar las gracias* : "to thank". *Da las gracias al señor, hijo mío* : "Say thank you to the gentleman, my son".
(4) *Le saluda atentamente* is the standard expression for ending a formal letter. We can also say *Muy atentamente*.
(5) *P.D.* is the abbreviation of *posdate* : "postscript".
P.S. also exists, but is somewhat rarer in Spain.

EXERCISE : 1. Please excuse me. – **2.** We will not be present at the next session. – **3.** We have the honour to announce to you... – **4.** According to what I have been told, the holidays start on Monday. – **5.** If you know something, let me know. – **6.** We possess a great deal of information. – **7.** Thank you in advance.

EJERCICIO DE CONTROL
Ponga las palabras que faltan

1 *Please be so kind as not to smoke.*

. . . .

. . . . .

2 *The director has informed me that he will be absent today.*

. . . .

. . . .

****

LECCION OCHENTA Y NUEVE

¡Hagan juego! (1)

1   Una de estas leyes está en vigor en una parte del mundo: ¿Cuál y dónde? **(2)**

2   Se prohibe: — volar sin alas. **(3)**

3 *Our centre has a very good library.*

. . . .

. . . .

4 *I remain at your full disposal.*

. . . .

5 *He always communicates his joy.*

. . . .

THE MISSING WORDS :   **1** tenga (or ¦ tengan) la extrema amabilidad de no fumar. **2** el director me ha comunicado que hoy estará ausente. *3* nuestro centro dispone de una biblioteca muy buena. **4** quedo a su entera disposición. **5** comunica siempre su alegría.

Segunda ola: lección 39

* *

LESSON EIGHTY-NINE

Place your bets (Play!)

1   One of these laws is in force (in vigour) in one part of the world : Which one? and where?

2   It is forbidden : to fly without wings.

NOTES
(1) *Hagan* is the polite plural imperative (present subjunctive) of *hacer.*
(2) This lesson is a list of amusing rules and regulations. One of them is not a joke : the game is to choose which one it is, and to guess where it is in force. The answer can be found in the next revision lesson.
(3) All the verbs are radical-changing verbs *(o to ue).* This group of verbs follows the same principles as the radical-changing verbs that we started to look at in lesson 85, where *e* changes to *ie (pensar, pienso).* Here, *o* changes to *ue (volar, vuelo).*

Lección 89

3 — morder la hamburguesa de otro.
4 — colgarse en ausencia de testigos.
5 — consolar a las viudas por la noche.
6 — demostrar que una ley es inútil.
7 — vender su propio cuerpo.
8 — apostarse dinero si no se tiene una perra.
9 — soñar con un aumento de salario.
10 — recordar malos recuerdos.
11 — probar que un político ha cambiado de chaqueta.
12 — invitar a almorzar cuando no se puede pagar. (4)
13 — encontrar a alguien que haya desaparecido.
14 — volverse a dormir a la hora de ir a trabajar.

EJERCICIO: 1. Teresa no encuentra trabajo. 2. Juan se acuesta tarde todos los días. 3. Me duelen las muelas. 4. Suele echarse la siesta. 5. Los coches ruedan. 6. Demuéstramelo. 7. Te encuentro cansado.

EJERCICIO DE CONTROL
Ponga las palabras que faltan

1 *I have found a place to park the car.*

. . . .

. . . .

2 *Does your dog bite ?*

¿ . . . . ?

3 *I dream of a boat trip.*

. . . . . con . . . .

4 *He has proved what he was saying.*

. . . .

3 — to bite the hamburger of somebody else.
4 — to hang oneself in the absence of witnesses.
5 — to console (to) widows at night.
6 — to prove (demonstrate) that a law is useless.
7 — to sell one's own body.
8 — to bet money if you don't have a copper.
9 — to dream of (with) an increase in salary.
10 — to remember bad memories.
11 — to prove that a politician has changed colours (changed of jacket).
12 — to invite [someone] to lunch when you cannot pay.
13 — to meet someone that has disappeared.
14 — to go back to sleep when it's time (at the time) to go to work.

NOTES

(4) *Almorzar* : "to have lunch". The Spanish generally say *comer* for the midday meal. *Almorzar* is more commonly used to refer to official luncheons, e.g., *el primer ministro almorzó con el embajador* : "the Prime Minister had lunch with the ambassador", or on special occasions : *después de la boda se almorzará en el restaurante* : "after the wedding, lunch will be at the restaurant".
El almuerzo is often used in reference to "elevenses" : the between-meals snack eaten between breakfast and lunch, during a break from the office or at school.

EXERCISE : 1. Teresa cannot find (does not find) any work. – **2.** Juan goes to bed late every day. – **3.** I have toothache. – **4.** He usually has a siesta. – **5.** The cars are driving along. – **6.** Prove it to me. – **7.** I find you tired.

5 *Do you want him to come back?*

¿ . . . . ?

THE MISSING WORDS : **1** he encontrado un sitio para aparcar el coche. **2** muerde su perro. **3** sueño - un viaje en barco. **4** ha probado lo que decía. **5** quieres que vuelva.

Segunda ola: lección 40

Lección 89

LECCION NOVENTA

Recuerdos

1 A veces, cuando me acuesto **(1)**
2 y, desde mi cama, veo brillar mis zapatos,
3 mientras espero la llegada del sueño, **(2)**
4 suelo dejarme envolver por el dulce recuerdo **(3)**
5 de aquella mujer, Julia, la madre de mi madre,
6 que, en los atardeceres en los que las gotas de lluvia **(4)**
7 resonaban en mis oídos al estrellarse **(5)**
8 contra los cristales de la cocina,
9 poblaba nuestra imaginación
10 — la de mis hermanos también —
11 con cuentos que nos volvían, durante unas horas,
12 los protagonistas de las hazañas
13 con las que se sueña en la infancia.

VAMOS A AMUEBLAR NUESTRA CASA

EJERCICIO: 1. Cuando he trabajado todo el día, me acuesto pronto. **2.** Las flores estaban envueltas con papel verde. **3.** Llueve mucho. **4.** Estamos amueblando nuestra nueva casa. **5.** Cuéntame lo que has visto. **6.** He tenido un sueño muy bonito. **7.** Suelo comprar en esa tienda.

LESSON NINETY

Memories

1   At times, when I go to bed
2   and, from my bed, I see my shoes shine
3   while I am waiting to go to sleep (await the arrival of the sleep)
4   I usually let myself be surrounded by the sweet memory
5   of that woman Julia, my mother's mother,
6   who, in the late evening when (in those which) the drops of rain
7   resounded in my ears as they crashed
8   against the window-panes of the kitchen.
9   inhabited our imagination
10   – that of my brothers too –
11   with tales that turned us, for a few hours, into
12   the protagonists of the exploits
13   of which (with which) one dreams in (the) childhood.

NOTES

(1) Just before you reach the revision lesson (lesson 91), have a close look at the radical-changing verbs in this lesson.
(2) *Sueño* means both "sleep" and "dream" ; *tengo sueño* : "I am sleepy". Note that the radical-changing verb *soñar* : "to dream" takes the conjunction *con* : *sueño contigo todas las noches* : "I dream of you every night".
(3) Spanish infinitives can be active or passive. In *suelo dejarme envolver,* we have translated *envolver* as "be surrounded".
(4) *Al atardecer* : "at the end of the day".
(5) *Oído* is used to mean "hearing" or "ear" in the sense of "to have a good ear". For the ear itself (the external part), we use *oreja.*

EXERCISE : 1. When I have worked all day, I go to bed early. – **2.** The flowers were wrapped up with green paper. – **3.** It is raining a lot. – **4.** We are furnishing our new house. – **5.** Tell me what you have seen. – **6.** I have had a very nice dream. – **7.** I usually buy in this shop.

EJERCICIO DE CONTROL
Ponga las palabras que faltan

1 *Do your remember her?*

¿ . . . . ?

2 *I like going for walks when it is raining.*

. . . .

3 *I usually clean the windows once a month.*

. . . .

al . . .

* *

LECCION NOVENTA Y UNA

LESSON NINETY-ONE

Revisión y notas

1. **Irregular verbs**
The Real Academia has drawn up a complete list of Spanish
irregular verbs. In this list, there are twelve categories, and
irregularities are constant within each category.

Outside these categories, there are 24 "irregular verbs
proper" with their own specific irregularities. You know
almost all of these already.

Naturally, we are not going to embark upon an exhaustive
study of all these verbs and their peculiarities. What we are
going to do, however, is to give you some basic points of
reference that will allow you to complete your Spanish
training in an pleasant manner, without going through the
long and tedious process of learning all the rules off by heart.

Over the last seven lessons, we have shown you most of the
commonest verbs in the first two groups.

4 *Will you be back late?*

¿ · · · · · · · · ·   · · · · · ?

5 *Do you dream in colour or in black and white?*

¿ · · · · · · ·   · ·   · · · · · · ·   · ·   · · · ·

· ·   · · · · · ?

THE MISSING WORDS :   **1** te acuerdas de ella. **2** me gusta
pasearme cuando llueve. **3** suelo limpiar los cristales una vez - mes. **4**
volverás tarde. **5** sueñas en color o en blanco y negro.

Segunda ola: lección 41

****

A. Groups 1 and 2

— Verbs in these groups are called "diphthong verbs"
because the pure vowel becomes a diphthong. Thus *e*
becomes *ie* and *o* becomes *ue* : *calentar* : "to heat" ; *yo
caliento* : "I heat" ; *llover* : "to rain" ; *llueve* : "it is raining".

— Verbs in these groups modify the last vowel of the stem
when the tonic accent falls on it (i.e., in the three persons
singular and third person plural of the present indicative
and present subjunctive, and in the imperative).

The table below gives details of three typical verbs in the first
group *(e to ie)* (*cerrar* : "to close" ; *perder* : "to lose" ;
pensar : "to think").

Present indicative	Present subjunctive	Present Imperative
cierro	pierda	
cierras	pierdas	piensa
cierra	pierda	piense
cerramos] reg.	perdamos] reg.	pensemos] reg.
cerráis	perdáis	pensad
cierran	pierdan	piensen

Lección 91

Examples of the group 2 verbs *soler* "to be in the habit of...", *renovar* : "to renovate" and *soñar* : "to dream" are given below :

Present indicative	Present subjunctive	Present Imperative
suelo sueles suele solemos] reg. soléis suelen	renueve renueves renueve renovemos] reg. renovéis renueven	sueña sueñe soñemos] reg soñad sueñen

Composite verbs are conjugated the same way as the simple verbs from which they are derived. Thus, *deshelar* : "to thaw" or "to unfreeze" is conjugated like *helar* "to freeze" *(hiela* : "it is freezing") ; *demostrar* : "to prove" or "to demonstrate" is conjugated like *mostrar* : "to show" (*muestran* : "they show").

B. **Peculiarities of group 1 (*e* to *ie*)**
– These verbs are either *-ar* or *-er* verbs, except *concernir* : "to concern" and *descernir* : "to discern".

– Verbs ending in *-irir* behave in the same way : the stem changes from *i* to *ie*. Example : *adquirir* : "to acquire" ; *adquiero* : "I acquire".

C. **Peculiarities of group 2 (*o* to *ue*)**
– These verbs are either *-ar* or *-er* verbs.

– The verb *jugar* behaves in the same way and changes its *u* into *ue*.

– Verbs ending in *-olver* all belong to this group. Thus *resuelvo* : "I resolve" (from *resolver),* *disuelva* : "it dissolves" (from *disolver*). Further, the past participle of all these verbs ends in *-uelto* : *disuelto* : dissolved ; *vuelto* : "returned", etc.

All the information given above is for reference only. Do not try to remember it all by heart. The best way to remember it is to see and hear real-life examples, and, little by little, you will become sufficiently accustomed to the general behaviour of the different groups of verbs to be able to predict what the correct form should be.

2. Solution to the game in lesson 89

Believe it or not, the correct solution is found in sentence 3. There is a law in Oklahoma forbidding in that State the practice of taking a bite out of somebody else's hamburger!

3. Writing in Spanish

1 Are you awake? - Your coffee is hot.
2 The pharmacist has asked me for the prescription. - Did you have it?
3 Without spectacles he cannot see very well.
4 Please take account of what I have said.
5 He has a very good memory of that trip.
6 We want to furnish our house with antique furniture.

4. Translation

1 ¿Estás despierta? — Tu café está caliente.
2 El farmacéutico me ha pedido la receta; — ¿La tenías?
3 Sin gafas, no distingue muy bien.
4 Le ruego que tome en cuenta lo que le he dicho.
5 Tiene muy buen recuerdo de ese viaje.
6 Queremos amueblar nuestra casa con muebles antiguos.

Segunda ola: lección 42

LECCION NOVENTA Y DOS

Turismo y viaje de estudios

1 — ¿Es la primera vez que usted viene a España?
2 — No, hace cinco años visité el País Vasco, Santander y Asturias.
3 Estuve un mes e hice muchos amigos.
4 Ahora, vengo sólo unos días para visitar un poco (1)
5 Toledo, Córdoba, Granada y Sevilla; es más bien un viaje de estudios.
6 — ¿Se interesa usted por el arte?
7 — Mucho, y ahora que hablo un poco el castellano, me atrae más.
8 — No me extraña, el arte de un país es más apreciado
9 cuando se conoce a la gente y su lengua.

Paternidad responsable

10 — Tomasín, ven aquí, tengo algo que decirte, hijo mío.
11 Si eres bueno, haces lo que se te diga, obedeces a tus mayores,
12 piensas como es debido y me amas... te daré un premio.
13 — ¿Cuál papá?
14 — No te daré una paliza.

*****

EJERCICIO: 1. Es la segunda vez que telefonea. 2. Hace un rato estaba aquí. 3. ¿Qué has hecho estas vacaciones? 4. He visitado la costa cantábrica. 5. Lo que dice nos interesa mucho. 6. Ese país me atrae mucho. 7. ¿Te gusta el arte?

LESSON NINETY-TWO

Tourism and educational trip[s]

1 — Is [this] the first time you [have] come to Spain?
2 — No, five years ago I visited the Basque country, Santander and Asturias.
3   I was [there] [for] a month and I made a lot of friends.
4   Now, I [have] come [for] only a few days to visit a little
5   Toledo, Cordoba, Granada and Seville ; it's more [like] an educational trip (voyage of studies).
6 — Are you interested in art? (Do you interest yourself by the art?)
7 — A lot, and now that I speak a little (the) Spanish, it attracts me more.
8 — I am not surprised ; a country's art is more appreciated
9   when one knows (to) the people and their language.

Responsible paternity

10 — Tomasín, come here ; I have something to tell you, my son.
11   If you are good, [and] do what you're told, obey your elders,
12   think as you ought (as is due), and love me... I'll give you a reward
13 — What (Which) [reward], Dad?
14 — I won't give you a beating.

NOTES
(1) Note the use of the present tense of *venir*. In English, we would say "I have come to visit you". In Spanish, we say *vengo para visitarte*. See also sentence A in the lesson, and sentence 1 in the exercise.

* * * * *

EXERCISE : 1. It is the second time he has telephoned. – **2.** He was here a while ago. – **3.** What have you done [during] these holidays? – **4.** I have visited the Cantabrican coast. – **5.** What he says interests us a lot. – **6.** That country attracts me a lot. – **7.** Do you like art?.

EJERCICIO DE CONTROL
Ponga las palabras que faltan

1 *Five years ago I was a student.*

. . . .

2 *I'm not surprised she hasn't come.*

. .   . . : . . . . .

3 *We have something for you.*

. . . .

USTED DEBE DE SER EXTRANJERO, SU LENGUA ES MUY RARA

****

LECCION NOVENTA Y TRES

Cuando la realidad sobrepasa la ficción

1 Suena el timbre y Abelardo, carnicero de enorme reputación,

2 deja el periódico, se levanta de la mesa y va a abrir.

3 — ¡Hombre! Pasa, llegas a tiempo,

4 *My elder brother is twenty.*

. . . .

5 *Will you give me your address?*

¿ . . . . ?

THE MISSING WORDS :   1 hace cinco años era estudiante. 2 no me extraña que no haya venido. 3 tenemos algo para vosotros. 4 mi hermano mayor tiene veinte años. 5 me darás tu dirección.

Note
At the beginning of the last revision lesson, we spoke about 24 irregular verbs that cannot be categorized because their irregularity is specific to each verb. In the next seven lessons, we will be looking at these verbs in greater detail. It is important for you to know these verbs, as almost all of them are very common. If you think about it, the commonest verbs in English are irregular, too.

Continue to leaf through the grammatical information in the back of the book.

Segunda ola: lección 43

****

LESSON NINETY-THREE

When fact (reality) surpasses fiction

1 The doorbell rings, and Abelardo, a butcher of enormous reputation
2 leaves the newspaper, gets up from the table and goes to open.
3 — Well! (Man!) Come in! (Pass), you have arrived just in time (you arrive in time)

4 íbamos a tomar ahora el café.
5 — Buenas tardes, ¿qué tal estáis?
6 — Ya ves, terminando de instalarnos. ¿Te gusta el piso? **(1)**
7 — Es muy moderno. Veo que tenéis una buena biblioteca.
8 — Estoy orgulloso; creo que el color de los libros **(2)**
9 hace juego con la pintura de la pared. **(3)**
10 La semana pasada compré dos metros y medio de Voltaire **(4)**
11 encuadernados en piel verde. Queda bonito ¿eh?
12 Como el formato era de dimensiones mayores
13 que el espacio disponible entre dos baldas
14 hemos tenido que serrar cuatro centímetros cada libro. **(5)**
15 — No se nota, te las has apañado muy bien. **(6)**

EJERCICIO: **1.** Abre, han llamado. **2.** Me levanto de la mesa. **3.** Íbamos a salir. **4.** Estoy orgulloso de mi trabajo. **5.** La camisa hace juego con el pantalón. **6.** La pintura no está seca. **7.** El piso es moderno.

EJERCICIO DE CONTROL
Ponga las palabras que faltan

1 *Their apartment is very modern.*

. . . .

4   we were going (now) to have a coffee (to take the coffee).
5 — Good afternoon. How are you?
6 — As you see (You see already), [we're] settling in (finishing installing ourselves). Do you like the flat?
7 — It is very modern. I see that you have a good library.
8 — I am proud : I think that the colour of the books
9   goes with (plays with) the paint of the wall.
10   Last week I bought two-and-a-half metres of Voltaire
11   bound in green leather. It's (It remains) nice, isn't it?
12   As the format was bigger (of greater dimensions)
13   than the available space between two shelves
14   we have had to saw off four centimetres [from] each book.
15 — You can't tell (It doesn't notice itself) ; you've managed very well.

NOTES
(1) *Terminando de :* "finishing". *Estamos terminando de cenar :* "we are finishing dinner". In sentence 6, the main verb *estamos* is understood.
(2) *Estar orgulloso de... :* "to be proud of" but *No soy orgulloso :* "I'm not proud".
(3) *Hacer juego con :* literally "to play with", means "to go with" when referring to colours.
(4) Strange as it may seem, certain antique dealers or booksellers really do sell books by the metre!
(5) *Ha habido que* is the perfect tense of *hay que* (see lesson 81, note 1).
(6) *Apañarse :* "to get by" or "to manage". *apañar* means "to patch up".

EXERCISE : 1. Open the door, the bell has gone. – **2.** I get up from the table. – **3.** We were going to go out. – **4.** I am proud of my work. – **5.** The shirt goes with the trousers. – **6.** The paint is not dry. – **7.** The flat is modern.

2 *Books bound in leather are expensive.*

. . . .

. . . . .

3 *We need four more shelves.*

. . .   .

4 *The doctor had to be called.*

. . .   .

****

LECCION NOVENTA Y CUATRO

Vamos al museo

1 — Os propongo ir al museo esta tarde.
2 — Excelente idea. ¿A qué hora abren? **(1)**
3 — No lo sé. Es posible que no cierren a la hora de comer.
4 — Podemos ir ahora y si está cerrado
5   entraremos a tomar algo en un bar o daremos un paseo.
6   En el museo: — Por favor, ¿puede indicarme en que dirección
7   se encuentra la sala de Goya?
8 — Con mucho gusto; Sigan hasta el fondo y luego a la derecha.
9 — Si habla tan deprisa no le entendemos.
10 — Perdonen. Había olvidado que eran extranjeros.
11   Es por allí. Quédense con mi plano, no lo necesito.
12 — Muchas gracias. Es usted muy amable.

5 *I noticed that he was proud.*

. . . .

THE MISSING WORDS :   1 su piso es muy moderno. 2 los libros encuadernados en piel son caros. 3 nos faltan cuatro baldas. 4 ha habido que llamar al médico. 5 he notado que estaba orgulloso.

Segunda ola: lección 44

* *

LESSON NINETY-FOUR

Let's go to the museum
or We are going to the museum

1 — I suggest we go (propose to you to go) to the museum this afternoon.
2 — [An] excellent idea. (At) What time do they open?
3 — I don't know (it). They may not (It is possible that they do not) close at lunchtime.
4 — We can go now and if it's closed
5 we'll go into a bar and have a drink, or go for a walk.
6 In the museum : — please, could you tell me (indicate me) in which direction
7 the Goya room is found?
8 — With pleasure (With much taste). Carry on (Follow) until the end and then [turn] (to the) right.
9 — If you speak so quickly, we cannot (do not) understand you.
10 — I'm sorry. I had forgotten that you were foreigners.
11 — It's over there. Keep (Remain with) my plan, I do not need it.
12 — Thank you very much. You are very kind.

NOTES
(1) *Abren* : "they open". This construction is also common in English, where "they" is impersonal (i.e., not "us").
Dicen que... : "they say that...".

Lección 94

Sensibilidad escultural

13 — ¡Oh! Esa escoba es maravillosa. Debe de ser
una escultura muy trabajada por Picasso o
Miró. Me interesan mucho esos artistas.

14 — No, señor. Es la escoba de la mujer de
la limpieza del museo que ha ido un
momento al servicio.

15 — ¡Ah!

EJERCICIO: **1**. El museo abre a las diez. **2**. Hoy está
cerrado. **3**. La sala que quiero ver está en esta dirección.
4.Hable despacio, por favor. **5**. ¿Es por aquí? **6**. Es por allí,
a la izquierda. **7**. Necesitamos un plano del museo.

EJERCICIO DE CONTROL
Ponga las palabras que faltan

1 *I would like to go to the Museum of Modern Art.*

. . . .

. . . .

2 *If you speak more slowly, I will be able to understand you.*

. . . .

. . . .

3 *In my room I have an Underground map.*

. . . . del

. . . . .

4 *Sit down. – Thank you. You are very kind.*

. . . .

5 *Where is the broom?*

¿ . . . . ?

Sculptural sensitivity

13 — Oh! This broom is marvellous. It must be a
sculpture long worked at (very worked) by Picasso
or Miró. Those artists interest me a lot.

14 — No, Sir. It's the broom of the cleaning lady, who has
gone to the toilet for a moment.

15 — Oh!

EXERCISE : 1. The museum opens at ten o'clock. – **2.** Today it is
closed. – **3.** The room that I want to see is in this direction. – **4.**
Speak slowly, please. – **5.** Is it this way? – **6.** It's over there on the
left. – **7.** We need a plan of the museum.

THE MISSING WORDS : **1** me gustaría ir al museo de Arte
Moderno. **2** si usted habla más despacio (or lentamente) podré
entenderlo. **3** en mi habitación tengo un plano - metro. **4** siéntese -
gracias es usted muy amable. **5** dónde está la escoba.

*We are getting close to the end, and you have picked up a
solid basis of Spanish. Your greatest need at this point is to
pay close attention to the verbs. There are not too many
problems in the texts of the lessons. This will give you more
time to look up the verb lists at the end of the book, or to
review the constructions that continue to give you trouble.*

Segunda ola: lección 45

Lección 94

LECCION NOVENTA Y CINCO

En la mesa, ante todo, buena educación

1 Aunque sólo sea para salvar las apariencias, **(1)**
2 nunca está de más el conocer unas cuantas **(2)**
3 fórmulas de cortesía. He aquí algunos ejemplos: **(3)**
4 Si en la mesa intentan pasarle una fuente
5 recién sacada del horno, siempre puede decir:
6 ''Usted primero''. Evitará, en general, quemarse y quedará bien. **(4)**
7 Si insisten puede añadir: ''De ninguna manera'' o ''Se lo ruego''
8 o ''Sírvase usted, por favor'' o ''Pásela a su señora''.
9 Intente que los otros comensales no se den cuenta **(5)**
10 de que usted recita de memoria; hace mal efecto.
11 No lleve su buena educación hasta el punto
12 de quedarse sin comer: el hambre
13 acarrea, a menudo, problemas de salud.

MAMÁ, ESE SEÑOR HA METIDO LA MANO EN LA FUENTE: YO, YA NO COMO

EJERCICIO: 1. Cada país tiene sus fórmulas de cortesía. 2. La fuente está demasiado caliente. 3. Ana se sabe la lección de memoria. 4. Usted primero. 5. Sírvase, por favor. 6. Es muy educado. 7. No tiene problemas de salud.

LESSON NINETY-FIVE

At (the) table, above all (before all), good manners (education)

1 Even if it is only for appearances' sake (to save appearances),

2 it is never too much to know (the knowing) a few

3 manners (formulas of courtesy). Here are some examples :

4 If at (the) table somebody tries (they try) to pass you a serving dish

5 just (taken) out of the oven, you (pol. sing.) can always say :

6 "After you" ("You first"). You will generally avoid burning (to burn) yourself, and you will be alright (remain well).

7 If they insist, you can add : "Not at all" ("In no way") or "I beg of you" ("I ask you it")

8 or "Help (serve) yourself, please" or "Pass it to your wife".

9 Try not to let the other guests realize (Try that the other commensalists might not realize)

10 (of) that you are reciting from memory ; it has (makes) a bad effect.

11 Do not take good manners (education) to the point

12 of not eating (of remaining without eating) : (the) hunger

13 brings with it, often, problems of health.

NOTES
(1) *Aunque sólo sea para* : "even if it is only for". (Hypothetical).
(2) *Estar de más* : "to be unnecessary" or "to be « de trop »".
(3) *Estar bien educado* literally means "to be well brought up" or "to be well educated". The word *educado* is often used to mean "polite".
(4) *Quedar bien* : "to do well" or "to leave a good impression".
(5) *Comensales* refers to the company at table ; *habrá 13 comensales* : "there will be 13 to dinner". (Cf. the biological term "commensalism", where two organisms live from the same food source).

EXERCISE : 1. Each country has its manners. – **2.** The dish is too hot. – **3.** Ana knows the lesson by heart. – **4.** After you. – **5.** Please help yourself. – **6.** He is very polite. – **7.** He has no health problems.

EJERCICIO DE CONTROL
Ponga las palabras que faltan

1 *Come to the beach, even if it's only for two hours.*

. . . .

. . . . .

2 *I beg of you.*

. . . .

3 *Wait a bit, it's too hot.*

. . . . , ...

. . . .

****

LECCION NOVENTA Y SEIS

Escándalo en casa de la condesa (1)

1 — Señorita, le he hecho venir porque me han contado
2 que mi hijo mantiene con usted relaciones particulares (2)
3 y como madre, de una antigua familia de alto rango,
4 me preocupo por el futuro de mi hijo,
5 para que esté a la altura que nuestra descendencia merece.
6 ¿Es verdad que su madre era peluquera? (3)

4 *Don't stay there without eating ; afterwards you won't have the time.*

. . .   .

. . . .

5 *The boss has submitted his report.*

. . .   . informe.

THE MISSING WORDS :   1 ven a la playa aunque sólo sea dos horas. 2 se lo ruego. 3 espera un poco, está demasiado caliente. 4 no te quedes sin comer, después no tendrás tiempo. 5 el jefe ha comunicado su -.

Segunda ola: lección 46

* *
# LESSON NINETY-SIX

Scandal at the countess's house

1 — Miss, I have made you come because I have heard (they have told me)
2   that my son is having (maintaining) [a] particular relationship(s) with you
3   and as [a] mother, of an old family of high rank,
4   I worry about (for) my son's future,
5   so that he might be worthy of our line (at the height that our descendance deserves).
6   Is it true that your mother was a hairdresser?

NOTES
(1) Notice that there are no words in Spanish that begin with *s* + consonant.
(2) *Mantener :* "to maintain" and "to keep". *Mantenga limpia España :* "Keep Spain clean". Here, *mantener* is used in the sense of "to sustain" or "to keep going".
(3) *Peluca :* "a wig". Originally, *peluquería* (note the spelling) was "a wig-maker's", but it has come to mean "a hairdressing salon". We can also say *voy al barbero :* "I'm going to the barber's".

Lección 96

7 — Sí, y además quiero a su hijo.

8 — Lo sabía, usted es de ésas que traen consigo el escándalo.

9 ¿Entonces no niega usted que sale con mi hijo?

10 — En efecto, hoy en día, no hay nada de extraño

11 en salir con el hombre con el que se vuelve.

12 — ¡Ah...! ¡Váyase...! ¡Ah...! ¡Fuera...! ¡Ramiro... me ahogo! **(4)**

13 — Sí, señora condesa. ¿Quiere la señora condesa que abra la ventana?

14 — ¡Imbécil! Me ahogo moralmente.

EJERCICIO: 1. Hágale pasar. 2. Con nuestros vecinos tenemos relaciones amistosas. 3. Nos preocupamos por el futuro de nuestros hijos. 4. Voy al peluquero. 5. ¿Sales o entras? 6. Se ahogaba de calor. 7. Abrid el balcón.

EJERCICIO DE CONTROL
Ponga las palabras que faltan

1 *He made us come in order to offer us some work.*

. . . .

. . . . . .

2 *His attitude deserves our respect.*

. . .   .

3 *This evening we are going out to dinner with some friends.*

. . . .

. . . . . .

4 *There was nothing strange in that film.*

. . .   .

. . . .

7	—	Yes, and furthermore I love your son.
8	—	I knew it. You are one of those who bring scandal with them (who bring themselves the scandal).
9		So you do not deny that you are out with my son?
10	—	Indeed I am. Nowadays, there is nothing (of) strange
11		about (in) going out with the man with which one goes home.
12	—	Oh! Go away!... Oh! Get out (outside!)... Ramiro... I'm suffocating!
13	—	Yes, Countess. Does the Countess want me to open the window?
14	—	Fool! I am suffocating morally.

NOTES

(4) *Ahogarse :* "to suffocate" or *to drown". Se ahogó porque no sabía nadar :* "he drowned because he didn't know how to swim". *Here, a better translation for* me ahogo *might have been "I'm overcome".*

EXERCISE : 1. Have him come in. – **2.** We have a friendly relationship with our neighbours. – **3.** We are worried about our children's future. – **4.** I'm going to the hairdresser's. – **5.** Are you going out or coming in? – **6.** He was suffocating from the heat. – **7.** Open the balcony.

5 *It is dangerous to bathe there.*

. . . .

THE MISSING WORDS : 1 nos ha hecho venir para proponernos trabajo. **2** su actitud merece nuestro respeto. **3** esta noche salimos a cenar con unos amigos. **4** no había nada de extraño en esa película. **5** es peligroso bañarse ahí.

Segunda ola: lección 47

LECCION NOVENTA Y SIETE

El progreso no se para (1)

1 El locutor: La noticia del día nos llega hoy del Museo del Prado.
2 Esta tarde, la joven promesa americana Jimmy-Jimmy
3 en presencia de numerosos espectadores,
4 ha batido el récord de velocidad de visita al Museo del Prado.
5 En efecto, 11 m 13 s y 2 décimas han bastado a Jimmy-Jimmy
6 para pulverizar el antiguo récord, 12 m 10 s 5 d,
7 que hasta esta mañana poseía el soviético Vasilov-Vasilov.
8 Numerosos expertos han manifestado que el joven americano
9 habría podido conseguir un mejor tiempo
10 si, cuando se disponía a pasar por la sala de Goya,
11 un inconsciente visitante
12 no hubiese dado dos pasos atrás para contemplar (2)
13 uno de los dibujos del pintor.
14 Telegramas de felicitación llegan a la Casa Blanca de todas las partes del mundo.

EJERCICIO: 1. ¿Está lejos la parada del autobús? 2. Tengo una buena noticia. 3. Había muchos espectadores. 4. Bastaba con telefonear. 5. Hemos conseguido comprar un equipo estereofónico barato. 6. Los visitantes eran numerosos. 7. Dibuja muy bien.

EJERCICIO DE CONTROL
Ponga las palabras que faltan

1 *All I need is a little salt.*

. . . . con . . . .

LESSON NINETY-SEVEN

You can't stop progress
(Progress doesn't stop)

1 The newsreader : The [main] news of the day comes (arrives) to us today from the Prado Museum.
2 This afternoon, the young American hope (promise) Jimmy-Jimmy
3 in [the] presence of numerous spectators,
4 beat (has beaten) the speed record for visiting (of visit to) the Prado Museum.
5 Indeed, 11 m, 13 s and 2 tenths were enough for Jimmy-Jimmy
6 to smash (pulverize) the previous (old) record [of] 12 m, 10 s, 5 tenths,
7 that until this morning the Soviet Vasilov-Vasilov held (possessed).
8 Numerous experts have stressed (manifested) that the young American
9 could have managed a better time
10 if, when he was getting ready (disposing himself) to pass through the Goya room
11 an unsuspecting (unaware) visitor
12 had not taken (given) two steps back to contemplate
13 one of the painter's drawings.
14 Congratulatory telegrams are arriving at the White House from all over the world.

NOTES
(1) *Parar* : "to stop" is a transitive verb. *El tren se paró* : literally "the train stopped itself".
(2) *No hubiese (si un visitante no hubiese dado)* : imperfect subjunctive of the auxiliary *haber*. The verb *dar* is used in the same way as *dar un paseo* : "to take a walk" ; *dar un paso atrás* : "to take a step backwards". Incidentally, *dar* is one of the irregular verbs that cannot be classified in the main groups of irregular verbs.

EXERCISE : 1. Is the bus-stop far? – 2. I have a piece of good news. – 3. There were a lot of spectators. – 4. Telephoning was sufficient. – 5. We have managed to buy a cheap stereo. – 6. The visitors were numerous. – 7. He draws very well.

2 *He has swum the hundred metres in record time.*

. . . .

. . . .

3 *If you want it to be a good photograph, take two steps back.*

. . . .

. . . .

4 *We are going to send them a congratulatory telegram.*

. . . .

. . . .

5 *Newspapers from all over the world arrive in big cities.*

. . . .

. . . .

. . . . .

****

LECCION NOVENTA Y OCHO
LESSON NINETY-EIGHT

Revisión y notas

1. "Irregular verbs proper" : see lesson 92.

This is our last look at the irregular verbs that do not fit into the 12 categories. However, remember you can always look them up in the grammatical appendix at the back of the book.

During the last seven lessons – which have not been particularly difficult – you have had the chance to look at how these "uncategorizable" verbs are used, and to realize how common many of them are.

THE MISSING WORDS : 1 me basta - un poco de sal. 2 ha nadado los cien metros en un tiempo récord. 3 si quieres que sea una buena foto da dos pasos atrás. 4 vamos a enviarles un telegrama de felicitación. 5 a las grandes ciudades llegan periódicos de todas las partes del mundo;

Segunda ola: lección 48

****

These 24 verbs are covered in greater detail in the grammatical index, but here we are going to give you a short list of the most common of these verbs, together with a sentence placing each one in context. To help you remember these important verbs, and to make sure you look at them in detail, they are also featured as the "Writing in Spanish" exercise for this lesson. The translation of each sentence is given on page 344, but test yourself before looking at the translation.

Apart from these 19 verbs, there are 5 others that can be found in the grammatical appendix, but which are not very common.

2. ¿Cuál? : see sentence 13, lesson 92.
¿Cuál? : "Which?" or "Which one?" ; *¿Cuáles? :* "Which?" or "Which ones?". Two points should be made about this interrogative :
- No article is used (Do not say *"¿El cuál?"*)
- It is only used when it is not followed by a noun : *¿Cuál es el tuyo? :* "Which is yours?". To say "which" followed by a noun, we use the invariable *que : ¿qué casa es la tuya? :* "Which house is yours?" or "Which is your house?".

3. Reflexive verbs
A. **Pronominal verbs.** The reflexive conjugation follows the model given below for all personal tenses of the verb :

me lavo	I wash (myself)
te lavas	You wash (yourself)
se lava	He / She washes (himself / herself)
nos lavamos	We wash (ourselves)
os laváis	You wash (yourselves)
se lavan	They wash (themselves)

B. **Remember the following points :**
- Pronominal verbs are conjugated with the reflexive pronoun (see lesson 21).
- In the infinitive, the gerundive and the imperative, these pronouns are stuck into the end of the verb.
- The reflexive pronoun for *Usted* is *se : ¿Quiere usted sentarse? :* "Do you want to sit down?"
- In compound tenses, reflexive verbs are always conjugated with the auxiliary *haber.*
- In the perfect infinitive and in the compound gerundive, the reflexive pronoun is placed with the auxiliary : *haberse lavado :* "to have washed (oneself)" ; *habiéndose lavado :* "having washed (oneself)".

C. **A few verbs** in Spanish can be conjugated either as simple verbs or as reflexives. The use of the reflexive conjugation with these verbs adds strength to the sense : *Quedó solo :* "he stayed on his own" ; *yo me quedo aquí :* "I'm staying here (and I'm not about to go anywhere else)" ; *guardar :* "to keep" ; *guardarse :* "to keep for oneself".

Similarly, when certain other verbs (e.g., *entrar :* "to go in", *bajar :* "to go down", *salir :* "to go out") are used reflexively, the sense implied is that the action was accomplished with some difficulty or despite obstacles.

A large number of verbs can thus be used reflexively, and it is hard to set any firm rules. Usage will show you how to employ this peculiarity of the Spanish language. In general, however, we can say that the use of the reflexive form with verbs that are not real reflexives *(lavarse,* etc.) very often implies that the subject exerts an effort, or particular attention or interest, to complete the action he is performing.

D. When the object of the verb is a part of the body or a piece of clothing, Spanish uses reflexive pronouns instead of possessive adjectives. Thus *me pone el sombrero :* "I put my hat on" (lit. "I put myself the hat") ; *abróchate la camisa :* "button your shirt" ; *me he cortado el dedo :* "I have cut my finger".

E. With verbs such as *comer :* "to eat", *beber :* to drink, *hacer :* "to make", reflexive pronouns are used if the object is quantified :
Me comí todo un pollo : "I ate a whole chicken".
Se bebieron tres botellas de vino : "They drank three bottles of wine".
Nos hicimos una tortilla : "We made (ourselves) an omelette".

If the object is not quantified, we use the verb on its own (without the reflexive pronoun) :
No bebo más que agua : "I only drink water".
Comemos muy poco : "We eat very little".

1 Anda más deprisa.
2 ¿Caben todas las maletas en el maletero?
3 Caen copos de nieve.
4 Dame su número de teléfono.
5 Dime algo bonito.
6 Estaremos en su casa hasta las ocho.
7 Había flores en la mesa.
8 Hace un día estupendo.
9 Iba a tomar el tren.

10 ¿Oyes algo?
11 ¿Puedo pasar?
12 Ponte un jersey, hace frío.
13 Queremos ir a verlo.
14 Sabía que estaba enfermo.
15 Es mi marido y éstos son mis hijos.
16 Tenemos alquilado un apartamento.
17 Trae también el periódico.
18 Ven al cine esta noche.
19 Veré lo que puedo hacer.

*****

****

4. **Translation**

1 Walk faster.
2 Do all the cases fit in the boot?
3 Snowflakes are falling.
4 Give me his telephone number.
5 Say something nice to me.
6 We will be at his house until eight o'clock.
7 There were flowers on the table.
8 It is a splendid day.
9 I was going to take the train.
10 Do you hear anything?
11 May I come in?
12 Put on a jersey, it's cold.
13 We want to go to see him.
14 I knew he was ill.
15 This is my husband, and these are my children. (sons)
16 We have a rented apartment.
17 Bring the newspaper too.
18 Come to the cinema tonight
19 I'll see what I can do.

Segunda ola: lección 49

* * * * *

* *

Lección 98

LECCION NOVENTA Y NUEVE

Verbos irregulares del tercer y cuarto grupo **(1)**

1 Conozco la carretera. **(2)**
2 Cuando el niño nazca, nos iremos al campo unos días. **(3)**
3 El sol ha lucido todo el día. **(4)**
4 Espero que, cuando anochezca, ya hayamos llegado.
5 ¿Te apetece un helado?
6 Después de la operación, se restableció rápidamente.
7 Los campos florecen, amanece más pronto
8 y oscurece más tarde: llega la primavera.
9 Conduzca con precaución. **(5)**
10 Tradujeron el discurso simultáneamente.

¡Justicia!

11 "... — Mujer, ¿qué quieres?
12 — Quiero justicia, señor.
13 — ¿De qué? — De una prenda hurtada. **(6)**
14 — ¿Qué prenda? — Mi corazón."

LESSON NINETY-NINE

Irregular verbs in the third and fourth groups

1   I know the road.
2   When the child is born, we will go to the country [for] a few days.
3   The sun has shone all day.
4   I hope that we will have arrived when night falls.
5   Do you want an ice-cream?
6   After the operation, he recovered (re-established himself) quickly.
7   The fields are in flower (flowering), the dawn is (it dawns) earlier
8   and it gets dark later : the spring is arriving.
9   Drive carefully.
10   They translated the speech simultaneously.

Justice!

11   – What do you want, woman?
12   – I want justice, sir.
13   – What for? - For a stolen object.
14   – What object? - My heart.

NOTES
(1) Here we are introducing the irregular verbs that make up the third and fourth groups. These verbs take a *z* in the three present tenses before the *c* preceding the ending *a* or *o*.
For example, *conocer* : "to know" (people) becomes *conozco* : "I know" instead of *"conoco"*. The second person *(conoces)* is completely regular. See details in revision lesson.
(2) The tonic accent of relevant verbs is still shown in boldface.
(3) *Nacer* : "to be born". Note that this is an active verb in Spanish but a passive verb in English.
(4) *Lucir* : "to shine" or "to glow". *La luz* : "the light".
(5) Verbs ending in -*ducir* behave like the group of verbs discussed in note 1. But the Real Academia has made a separate group out of them, because they also change in the past tenses (imperfect and preterite) : instead of "conduci", we say *conduje*. The verbs *producir* : "to produce", *traducir* : "to translate" and several other verbs behave in the same way.
(6) *Una prenda* usually means "a pledge", but is used here figuratively in this short dialogue taken from the work of the Spanish Romantic poet José Zorrilla (1817 - 1893).

EJERCICIO: 1. Conozco a alguien que podrá informarte.
2. Nací en el pueblo de mis padres. **3.** Me apetece ir a la
playa. **4.** Cuando amanezca, saldremos. **5.** Conduce muy
bien. **6.** Tradujimos sin dificultad. **7.** Se introdujo por la
ventana.

EJERCICIO DE CONTROL
Ponga las palabras que faltan

1 *I have heard of her, but I do not know her.*

. . oído . . . .

. . . .

2 *He recovered little by little.*

. . . .

****

LECCION CIEN

¡Sálvese quien pueda!

Olvido.

1 — Doctor, tengo trastornos de memoria.
2 — ¿Desde cuándo?
3 — ¿Desde cuándo, qué?

Sentido de la responsabilidad.

4 — En la mesa de operaciones: — Doctor, sea
sincero,
5 ¿está a favor o en contra de la pena de
muerte?
6 — Estoy a favor, pero... tranquilícese, no suelo
7 hacer política en el trabajo.

EXERCISE : 1. I know someone who will be able to inform you. – 2. I was born in my parents' village. – 3. I feel like going to the beach. – 4. When it starts to get light, we will go out. – 5. He drives very well. – 6. We translated without difficulty. – 7. He got in through the window.

3 *He offered me his house.*

. . . .

4 *As it was raining, he did not drive fast.*

. . . .

5 *Insert a five-peseta coin in the machine.*

. . . . moneda . . . .

. . . .

THE MISSING WORDS : 1 he - hablar de ella pero no la conozco. 2 se restableció poco a poco. 3 me ofreció su casa. 4 como llovía no condujo deprisa; 5 introduzca una - de cinco pesetas en la máquina.

Segunda ola: lección 50

****

LESSON ONE HUNDRED

Every man for himself!
(Let him who can, save himself!)

Forgetfulness

1 — Doctor, I have memory problems (disorders).
2 — Since when?
3 — Since when what?

Sense of responsibility

4 — On the operating table : - Doctor, be sincere,
5 are you in favour or against the death penalty?
6 — I am in favour, but... calm down (tranquillize yourself), I don't usually
7 practice (do) (the) politic[s] during work (in the work).

Lección 100

Palabras de ánimo.

8 La enfermera: — Intente poner buena cara **(1)**

9 y sonreír cuando el doctor pase; últimamente

10 todo el equipo de médicos está muy preocupado por su salud.

Desprendimiento y altruismo.

11 — Pero... ¡doctor! la muela que me ha sacado

12 no es la que me duele. **(2)**

13 — Bueno, bueno, no se preocupe

14 por tratarse de usted, no se la cobraré. **(3)**

EJERCICIO: 1. Me duele mucho la cabeza. 2. Toma una pastilla. 3. ¿Quieres que telefonee al médico? 4. No muy lejos de aquí, hay una farmacia de guardia. 5. La enfermera es muy simpática. 6. Su estado de salud es muy bueno. 7. La operación fue un éxito.

EJERCICIO DE CONTROL
Ponga las palabras que faltan

1 *Where does it hurt you?*

¿ . . . . ?

Words of encouragement

8 The nurse : - Try to put a brave (good) face [on it].
9 and smile when the doctor comes past (passes) ; lately
10 the whole team of doctors is very worried about your health.

Disinterestedness and altruism

11 — But... Doctor! The tooth (molar) that you took out [for] me
12 is not the one that hurts (me).
13 — Very well. Don't worry.
14 As it's you, I won't charge (it to) you.

NOTES
(1) *Cara :* "face". *Lávate la cara :* "wash your face" ; *tienes mala cara :* "you don't look very well" ; *hacer cara a algo :* "to face up to something". *Cara o cruz :* literally "face or cross" is the Spanish for "heads or tails".
(2) *Doler :* "to hurt". This is a radical-changing verb in group 2 *(o to ue)*. It always takes an indirect personal object ("it hurts to me").
(3) *Por tratarse de usted :* "through involving you" or "as it's you". *Cobrar* has many meanings, the most common of which are "to charge" and "to earn". *Me han cobrado demasiado :* "I was overcharged" ; *¿Cuánto cobras al mes? :* "How much do you earn a month?".

EXERCISE : 1. I have a bad headache. – **2.** Take a tablet. – **3.** Do you want me to phone the doctor? – **4.** Not very far from here, there is a late-night chemist. – **5.** The nurse is very nice. – **6.** Your state of health is very good. – **7.** The operation was a success.

2 *We have a good doctor.*

. . . .

3 *I do not understand this prescription.*

. . . .

4 *I am a doctor. Can I help you?*

. . . . , ¿ . . . . ?

5 *Sit down. I will call you in straight away.*

. . . .

****

LECCION CIENTO UNA

Escribir

Crimen.

1 — ¿Sabes? la policía ha arrestado al autor del libro

2 que compraste el otro día. Varias personas lo han denunciado. **(1)**

3 — No me extraña. Sus libros son carísimos.

4 — No, la razón no es ésa. Lo acusan de asesinato.

5 Parece ser que varias personas que leían sus libros **(2)**

6 han muerto de aburrimiento.

La cultura es como la mermelada, cuanto menos se tiene más se extiende. **(3)**

7 — Vengo de la charcutería y he comprado para el cuerpo y para el espíritu.

8 Para comer: salchichón, tres latas de sardinas y cuatro latas de bonito.

9 Para instruirnos: dos "latas de palabras".

10 — No sabía que se vendían libros en las tiendas de alimentación.

11 — Sí, es la nueva política: "Por una cultura al alcance de todos".

THE MISSING WORDS : 1 dónde te duele. 2 tenemos un buen médico. 3 no entiendo esta receta. 4 soy médico, ¿puedo ayudarle? 5 siéntese, le haré entrar enseguida.

Segunda ola: lección 51

****

LESSON ONE HUNDRED AND ONE

Writing (To write)

Crime.

1 — Guess what! (Do you know). The police have (has) arrested (to) the author of the book
2 that you bought the other day. Several (various) people have denounced him.
3 — I'm not surprised. His books are extremely expensive.
4 — No, that isn't the reason. He is accused of murder.
5 It appears that several people who read his books
6 have died of boredom.

Culture is like jam (marmalade), the less one has, the more it is spread out.

7 — I have just been to the (I come from the) pork-butcher's and I have bought for the body and for the spirit.
8 To eat : sausage, three tins of sardines and four tins of tuna-fish.
9 To educate (instruct) ourselves : two "tins of words".
10 — I didn't know that books were sold in food shops.
11 — Yes, it's the new policy : "For (a) culture in the reach of everyone".

NOTES
(1) *Denunciar :* "to report to the police" or "to denounce".
(2) *Parece ser que* means the same as *parece que :* "apparently".
(3) *Cuanto menos... más :* "the more... the less".
Aburrimiento : "boredom". The reflexive verb *aburrirse :* "to be bored" can be found in the exercise.

Lección 101

La delicadeza del editor. **(4)**

12 — Los manuscritos que nos son sometidos a revisión,

13 son en general tan malos

14 que tachamos la mitad antes de tirarlos a la papelera.

EJERCICIO: 1. Varias personas han sido arrestadas. **2.** ¿Por qué razón? **3.** Parece ser que se aburrían. **4.** El mes pasado leí tres novelas. **5.** He visto libros en el supermercado. **6.** No me gusta ese bonito. **7.** La comida estaba muy buena.

EJERCICIO DE CONTROL
Ponga las palabras que faltan :

1 *We have spent a lot of money on books.*

. . . .

****

The tact (delicacy) of the editor.

12 — The manuscripts that are submitted to us for revision,

13 are generally so bad

14 that we cross out (the) half before throwing (to throw) them in the waste-paper bin.

EXERCISE : **1.** Several people have been arrested. – **2.** What for? – **3.** Apparently they were bored. – **4.** I read three novels last month. – **5.** I have seen books in the supermarket. – **6.** I don't like that tuna. – **7.** The food was very good.

2 *We are going to ask him for advice.*

. . . .

3 *We have jam for breakfast.*

. . . .

4 *The pork butcher does not sell fish.*

. . . .

5 *In summer I read much more than in winter.*

. . . .

. . . .

THE MISSING WORDS : **1** hemos gastado mucho dinero en libros. **2** vamos a pedirle consejo. **3** desayunamos con mermelada . **4** el charcutero no vende pescado. **5** en verano leo mucho más que en invierno.

Segunda ola: lección 52

* *

Lección 101

LECCION CIENTO DOS

Verbos irregulares del quinto, sexto y séptimo grupo (1)

1   Julia tañe la guitarra con muchísima habilidad. (2)
2   Van al jardín a mullir el colchón. (2)

En el restaurante

3 — Si ya has elegido déjame la carta.
4 — ¿Qué vas a pedir? (3)
5 — Papá, yo quiero un helado.
6 — De acuerdo, pero después de comer.
7 — Si le pides ahora se va a derretir.
8 — Yo pediré unas chuletas de cordero.
9 — ¿Crees que tardarán en servirnos?
10 — No creo, la gente come más tarde (4)
11   y a esta hora en los restaurantes todavía no hay mucho trabajo.
12 — Espero que tengas razón porque tengo mucho hambre.

¿SI ADEMÁS TOMO EL SOL, TENDRÉ QUE PAGAR MÁS?

102

LESSON ONE HUNDRED AND TWO

Irregular verbs of 5th, 6th and 7th groups

1   Julia plays the guitar extremely well (with very much skill).
2   They are going to the garden to beat the mattress.

In the restaurant

3 — If you have already chosen, leave me the menu.
4 — What are you going to ask for?
5 — Daddy, I want an ice-cream.
6 — OK, but after eating.
7 — If you ask for it now, it is going to melt.
8 — I will ask for a few lamb chops.
9 — Do you think they will be long in serving us?
10 — I don't think so. People eat later
11   and at this time in the restaurants there is still not much work.
12 — I hope you're right because I am very hungry.

NOTES
(1) Here we are continuing with our classification of the irregular verbs. Sentences 1 and 2 have verbs from group 5 ; sentences 3, 4, 7, 8 and 9 have verbs from group 6, and the verb *reír* : "to laugh" in sentence 12 is from group 7. Note also how to say the ordinal numbers.

(2) *Tañer* : "to play (music)". As we have already seen, *tocar* is more commonly used. *Mullir* : "to beat" and *tañer* : "to play" belong to the fifth group of irregular verbs, which are not very common. (See grammatical index).

(3) Verbs in the sixth group, on the other hand, are very common. The most important of these are : *pedir* : "to ask for" ; *seguir* : "to follow" ; *vestir* : "to dress" ; *servir* : "to serve". We will see the irregularities of these verbs in more detail in the next revision lesson.

(4) Remember that meal times in Spain are considerably later than in Britain. Lunch is eaten between 2 and 3 pm, and the evening meal around 9 or 10 pm. And don't forget the 24-hour clock system, which is sometimes used in conversation as well as in train timetables, etc.

Por el momento no se paga por reír o cuando el sol no es rentable.

13 En la terraza de la cafetería: — Buenos días, ¿qué desean tomar?

14 — El sol. — ¡Fuera!

EJERCICIO: **1.** Pidió una botella de vino de Rioja. **2.** Pide dos helados y una cerveza. **3.** Se vistió con el pantalón que le compraste. **4.** Esta rueda no sirve para mi bicicleta. **5.** Elige lo que quieras. **6.** ¿Te sirvo el aperitivo? **7.** Se rió cuando le dije lo que pasó.

EJERCICIO DE CONTROL
Ponga las palabras que faltan

1 *Have you managed to find some work?*

¿ . . . conseguido encontrar . . . . ?

2 *They chose a very modern dress.*

. . . .

3 *It's this way ; follow me.*

. . . . , ...

****

LECCION CIENTO TRES

Precisiones

1 De los tres grupos de verbos que hemos presentado

2 en la lección precedente, el grupo sexto es el que más nos interesa. **(1)**

For the moment one doesn't pay to laugh or when the sun is not worthwhile.

13 On the cafe terrace : - Good morning. What would you like (to take)?

14 — The sun. - Get out!

EXERCISE : 1. He asked for a bottle of Rioja wine. – **2.** Ask for two ice-creams and a beer. – **3.** He dressed in the trousers you bought him. – **4.** This wheel is no use for my bicycle. – **5.** Choose what you want. – **6.** Shall I serve you the aperitif? – **7.** He laughed when I told him what happened.

4 *He asked me for a piece of information.*

. . . .

5 *They made us smile.*

. . . .

THE MISSING WORDS : 1 has - - trabajo. **2** "el grupo incluyendo "pedir" es el que más nos interesa". **3** es por aquí, sígame. **4** me pidió una información. **5** nos hacían sonreír.

Segunda ola: lección 53

****

LESSON ONE HUNDRED AND THREE

Further details (precisions)

1
2 Of the three groups of verbs that we have presented in the last (preceding) lesson, group six is the one that interests us most.

NOTES
(1) The irregular verbs in the sixth group change the *e* into *i* (in the three present tenses, the preterite, and thus the rest of the subjunctive, and in the gerundive) when the tonic accent falls on the *e : sirvo :* "I serve" instead of *"servo",* or when the ending begins with an *a* or a diphthong – *sirvió :* "he served" instead of *"servio",* and *sirva :* "I serve" (subj.) instead of *"serva".* More details are given in lesson 105.

Lección 103

3 Veamos algunas frases corrientes construidas con esos verbos:

4 Fueron a despedirnos a la estación. **(2)**

5 Nos siguen escribiendo regularmente. **(3)**

6 Por favor, corríjame cuando haga faltas, así aprenderé más rápido.

7 Eligieron un pequeño hotel cerca de la costa.

8 Se viste a la última moda.

9 Cuando nos sirvieron ya no teníamos casi hambre.

10 Yo mido un metro setenta y cinco y tú ¿cuánto mides?

*****

"... delicada fue la invención de la taberna

11 porque allí llego sediento

12 pido vino de lo nuevo

13 mídenlo, dánmelo (me sirven), bebo, **(4)**

14 págolo y me voy contento."

(Baltasar de Alcázar)

ELIGIERON UN PEQUEÑO HOTEL CERCA DE LA COSTA

EJERCICIO: 1. ¿Vendrás a despedirnos? **2.** Les escribimos en la playa. **3.** Me corregía la pronunciación. **4.** Vístete porque vamos a salir. **5.** ¿Quieren que les sirva? **6.** Voy a tomar las medidas. **7.** Le queremos pedir un favor.

3	Let us look at a few common sentences constructed with those verbs.
4	They went to say goodbye [to] us at the station.
5	They continue to write to us regularly.
6	Please correct me when I make mistakes ; that way I will learn more quickly.
7	They chose a small hotel near the coast.
8	He dresses (himself) in (at) the latest fashion[s].
9	When they served us we were hardly hungry any more (already we didn't have almost hunger).
10	I measure one metre seventy-five. And you, how much do you measure?
	"... the invention of the tavern was delicate
11	because I arrive there thirsty,
12	ask for some new wine
13	they measure it, they give it to me (they serve me), I drink,
14	I pay [for] it and I go away content."
	(Baltazar de Alcázar)

NOTES
(2) The verb *despedir* has various meanings : "to say goodbye", "to send away", "to sack". *Despedirse a la francesa :* "to sneak off". See sentence 1 in the *ejercicio de control.*
(3) *Siguen escribiendo :* "they continue writing". *Seguir* can be used with any infinitive to express continuation of an action. *seguía comiendo :* "he carried on eating".
(4) The construction of this text from Baltazar de Alcázar is somewhat old fashioned : in modern Spanish, we would tend to say *lo miden, me lo dan, lo pago,* but the meaning is identical. Notice the word order, always rather more flexible in poetic writing.

***** *****

EXERCISE : 1. Will you come to say goodbye to us? – **2.** We wrote to them at the beach. – **3.** He was correcting my pronunciation. – **4.** Get dressed because we are going to go out. – **5.** Do you want me to serve you (pol. pl.)? – **6.** I am going to take the measurements. – **7.** We want to ask him a favour.

EJERCICIO DE CONTROL
Ponga las palabras que faltan

1 *We said goodbye to each other at the airport.*

. . .   .

2 *I have chosen a little "typical" restaurant to go to have dinner tonight.*

. . .   .

. . . .

3 *The hotel was near the beach.*

. . .   .

* *

LECCION CIENTO CUATRO

Parábola (1)

1 Era un niño que soñaba
  un caballo de cartón.
2 Abrió los ojos el niño
  y el caballito no vió. (2)
3 Con un caballito blanco
  el niño volvió a soñar; (3)
4 y por la crin lo cogía...
  ¡Ahora no te escaparás!
5 Apenas lo hubo cogido,
  el niño se despertó.
6 Tenía el puño cerrado.
  ¡El caballito voló!

4 *He was thirsty and asked for water.*

. . . .

5 *He was served wine.*

. . . .

THE MISSING WORDS : **1** nos despedimos en el aeropuerto. **2** he elegido un pequeño restaurante típico para ir a cenar esta noche. **3** el hotel estaba cerca de la playa. **4** estaba sediento y pidió agua. **5** le sirvieron vino.

Segunda ola: lección 54

****

LESSON ONE HUNDRED AND FOUR

Parable

1 There was (He was) a child who dreamed [of] a cardboard horse.
2 The child opened his eyes and he didn't see the little horse.
3 Of (With) a little white horse the child dreamed again ;
4 and by the mane he caught it... Now you won't escape!
5 Hardly had he taken hold of it the child woke up.
6 He had his (the) fist clenched. The little horse flew!

NOTES
(1) Read these lines from Antonio Machado once without looking at the English translation. The language shouldn't pose any problems now, but study tenses!
(2) *Vio :* third person singular preterite of *ver*.
(3) *Volver :* "to return" (intransitive) ; *volver a escribir :* "to write again".

7 Quedóse el niño muy serio
pensando que no es verdad
8 un caballito soñado.
Y ya no volvió a soñar.
9 Pero el niño se hizo mozo **(4)**
y el mozo tuvo un amor, **(5)**
10 y a su amada le decía:
¿Tú eres de verdad o no?
11 Cuando el mozo se hizo viejo
pensaba: Todo es soñar,
12 el caballito soñado
y el caballo de verdad.
13 Y cuando vino la muerte,
el viejo a su corazón
14 preguntaba: ¿Tú eres sueño?
¡Quién sabe si despertó!

EJERCICIO: **1.** Fuimos a pasear a caballo. **2.** Volví a verlo el mes pasado. **3.** El perro se ha escapado. **4.** Se hirió en el puño. **5.** Se ha quedado en el jardín. **6.** He soñado contigo. **7.** El viejo estaba sentado.

EJERCICIO DE CONTROL
Ponga las palabras que faltan

1 *We are going to stay with the horses.*

. . . .

7	The child was (remained) very serious
	thinking that it isn't true,
8	a little horse in a dream (dreamed of).
	And he never dreamed of it again.
9	But the child turned into a young man
	and the young man had a love
10	and to his loved one he said
	Are you true or not?
11	When the young man became (made himself) old
	He thought : Everything is dreaming (to dream)
12	the little horse of my dreams (dreamed of)
	and the real horse [as well].
13	And when (the) death came,
	The old man to his heart
14	asked : Are you a dream?
	Who knows if he woke up!

NOTES

(4) *Se hizo viejo* : "he became old". *Hacerse* is used for more gradual changes than *volverse* (e.g., *se ha vuelto loco* : "he has gone crazy").

(5) *Mozo* : "a young man". The word is falling out of common use, in favour of *joven*. Certain common expresions are still used, however : *mozo de café* : "waiter", *mozo de caballos* : "stable boy", etc.

This lesson gives you an opportunity to revise many of the "uncategorizable" verbs. At the same time it reviews the verbs in groups 1 and 2 — which we began to look at formally in lesson 85 : *cerrar* : "to close" ; *pensar* : "to think" ; *volar* : "to fly" ; *soñar* : "to dream", etc.

EXERCISE : **1.** We went for a horse-ride. – **2.** I saw him again last month. – **3.** The dog has escaped. – **4.** He injured himself on the knuckle. – **5.** He has stayed in the garden. – **6.** I have dreamed of you. – **7.** The old man was sitting down.

2 *He has called back this morning.*

. .   .   .

3 *Is it true or not?*

¿ · ·   . . . . ?

4 *They have big hearts.*

. . . .

5 *He woke up late.*

. .   . .

****

LECCION CIENTO CINCO

LESSON ONE HUNDRED AND FIVE

Revisión y notas

1. Verbos irregulares del tercer y cuarto grupo
A. **Third group :** this group includes verbs ending in *-acer,
-ecer, -ocer* and *-ucir* (for the rare exceptions, see
grammatical appendix) : *nacer :* "to be born" ; *crecer :* "to
grow" ; *conocer :* "to know" ; *lucir :* "to shine", etc.

B. **Fourth group :** this group includes verbs ending in
-ducir : conducir : "to drive" ; *traducir :* "to translate" ;
seducir : "to seduce", etc.

C. **Points common to both groups** (see lesson 99).
– In the three present tenses (present indicative, present
subjunctive and imperative), the verbs take a *z* in front of
the *c* preceding the ending when that *c* is followed by an *o*
or an *a*. Examples : *parecer :* "to appear" ; *conocer :* "to
know" ; *conducir :* "to drive".

Present indicative	Present subjunctive	Imperative
parezco	conozca	
pareces	conozcas	conduce
parece	conozca	conduzca
parecemos	conozcamos	conduzcamos
parecéis	conozcáis	conducid
parecen	conozcan	conduzcan

THE MISSING WORDS : 1 vamos a quedarnos con los caballos. **2** ha vuelto a telefonear esta mañana. **3** es verdad o no. **4** tienen un gran corazón. **5** se despertó muy tarde.

Segunda ola: lección 55

* *

D. Specific aspects of the third group
— These verbs belong to the second and third conjugations.
— Verbs ending in *-ecer* are generally derived from adjectives : *entristecer :* "to sadden" (derived from *triste :* "sad") ; *embellecer :* "to grow more beautiful" (derived from *bello :* "beautiful"), etc.

E. Specific aspects of the fourth group (see lesson 99)
— These verbs end in *-ducir,* and thus all belong to the third conjugation.
— In addition to the irregularities in the present tense, which we mentioned above, these verbs take the form *-duje* in the preterite - - and thus also in the imperfect subjunctive. Examples : *conducir :* "to drive" ; *traducir :* "to translate".

Preterite	Imperfect subjunctive		
con**duje**	tra**dujera**	(or)	tra**dujese**
con**duji**ste	tra**dujeras**		tra**dujeses**
con**dujo**	tra**dujera**		tra**dujese**
con**duji**mos	tra**dujéramos**		tra**dujésemos**
con**duji**steis	tra**dujerais**		tra**dujeseis**
con**dujeron**	tra**dujeran**		tra**dujesen**

3. This brief resumé of the main different types of verb might seem complicated, and it is true that many parameters must be taken into account. Recent lessons have given examples of many of the categories of irregular verbs, and you can pick up the most commonly used forms by looking back through the sentences in those lessons. If you feel that a more systematic approach would help clarify the situation, look at the complete verb lists at the back of the book. Use these lists for reference only : learning by heart is only helpful for parrots or computers!

2. Verbos irregulares del quinto grupo (see lesson 102)
The verbs in this group are so rare that we are not going to look at them here. However, just for the record, they are covered in the grammatical appendix.

3. Verbos irregulares del sexto grupo (see lessons 102 and 103)
— This group includes *servir :* "to serve" ; *pedir :* "to ask for" ; *seguir :* "to follow" ; *vestir :* "to dress" ; *repetir :* "to repeat" as well as verbs ending in *-ebir, -edir, -egir, -eguir, -emir, -enchir, -endir, -estir* and *-etir*.
— The irregularities of this group of verbs involve the vowel change *e* to *i* in the stressed persons or when the ending begins with an *a* or a diphthong. The irregularity thus appears in the three present tenses, the preterite, the imperfect subjunctive and the gerundive. Examples : *servir :* "to serve" ; *pedir :* "to ask for" ; *vestir :* "to dress".

Present indicative	Present subjunctive	Imperative
sirvo	pida	
sirves	pidas	viste
sirve	pida	vista
servimos	pidamos	vistamos
servís	pidáis	vestid
sirven	pidan	vistan

Preterite	Imperfect subjunctive		Gerundive
serví	pidiera (or)	pidiese	
serviste	pidieras	pidieses	
sirvió	pidiera	pidiese	pidiendo
servimos	pidiéramos	pidiésemos	
servisteis	pidierais	pidieseis	
sirvieron	pidieran	pidiesen	

4. Verbos irregulares del séptimo grupo:

— Appartiennent à ce groupe les verbes finissant en *-eir*

4. Verbos irregulares del séptimo grupo
– This group includes verbs ending in *-eir* and *-eñir* : *freír* : "to fry" ; *reír* : "to laugh" ; *teñir* : "to dye".
– There are relatively few verbs in this group. The most commonly used is *reír*.
– These verbs have the irregularities of both group 5 (see grammatical appendix) and group 6 (see above).

5. Note. Here we should repeat what we said about irregular verbs in earlier revision lessons : do not learn them all by heart - we are simply trying to give you a point of reference that you will find useful when you come across specific problems. Just remember the main points, without spending unnecessary time learning verb lists. If you have a problem later, you'll know where to refer back to.

6 Writing in Spanish

1   I know a very pleasant little restaurant near the beach.
2   When I went past, I said goodbye to him and smiled at him.
3   I think it is going to rain.
4   I haven't seen the wines on the menu.
5   I have to correct my pronunciation.
6   Before serving me, he asked me if I was hungry.

7. Translation

1   Conozco un pequeño restaurante muy agradable cerca de la playa.
2   Cuando pasé le dije adiós y le sonreí.
3   Me parece que va a llover.
4   No he visto los vinos en la carta.
5   Tengo que corregir mi pronunciación.
6   Antes de servirme me preguntó si tenía hambre.

Segunda ola: lección 56

Lección 105

LECCION CIENTO SEIS

Ultimas advertencias

1 El fin del principio de su aprendizaje se acerca.
2 En lo que concierne a los verbos, aún nos quedan
3 algunas precisiones que hacer.
4 Como no son numerosas y se refieren a verbos
5 que ya hemos visto en el curso de las lecciones precedentes,
6 nos contentaremos con advertirle en las notas **(1)**
7 y le sugeriremos que se dirija directamente al apéndice gramatical.

Proverbios **(2)**

8 ¡Malo, malo! dice el comprador,
   pero al marchar se felicita. **(3)**
9 Para el asno la brida,
   para la espalda de los necios la vara.
10 Como ramo de espino en la mano del borracho
   es el proverbio en la boca de los necios.

LESSON ONE HUNDRED AND SIX

Last pieces of advice

1   The end of the beginning of your apprenticeship is approaching. ·
2   As far as verbs are concerned (In that which concerns verbs), we still have (still remain to us)
3   a few details to clear up (precisions to make).
4   As they are not numerous and refer to verbs
5   that we have already seen during (in) the course of the previous lessons,
6   we will content ourselves with pointing them out to you in the notes
7   and we will suggest that you turn (direct yourself) directly to the grammatical appendix.

Proverbs

8   Terrible! Terrible! says the buyer
    But congratulates himself on leaving.
9   The bridle for the donkey
    The rod for the backs of fools.
10 Like [a] branch of hawthorn in the hand of the drunkard is the proverb in the mouth of (the) fools.

NOTES
(1) This lesson concentrates on verbs belonging to the eighth group of irregular verbs. In the present tenses (present indicative, present subjunctive and imperative), these verbs have the same irregularities as the verbs in group 1 (see lesson 91). They make up a separate group because they also demonstrate the irregularity we mention in the grammatical appendix.

We are not going to spend too much time on these verbs here, because we have already seen the most common ones in earlier lessons. The stressed syllable is given in boldface. Most of these verbs are contained in the "Missing words" exercise.
(2) These three proverbs about fools are attributed to King Solomon.
(3) *Al marchar :* remember the *al* + infinitive construction (See Note 2 to lesson 22).

EJERCICIO: 1. Hemos llegado los últimos. **2.** Al principio no sabíamos qué decir. **3.** Aún tengo tiempo. **4.** ¿Te queda dinero suelto? **5.** Han enviado un telegrama para advertirnos de su llegada. **6.** Diríjase a aquella ventanilla. **7.** Me duele la espalda.

EJERCICIO DE CONTROL
Ponga las palabras que faltan

1 *We don't know what to do. What do you suggest to us?*

. . . . , ¿ . . . .

. . . . ?

2 *I am sorry not to have been able to take that train.*

Siento . . . .

****

LECCION CIENTO SIETE

El arte de saber distanciarse

1 José era carpintero y desde hacía muchos años

2 vivía de su trabajo,

3 que no era otro que el de construir las casas **(1)**

4 de aquellos que querían instalarse al borde del río.

*****

EXERCISE : 1. We were the last to arrive. – **2.** At first we did not know what to say. – **3.** I still have time. – **4.** Do you have some change left? – **5.** They sent a telegram to warn us of his arrival. – **6.** Go to that window over there. – **7.** I have backache.

3 We enjoyed ourselves a lot.

. . .   .

4 *I would rather you came with me.*

. . . .

5 *The water is boiling.*

. . . .

THE MISSING WORDS :   **1** no sabemos qué hacer – ¿qué nos sugieres? **2** – no haber cogido ese tren. **3** nos hemos divertido mucho. **4** prefiero que me acompañes. **5** el agua está hirviendo.

Segunda ola: lección 57

* *

LESSON ONE HUNDRED AND SEVEN

The art of keeping one's distance

1   José was a carpenter and for (since) several years
2   had lived (was living) from his work,
3   that was none other than constructing the houses
4   of those who wanted to live (install themselves) at
      the edge of the river.

NOTES
(1) In this lesson we will continue to look at the different types of irregular verbs. *Construir :* "to build", like all verbs ending in *-uir*, is in group 10. These verbs take a *y* after the *u* of the stem when followed by a strong vowel *(a, e, o)*. The irregularity thus appears in the present indicative, the present subjunctive and the imperative. There are also spelling changes in these verbs : look at the table in the grammatical appendix.

5   De todos era temido y respetado.

6   Se le atribuían poderes extraños.

7   Las gentes hablaban de su maravillosa capacidad de ver de lejos.

8   Cuentan que un día alguien oyó un gran ruido

9   en la habitación en la que él dormía **(2)**

10   y asustados preguntaron desde fuera:

11   — ¿Qué ha sido eso? ¿Qué ha pasado?

12   — No os preocupéis, salgo enseguida, - respondió- ha sido mi pijama que se ha caído. **(3)**

13   Perplejos, los vecinos gritaron: — Es imposible, un pijama no hace tanto ruido.

14   Y con voz tranquila José respondió: — ¡Claro! Es porque yo estaba dentro.

EJERCICIO: 1. Construyo una casa. **2.** Se durmió en la playa. **3.** Este cuadro se atribuye a Murillo. **4.** Voy a salir. **5.** Esos zapatos no te valen. **6.** Fue excluido de la lista. **7.** Todos contribuimos a la construcción de la casa.

*****

5	He was feared and respected by everyone.
6	He was attributed strange powers.
7	People spoke of his marvellous capacity to see from afar.
8	It is said that one day somebody heard a great noise
9	in the room where (in that which) he was sleeping
10	and, frightened, asked him from outside :
11 —	What was that? What has happened?
12 —	"Don't worry. I'm coming out straight away", he replied, "It was my pyjama[s] falling"
13	Perplexed, the neighbours shouted : "It's impossible, a [pair of] pyjama[s] doesn't make so much noise."
14	And in (with) a quiet voice José replied : "Of course! It's because I was in them (inside)".

NOTES
(2) *Dormir* : "to sleep". We've already seen a lot of this verb, and you probably have no problems with it by now. But remember that *dormir* and *morir* : "to die" make up the eleventh group of irregular verbs.
(3) *Salir* : "to go out" is a very common verb in Spanish, and you will already be familiar with it by now. Together with *valer* : "to be worth", it makes up the twelfth (and final) group of irregular verbs.
To find out more about these last two groups of verbs, you should refer to pages 447 to 450 in the grammatical appendix. Reference to this section will help you to do exercises – indeed the exercises only include verbs from the three groups we speak about in this lesson.

EXERCISE : 1. I am building a house. – **2.** He fell asleep on the beach. – **3.** This picture is attributed to Murillo. – **4.** I am going to go out. – **5.** Those shoes do not fit you. – **6.** He was left off the list. – **7.** We all helped build the house.

*****

Note : *Remember the verbs belonging to the ninth group that were dealt with in lesson 91.*

EJERCICIO DE CONTROL
Ponga las palabras que faltan

1 *Which room are you sleeping in?*

¿ . . . .?

2 *They are building a motorway.*

. . . .

3 *Tell me when you go out.*

. . . .

****

*****

LECCION CIENTO OCHO

"Vientos del pueblo me llevan" **(1)**

...
1 Asturianos de braveza,
vascos de piedra blindada, **(2)**
2 valencianos de alegría
y castellanos de alma,
3 labrados como la tierra
y airosos como las alas;
4 andaluces de relámpagos,
nacidos entre guitarras
5 y forjados en los yunques
torrenciales de las lágrimas;
6 extremeños de centeno,
gallegos de lluvia y calma,

4 *How much is that bike worth?*

¿ . . . . ?

5 *Can you go out for a moment?*

¿ . . . . ?

THE MISSING WORDS :   **1** en qué habitación duermes. **2** están construyendo una autopista. **3** adviérteme cuando salgas. **4** cuánto vale esa bici. **5** puedes salir un momento.

Segunda ola: lección 58

* *

LESSON ONE HUNDRED AND EIGHT

Winds of the people carry me off

1	Asturians of bravery
	Basques hard as stone (of armoured stone)
2	Valencians of happiness
	and Castilians of soul
3	ploughed like the earth
	and gracious as (the) wings ;
4	Andalucians of lightning flashes
	born amidst guitars
5	and forged amidst the anvils
	[of] torrential (of the) tears ;
6	Extremadurans of rye,
	Gallicians of rain and calm

NOTES
(1) These lines are from the poem entitled *"Vientos del pueblo me llevan"* by Miguel Hernández. We advise you to read the Spanish without referring to the English translation, even if you have to read it several times. This will allow you to familiarize yourself with the names of the inhabitants of the different regions of Spain. Inhabitants of Madrid, incidentally, are called *madrileños* (cf. *estremeños* in sentence 6 : "inhabitants of Extremadura").

(2) *Blindada* comes from the verb *blindar* : "to shield" or "to armour-plate", which is mainly used today in technical and military contexts.

7   catalanes de firmeza,
      aragoneses de casta,
8   murcianos de dinamita
      frutalmente propagada,
9   leoneses, navarros, dueños
      del hambre, el sudor y el hacha,
10   reyes de la minería,
      señores de la labranza,
11   hombres que entre las raíces,
      como raíces gallardas,
12   vais de la vida a la muerte,
      vais de la nada a la nada
      ...

EJERCICIO: 1. Asturias es una región minera; 2. El Teide es un volcán que está en las islas Canarias. 3. Extremadura limita al oeste con Portugal. 4. Goya nació en Aragón. 5. Galicia es una región pesquera y ganadera. 6. Murcia tiene dos provincias y un puerto importante. 7. El olivo es cultivado, principalmente, en Andalucía.

EJERCICIO DE CONTROL
Ponga las palabras que faltan

1 *There is a lot of wind these days.*

. . . .

7	Catalans of firmness
	Aragonese of race (caste),
8	Murcians of dynamite
	fruitfully spread out (propagated)
9	Leonese, Navarrans, masters
	of (the) hunger, sweat and the axe,
10	kings of (the) mining
	lords of labour
11	men who between the roots
	like gallant roots
12	go from life to death
	go from nothingness to nothingness.
	...

EXERCISE : 1. Asturias is a mining region. − **2.** El Teide is a volcano that is in the Canary Islands. − **3.** To the West Estremadura borders on Portugal. − **4.** Goya was born in Aragón. − **5.** Galicia is a fishing and livestock-breeding region. − **6.** Murcia has two provinces and an important port. − **7.** The olive is cultivated mainly in Andalucia.

2 *The rain helped the farm labourer (ploughman).*

. .   . .

3 *The roots of the tree are deep.*

. . .   .

4 *Flashes of lightning were illuminating the sky.*

. . .   .

5 *The stream crosses the orchard.*

. .   riachuelo . . . .

THE MISSING WORDS : **1** estos días hace mucho viento. **2** la lluvia ayudó al labrador. **3** las raíces del árbol son profundas. **4** los relámpagos iluminaban el cielo. **5** el - atraviesa el huerto.

Segunda ola: lección 59

PERSONAL NOTES

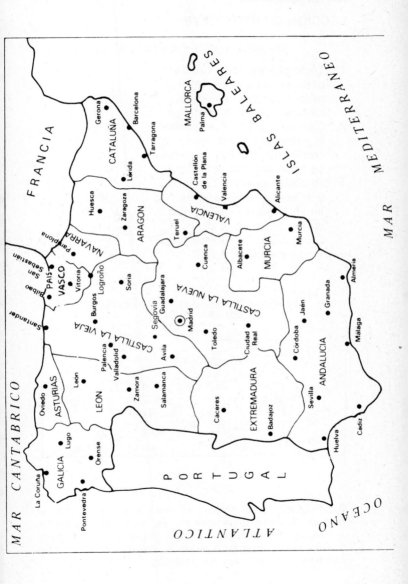

LECCION CIENTO NUEVE

"PROVERBIOS Y CANTARES" (1)

1 Todo pasa y todo queda,
   pero lo nuestro es pasar,
   pasar haciendo caminos,
   caminos sobre la mar.
2 Caminante, son tus huellas
   el camino, y nada más;
   caminante, no hay camino,
   se hace camino al andar.
3 Al andar se hace camino,
   y al volver la vista atrás
   se ve la senda que nunca
   se ha de volver a pisar.
   Caminante, no hay camino,
   sino estelas en la mar.

CAMINANTE NO HAY CAMINO, SINO ESTELAS EN LA MAR.

EJERCICIO: **1.** El viajero se paraba a contemplar el paisaje. **2.** Pasó unos días en làs montañas. **3.** En un pueblo le ofrecieron pan y vino. **4.** El camino era de tierra. **5.** Dejó sus huellas en la nieve. **6.** Volvió a casa por otro sendero. **7.** El mar estaba tranquilo.

LESSON ONE HUNDRED AND NINE

"Proverbs and Songs"

1   All passes and yet all remains
but our fate is to pass
making tracks
tracks over sea.

2   Traveller, your footprints are
the track, and nothing else ;
traveller, there is no track,
the track is made by walking

3   The track is made by walking
and, on glancing back, you see
the path that will never
never again be trod.
Traveller, there is no track
just trails in the sea.

NOTE
(1) We are ending on these lines of Antonio Machado's
"Proverbios y cantares". *(Un cantar :* "a poem set to music".)
Read the Spanish without looking at the translation : the
beauty of the original is worth more than any translation.

EXERCISE : **1.** The traveller stopped to contemplate the
countryside. – **2.** He spent a few days in the mountains. – **3.** In a
village, he was offered bread and wine. – **4.** The track was made of
earth. – **5.** He left his footsteps in the snow. – **6.** He came home by
another path. – **7.** The sea was calm.

* * * * *

EJERCICIO DE CONTROL
Ponga las palabras que faltan

1 *Sing me a song.*

. . . .

2 *Has she been past here?*

¿ . .   . . ?

3 *He didn't look back when he was leaving.*

. .   . .   se

. . .

4 *He will never return.*

. .   . .

****

5 *Can you see the track?*

¿ . . . . ?

THE MISSING WORDS : **1** cántame una canción. **2** ha pasado por
aquí. **3** no volvía la vista atrás cuando   iba. **4** no volverá nunca. **5** ves el
camino.

Segunda ola: lección 60

* *

*We have reached the end of the lessons, but you should
continue with the "second wave" from lesson 50 to lesson
109 at your normal rhythm.*
*In the pages that follow, you will find short lists of expressions
used in different Latin American countries.*

*We hope that you have enjoyed your introduction to Spanish,
and that you have had a first chance to grasp the special
feeling of Spain and its language. Carry on practising!*

See you soon!

THE LANGUAGES OF LATIN AMERICA

Spanish is an official language of the following countries :

Argentina	Argentina	argentino
Colombia	Colombia	colombiano
Costa Rica	Costa Rica	costarriquense or costarricense
Cuba	Cuba	cubano
Chile	Chile	chileno
Ecuador	Ecuador	ecuatoriano
Guatemala	Guatemala	guatemalteco
Honduras	Honduras	hondureño
Mexico	Méjico	mejicano
Nicaragua	Nicaragua	nicaragüense or nicaragüeño
Panama	Panamá	panameño
Paraguay	Paraguay	paraguayo or paraguayano
Peru	Perú	peruano
El Salvador	El Salvador	salvadoreño
Dominican Republic (Santo Domingo)	Dominican Republic (Santo Domingo)	dominicano
Uruguay	Uruguay	uruguayo
Venezuela	Venezuela	venezolano
Puerto Rico	Puerto Rico	puertorriqueño or portorriqueño

It is also spoken in the Philippines (Filipinas), and in certain former Spanish colonies in Africa. Certain parts of the United States have more Spanish-speakers than English-speakers, although official acceptance of Spanish as an official language is still far away. In various Caribbean islands, Spanish and Spanish-based creoles are spoken, and in certain Jewish colonies in Africa, the Balkans and the Near East, an archaic form of Castilian – Sefaraddi – is widely spoken.

Remember, however, that Spanish is only a second language for many indigenous populations, and that the rate of illiteracy is very high in many countries. Major Indian languages include Quechua and Nahuatl. There are also a large number of minor Indian languages, whose syntax has never been formalized. In Guatemala, for instance, locals will tell you that no fewer than nineteen languages are spoken in their country. The influence of indigenous languages on the spoken Spanish of many population groups is one of the causes of the differences between Latin American Spanish and Castilian Spanish. However, with up to 200 million individuals using Spanish as their official means of communication, it can be considered a genuine universal language.

A language is like a living being, constantly reflecting socio-cultural changes, and evolving in response to contact with other peoples and languages. Nobody can effectively dictate or predict the development of a language, since language evolves only on the lips and under the pens of its users. Every language user has something to add : indeed, the creativity of writers and speakers depends to a large extent on their personal interpretation of the intrinsic structure of the language.

Let us venture no further into the perilous straits of psycholinguistics. Suffice it to say that the less contact there is between two groups of language users, the more their respective languages will differ. Before the colonial era ended in Latin America, the standard Spanish spoken in that continent was much the same as that spoken in Spain at the time. While a certain degree of contact has been maintained to this day, Latin American countries have naturally put more weight on dialogue with their immediate neighbours. As a result, the Spanish that is used there has slowly evolved in its own way, becoming increasingly autonomous and independent of its Castilian roots. Certain old Castilian words and structures have remained in Latin America, while they have been renewed or replaced in Spain. Similarly, certain neologisms or borrowings have become standard in Latin American countries while they are often not employed in Spain.

The specific features of Latin American Spanish can add to the culture shock experienced by the tourist or traveller arriving in Latin America for the first time, yet speaking fairly good Castilian Spanish. The most common are listed in the pages that follow. These include :

– 8 phonetic differences (pronunciation) ;
– 8 morpho-syntactic ("grammatical" differences) ;
– lexical differences (vocabulary).

It should be stressed that while "standard" Spanish is by and large defined by reference to the Real Academia, the spoken language can vary quite considerably. People will understand you... but will you understand the people? Do not be put off! Give yourself time to become accustomed to the environment, and to the "music" in the language. The intonation patterns of Spanish in Latin America are quite different from those in Spain, and can make the language sound not only quite different, but also, very soon, irresistibly attractive.

The lists of words (lexical differences) given in the pages that follow are far from exhaustive, and the geographical classification is not as cut and dried as it may look. Thus, for example, some of the words in the Venezuela list are also used in Colombia, and certain words in the Chile list are also used in Uruguay. On the other hand, local rivalries will further differentiate the vocabularies of certains neighbours (Mexico and Guatemala, for instance). The lists are reproduced here for guidance and interest, and should not be taken as an attempt to crystallize what is essentially a highly fluid process.

Phonetic differences
By and large, the Spanish spoken in Latin America is closer to Andalusian Spanish than Castilian Spanish.

1. The **seseo** : *c* and *z* are pronounced like the English "s", and not like the English "th".

2. The **yeismo** : *ll* is pronounced like *y*. In certain countries (including Argentina and Colombia), the *y* sound becomes almost like an English soft "j" (as in "television).

3. **Confusion between *r* and *l* :** e.g., *calne* instead of *carne* "meat", *pielna* instead of *pierna* : "leg", etc.

4. **Aspiration or loss of the final *s* of a syllable or word :** e.g., *lojombre* instead of *los hombres*, *la mohca* instead of *las moscas*, etc.

5. **Loss of certain vowels :** e.g., *cafcito* instead of *cafecito*. Certain researchers have linked this phenomenon to altitude.

6. **Loss of the final *r* :** e.g., *voy a comé* instead of *voy a comer*.

7. **Loss of the *d* between vowels :** e.g., *pejcao* instead of *pescado*, *el deo* instead of *el dedo*.

8. **Aspiration of the initial *h*,** e.g. in *hilo* or *hora*.

Morpho-syntactic differences
1. **Extension of the plural :** e.g., *¿Qué horas son?, los tiempos están lluviosos*.

2. **Use of the pronoun *yo* with a preposition :** e.g., *a yo* instead of *a mí*, *con yo* instead of *conmigo*.

3. Increased use of the **preterite in place of the perfect.** Latin American usage of these tenses resembles United States usage in English.

4. Use of **the reflexive pronoun with intransitive verbs** : e.g., *subióse* instead of *subió* : "he went up", *entróse* instead of *entró*, etc.

5. Use of **auxiliaries in the present tense to express the future** : e.g., *han de querer* instead of *querrán, he de ir yo* instead of *yo iré*.

6. Increased and different **usage of the adverb recién** : *llegó recién* : "he has just arrived" *(acaba de llegar)* ; *recién hoy* : "only today" *(sólo hoy)* ; *recién llegará mañana* : "he's only arriving tomorrow" *(no llegará hasta mañana)* ; *lo vi recién llegó* : "I saw him when he had just arrived" *(lo vi apenas llegó)*.

7. Wider **use of diminutives** : *ahorita, prontito,* but also *enterito* and *grandito*.

8. **The "voseo"** : The use of the word *vos* instead of *tú*. Thus *tú tienes* becomes *vos tenés, contigo* becomes *con vos*. The problems involved with the use of *vos* thus involve the introduction of new verb forms. However the overall picture is simpler than in Castilian Spanish. The use of *vosotros* (second person familiar plural) disappears, and *ustedes* covers all cases. Thus *vos* is familiar singular, *usted* polite singular, and *ustedes* plurals of all kinds. Note, however, that *te* is used : *¿Cómo te llamas?*, etc.

Lexical differences

Vocabulary is by and large the same in Latin America and Spain and regional differences are as noticeable within Spain as they are in America. There are many instances where the same concept is expressed differently in different regions, and innumerable examples of "faux amis" between different Hispanic vocabularies can be found.

Leaf through the lists in the pages that follow. Be ready to understand them, but do not try – for the time being – to emulate them.

By way of introduction, here are ten words that are common in many regions of Latin America. The Castilian Spanish equivalent is given in the middle column, and an English translation appears in the right-hand column :

bolillos	panecillos	small loaves, buns
camión	autobús	bus
chancleta	acelerador	accelerator
droga	deuda	debt
exigir	rogar	to ask
luego	al instante	straight away
palo	trago	a drink
parquear	aparcar	to park
ruletero	taxista	taxi driver
tinto	café negro	black coffee
etc.		

trescientas noventa y dos **392**

Archaic Castilian still common in Latin America

amargoso	amargo	bitter
fatiga	agonía	agony
despacharse	darse prisa	to hurry
recordarse	despertarse	to wake up
saber	soler	to be used to
taita	padre	father
candela	fuego	fire, a light for a cigarette
catar	mirar	to look at
bregar	trabajar	to work
mercar	comprar	buy
etc.		

Neologisms and borrowings

The following are just a few examples of the many words
borrowed from English :

computador	ordenador	computer
masacrar	matar	to kill
ultimar	matar	to kill
closet	armario	cupboard
rentar	alquilar	to rent

WORDS USED THROUGHOUT
LATIN AMERICA

arrancarse	despedirse	to take time off
balaceo	tiroteo	gunfight
bestia	caballo	horse
diarismo	periodismo	journalism
eleccionario	electivo, elector	voter
esportivo	deportivo	sporting
estampilla	sello	stamp
expeditar	despachar, hacer algo con prontitud	to hurry along, expedite
expendio	local de venta al por menor	retailer
foja	hoja de papel	sheet of paper
frazada	manta	blanket
lindo	bonito	pretty
manejar	conducir un coche	to drive a car
memorias	recuerdos, saludos	memories
pararse	ponerse en pie	to stand up
plata	dinero	money
quedadizo quedado	lento, indolente	slow, indolent
sabana	llanura	plain, savanna
saco	chaqueta	jacket
ubicar	colocar en un sitio preciso	to put in a specific place

CENTRAL AMERICA

abreviarse	apresurarse	to hurry
acogencia	acogida, aceptación	welcome, acceptance
acuerpar	defender	to defend
afanar	ganar dinero	to earn money
cobija	manta	blanket
de juro	sin remedio, a la fuerza	truly, by force
de pie	constantemente	constantly
estacón	pinchazo	puncture
festinar	festejar	to celebrate
marfil	peine	comb
mercar	comprar	to buy
¿qué tanto?	¿cuánto?	how much? how many?
rajar	gastar mucho dinero	to spend a lot of money
rango	lujo	luxury
sentirse	resentirse, estar dolido	to be upset
tajarrazo	herida	injury
vallunco	rústico, burdo	vulgar
venduta	venta pública	sale to the public
zipote	muchacho	young man

ARGENTINA

apolillar	dormir	to sleep
auto	coche	car
colectivo, omnibús	autobús	bus (*colectivo* is most common in cities)
con fantasía	con ganas, mucho	with pleasure
correo	correos	the mail
desilo, desíselo	díselo	tell him so
escobilla	cepillo	brush
exprés, expreso	café exprés	expresso (coffee)
fósforos	cerillas	matches
kiosko	lugar en el que se venden los periódicos y el tabaco	kiosk
laburo	trabajo	work
lunfardo		slang, originally from Buenos Aires, but now more widespread
morfar	comer	eat
pollera	falda	skirt
puchos	cigarrillos	cigarettes
tomar	beber	to have a drink
viejo, a	padre, madre	father, mother
¿viste?	¿ves? ¿entiendes?	Do you see?

BOLIVIA

anque	aunque	although
aplicarle	comer o beber algo con gusto	to enjoy eating or drinking something
corre, haz corre este trabajo	deprisa haz deprisa este trabajo	hurry up, do this work quickly
desecho	atajo	short cut
¿diande?	¿cómo?	Pardon?
fachada	cara, rostro	face
futre	elegante	elegant
¿hay?	¿cómo dice usted? ¿qué?	Pardon?
guagua	niño pequeño, bebé	baby, little child
limpio	vacío	empty
monis	dinero	money
mi negocio camina bien	mi negocio marcha bien	My business is going well.
no más	solamente	only
no le hace	no importa	it doesn't matter
pajuela	cerilla	match
peyor, más peyor	peor	worse
pulmón, he trabajado tanto que me duele el pulmón	espalda, he trabajado tanto que me duele la espalda	back, I have worked so much I have a bad back.
quija	hambre, apetito	hunger
sobre	cama	bed
suplementero	persona que vende periódicos y revistas	newspaper seller
tata	señor	sir
trabajo	difícil, penoso	difficult

COLOMBIA

antier	anteayer	the day before yesterday
amañarse	estar a gusto en un sitio	to be at home somewhere
agente viajero	viajante	travelling salesman
china	mujer indígena en general bella y simpática	indian woman (usually good looking and friendly)
finir	acabar, terminar	to finish
parquear	aparcar, estacionar	to park
pase	permiso de conducir	driving licence
patilla	sandía	water melon
peluquear	cortar el pelo	to have one's hair cut
querido	persona simpática, amable	nice, friendly person
saco	chaqueta	jacket
sifón	cerveza de barril	draught beer
taita	padre	father
tanque	depósito de gasolina del coche	petrol (gas) tank
teatro	sala de cine	cinema
televidente	telespectador	viewer (TV)
tener afán	tener prisa	to be in a hurry
trastearse	mudarse	to move house
sesionar	reunirse para celebrar una sesión	to hold a meeting

CHILE

al tiro	inmediatamente	immediately
arrancarse	irse	to go away
botar	tirar	throw away
bus	autobús	bus
cierro	sobre	envelope
farsear	bromear	to joke
finir	acabar	to finish
fundo	finca rústica	country estate
garson	camarero	waiter (in a bar)
guagua	niño pequeño, bebé	baby, small child
harto	mucho	a lot
individual	idéntico	identical
¡oye che!	¡oye tú!	Hey! Listen!
regana	gana muy grande	great desire
¿tenís tabaco?	¿tienes cigarros?	Do you have a cigarette?
zoquetes	calcetines	socks

MEXICO

abarrotes	artículos de comercio	groceries
abrirse	retirarse	to leave, slip away
adición	cuenta	bill
banqueta	acera	pavement (sidewalk)
carro	coche	car
cerillos	cerillas	matches
chequeo	examen, revisión	check-up
¡esquina!		used by bus passengers to indicate that they want to get off.
destanteado	confundido, indeciso, desorientado	confused, undecided, disoriented
gringo	norteamericano	gringo (originally a North American ; now used throughout the continent to refer to all Westerners)
hallarse	acostumbrarse, estar a gusto	To be at ease, to get used to something
ni modo	imposible a pesar del esfuerzo	no way (impossible despite our efforts)
palabrar ou palabrear	hablar por teléfono	talk on the telephone
pendejo	torpe	clumsy

petrolero	petrolífero, persona que trabaja en ese dominio	roustabout (oil worker)
ruletero	taxista	taxi driver
rutero	conductor de autobús	bus driver
tener leche	tener suerte	to be lucky
tortilla		staple diet of much of the population (with *ají* (hot pepper) and *frijoles* (red beans)
trabajoso	difícil, complicado	difficult

PERU

agarrar	coger, tomar	to take
asomarse	acercarse	to approach
botar	arrojar, echar fuera con violencia	to throw out violently
cachete	carrillo, mejilla	cheek
candela	fuego, llama	fire, flame
cigarrería	estanco	tobacconist
cocinar	cocer	to cook
cubierta de la carta	sobre	envelope
díceselo	díselo	tell him so
donde fulano de donde fulano	a casa de fulano de casa de fulano	at so-and-so's house ; from so-and-so's house
dulcería	confitería	sweet shop (candy store)
palo	madera	wood
pellejo	piel	skin
pitar	fumar	to smoke
tener moneda sencilla	tener dinero suelto	to have change
vereda	acera	pavement (sidewalk)
voltear	volver	to turn, to turn upside down
vuelto (el)	vuelta (la)	change

PUERTO RICO

azuquita	diminutivo familiar de azúcar	popular diminutive of sugar
cada vez más	cada día más	more every day
camarero	delegado elegido a la cámara de representantes (diputado)	elected member of the house of representatives
en un bendito	en un santiamém	in an instant
explicotear	explicar	explain
faculto	entendido, experto	expert
¡gana!	es imposible, es inútil empeñarse en ello	It's impossible. It's no use trying.
llorarle a uno una cosa	sentarle a uno mal una cosa, irle mal	not to suit someone (clothes, etc.)
maduro	plátano	banana
mandar	dar, tirar	to give away, to throw away
carro, máquina, auto	coche	car
mantequero	dueño de una pequeña tienda de comestibles	grocer
pluma	grifo	tap (faucet)
pollería	edad de la niñez o grupo de niños	childhood or group of children
regar	dar	to give
remojar	dar una propina	to give a tip
rosario	cuento, chisme, historia	tale, story
tertuliar	estar en reunión conversando, hablando	to chat
traficar	trajinar	to come and go, to be busy

VENEZUELA

banqueta	cuneta	ravine
boleto	billete	ticket (plane, train, etc.)
botar	tirar	to throw away
comida	cena	dinner
chancleta	acelerador	accelerator
escaparate	ropero	wardrobe
estupendoso	estupendo	great, fantastic
exigir	rogar	to request
exigencia	ruego cortés	polite request
flux	traje	suit
galleta	atasco	traffic jam
guindar	colgar	hang, hang up
musiú, a	todo extranjero, a	all foreigners
palo	trago	drink
pegar	empezar a hacer algo	to start to do something
remojo	propina	tip
tripa	neumático del coche	car tyre

GRAMMATICAL APPENDIX
AND VERB LISTS

Grammatical Appendix

CONTENTS

* * * * *

BASIC NOTIONS

1. Simple verb tenses
Simple verb tenses in Spanish are formed as follows :

A. The root of the verb   present indicative
present subjunctive
imperative
imperfect indicative
gerundive
past participle

B. The infinitive   future indicative
conditional

C. Preterite   imperfect subjunctive (both forms)
future subjunctive

2. Irregular verbs
There is an easy way of deciding whether a verb is irregular
or not : compare it with the models of *-ar, -er* or *-ir* verbs, and
check the singular forms of the following tenses :

a) present indicative   — first person
b) preterite   — third person
c) future   — first person

If the verb is regular in these three instances, then it will be
regular everywhere.

But if the verb is irregular in (a) the first person singular of the
presente indicative, then it will also be irregular in the present
subjunctive and the imperative. If it is irregular in (b) the third
person singular of the preterite, it will also be irregular in the
imperfect subjunctive and the future subjunctive. If the first
person singular of the future indicative is irregular, the
conditional tense will be irregular also.

We can call these three groups (a) the present group, (b) the
preterite group and (c) the future group.

The imperfect indicative forms a separate group, but only for
the following verbs and their derivatives : *ir :* "to go", *ser :* "to
be" and *ver :* "to see".

3. Compound verbs

Compound verbs are conjugated like the simple verb from which they are derived. Thus, for example, *satisfacer* : "to satisfy" is conjugated like *hacer ; disponer de* : "to have at one's disposal" is conjugated like *poner*.

The only exception to this is *decir* and its derivatives :

— in the future, the derivatives are regular : *maldecir* : "to slander" ; *bendecir* : "to bless", etc. ;

— in the imperative, derivatives end in *dice* : e.g., *predice* : "predict!" ; *bendice* : "bless!", etc.

— in the past participle, *precedir* : "to predict" and *desdecir* : "to clash" or "not to be up to the expected standard" follow the *decir* model, i.e., their past participles are *predicho* and *desdicho*. On the other hand, *contradecir* : "to contradict" is regular, and has *contradecido* as its past participle. *Bendecir* and *maldecir* have two past participles each : *bendecido* and *maldecido,* which are used to conjugate compound tenses, and *bendito* and *maldito,* which are used as adjectives or with the verbs *estar* or *tener*.

Note :
In the grammatical appendix, the imperative is given only in the two familiar forms (singular and plural). As we have said before, the polite imperative forms are the same as the present subjunctive. The same is true of imperatives preceded by a negative. So when, for example, we refer to an irregularity in the present group — and thus also in the imperative — and you don't find the irregularity in boldface in the subjunctive in the table, you will have to think of the other persons that use the present subjunctive as their imperative forms — at least one of which will be irregular. If you're not clear on this matter, look at paragraph on in Lesson 84.

*****

HABER : to have (1)

Impersonal forms

Simple forms

Infinitive	— hab	er
Gerundive (pres. part.)	— hab	iendo
Past participle	— hab	ido

Compound forms

Infinitive	— haber habido
Gerundive (pres. part.)	— habiendo habido

Indicative

present		perfect		
he		he	hab	ido
has		has	hab	ido
ha		ha	hab	ido
hemos		hemos	hab	ido
habéis		habéis	hab	ido
han		han	hab	ido

imperfect		pluperfect		
hab	ía	había	hab	ido
hab	ías	habías	hab	ido
hab	ía	había	hab	ido
hab	íamos	habíamos	hab	ido
hab	íais	habíais	hab	ido
hab	ían	habían	hab	ido

preterite		past anterior		
hub	e	hube	hab	ido
hub	iste	hubiste	hab	ido
hub	o	hubo	hab	ido
hub	imos	hubimos	hab	ido
hub	isteis	hubisteis	hab	ido
hub	ieron	hubieron	hab	ido

future		future perfect		
hab	ré	habré	hab	ido
hab	rás	habrás	hab	ido
hab	rá	habrá	hab	ido
hab	remos	habremos	hab	ido
hab	réis	habréis	hab	ido
hab	rán	habrán	hab	ido

Conditional

	hab	ría		habría	hab ido
	hab	rías		habrías	hab ido
present	hab	ría	past	habría	hab ido
	hab	ríamos		habríamos	hab ido
	hab	ríais		habríais	hab ido
	hab	rían		habrían	hab ido

Subjunctive

	hay	a		haya	hab ido
	hay	as		hayas	hab ido
present	hay	a	past	haya	hab ido
	hay	amos		hayamos	hab ido
	hay	áis		hayáis	hab ido
	hay	an		hayan	hab ido

	hub	iera	(or)	iese
	hub	ieras		ieses
imperfect	hub	iera		iese
	hub	iéramos		iésemos
	hub	ierais		ieseis
	hub	ieran		iesen

	hubiera	(or)	hubiese	hab ido
	hubieras		hubieses	hab ido
pluperfect	hubiera		hubiese	hab ido
	hubiéramos		hubiésemos	hab ido
	hubierais		hubieseis	hab ido
	hubieran		hubiesen	hab ido

	hub	iere		hubiere	hab ido
	hub	ieres		hubieres	hab ido
future	hub	iere		hubiere	hab ido
	hub	iéremos	future perfect	hubiéremos	hab ido
	hub	iereis		hubiereis	hab ido
	hub	ieren		hubieren	hab ido

Imperative

he

—

—

hab ed

(1) The verb **haber** is an auxiliary verb. It is the only Spanish verb used to form compound tenses of verbs.

TENER : to have (possess)

Impersonal forms

Simple forms

Infinitive	— ten	er
Gerundive (pres. part.)	— ten	iendo
Past participle	— ten	ido

Compound forms

Infinitive	— haber tenido
Gerundive (pres. part.)	— habiendo tenido

Indicative

present		perfect		
teng	o	he	ten	ido
tien	es	has	ten	ido
tien	e	ha	ten	ido
ten	emos	hemos	ten	ido
ten	éis	habéis	ten	ido
tien	en	han	ten	ido

imperfect		pluperfect		
ten	ía	había	ten	ido
ten	ías	habías	ten	ido
ten	ía	había	ten	ido
ten	íamos	habíamos	ten	ido
ten	íais	habíais	ten	ido
ten	ían	habían	ten	ido

preterite		past anterior		
tuv	e	hube	ten	ido
tuv	iste	hubiste	ten	ido
tuv	o	hubo	ten	ido
tuv	imos	hubimos	ten	ido
tuv	isteis	hubisteis	ten	ido
tuv	ieron	hubieron	ten	ido

future		future perfect		
ten	dré	habré	ten	ido
ten	drás	habrás	ten	ido
ten	drá	habrá	ten	ido
ten	dremos	habremos	ten	ido
ten	dréis	habréis	ten	ido
ten	drán	habrán	ten	ido

Conditional

	present			past		
	ten	dría		habría	ten	ido
	ten	drías		habrías	ten	ido
	ten	dría		habría	ten	ido
	ten	dríamos		habríamos	ten	ido
	ten	dríais		habríais	ten	ido
	ten	drían		habrían	ten	ido

Subjunctive

	present			past		
	teng	a		haya	ten	ido
	teng	as		hayas	ten	ido
	teng	a		haya	ten	ido
	teng	amos		hayamos	ten	ido
	teng	áis		hayáis	ten	ido
	teng	an		hayan	ten	ido

	imperfect		(or)			
	tuv	iera	(or)	iese		
	tuv	ieras		ieses		
	tuv	iera		iese		
	tuv	iéramos		iésemos		
	tuv	ierais		ieseis		
	tuv	ieran		iesen		

	pluperfect	(or)			
	hubiera	(or)	hubiese	ten	ido
	hubieras		hubieses	ten	ido
	hubiera		hubiese	ten	ido
	hubiéramos		hubiésemos	ten	ido
	hubierais		hubieseis	ten	ido
	hubieran		hubiesen	ten	ido

	future			future perfect		
	tuv	iere		hubiere	ten	ido
	tuv	ieres		hubieres	ten	ido
	tuv	iere		hubiere	ten	ido
	tuv	iéremos		hubiéremos	ten	ido
	tuv	iereis		hubiereis	ten	ido
	tuv	ieren		hubieren	ten	ido

Imperative

ten

—

—

tened

SER : to be (1)

Impersonal forms

Simple forms

Indicative	— s	er
Gerundive (pres. part.)	— s	iendo
Past participle	— s	ido

Compound forms

Infinitive	— haber sido
Gerundive (pres. part.)	— habiendo sido

Indicative

present		perfect		
	soy		he	s ido
	eres		has	s ido
	es		ha	s ido
	somos		hemos	s ido
	sois		habéis	s ido
	son		han	s ido

imperfect		pluperfect		
	era		había	s ido
	eras		habías	s ido
	era		había	s ido
	éramos		habíamos	s ido
	erais		habíais	s ido
	eran		habían	s ido

preterite		past anterior		
	fui		hube	s ido
	fuiste		hubiste	s ido
	fue		hubo	s ido
	fuimos		hubimos	s ido
	fuisteis		hubisteis	s ido
	fueron		hubieron	s ido

future			future perfect		
	s	eré		habré	s ido
	s	erás		habrás	s ido
	s	erá		habrá	s ido
	s	eremos		habremos	s ido
	s	eréis		habréis	s ido
	s	erán		habrán	s ido

Conditional

	s	ería		habría	s	ido
	s	erías		habrías	s	ido
present	s	ería	past	habría	s	ido
	s	eríamos		habríamos	s	ido
	s	eríais		habríais	s	ido
	s	erían		habrían	s	ido

Subjunctive

	se	a		haya	s	ido
	se	as		hayas	s	ido
present	se	a	past	haya	s	ido
	se	amos		hayamos	s	ido
	se	áis		hayáis	s	ido
	se	an		hayan	s	ido

	fu	era	(or)	ese
	fu	eras		eses
imperfect	fu	era		ese
	fu	éramos		ésemos
	fu	erais		eseis
	fu	eran		esen

	hubiera	(or)	hubiese	s	ido
	hubieras		hubieses	s	ido
pluperfect	hubiera		hubiese	s	ido
	hubiéramos		hubiésemos	s	ido
	hubierais		hubieseis	s	ido
	hubieran		hubiesen	s	ido

	fu	ere		hubiere	s	ido
	fu	eres		hubieres	s	ido
future	fu	ere	future perfect	hubiere	s	ido
	fu	éremos		hubiéremos	s	ido
	fu	ereis		hubiereis	s	ido
	fu	eren		hubieren	s	ido

Imperative

s é

——

——

s ed

(1) The verb **ser** is, like **haber,** also an auxiliary verb. It is used to express the passive voice.

ESTAR : to be (state or location)

Impersonal forms

Simple forms

Infinitive	— est	ar
Gerundive (pres. part.)	— est	ando
Past participle	— est	ado

Compound forms

Infinitive	— haber estado
Gerundive (pres. part.)	— habiendo estado

Indicative

present	est	oy	**perfect**	he	est	ado
	est	ás		has	est	ado
	est	á		ha	est	ado
	est	amos		hemos	est	ado
	est	áis		habéis	est	ado
	est	án		han	est	ado
imperfect	est	aba	**pluperfect**	había	est	ado
	est	abas		habías	est	ado
	est	aba		había	est	ado
	est	ábamos		habíamos	est	ado
	est	abais		habíais	est	ado
	est	aban		habían	est	ado
preterite	estuv	e	**past anterior**	hube	est	ado
	estuv	iste		hubiste	est	ado
	estuv	o		hubo	est	ado
	estuv	imos		hubimos	est	ado
	estuv	isteis		hubisteis	est	ado
	estuv	ieron		hubieron	est	ado
future	est	aré	**future perfect**	habré	est	ado
	est	arás		habrás	est	ado
	est	ará		habrá	est	ado
	est	aremos		habremos	est	ado
	est	aréis		habréis	est	ado
	est	arán		habrán	est	ado

Conditional

	est	aría	habría	est ado
	est	arías	habrías	est ado
present	est	aría	past habría	est ado
	est	aríamos	habríamos	est ado
	est	aríais	habríais	est ado
	est	arían	habrían	est ado

Subjunctive

	est	é	haya	est ado
	est	és	hayas	est ado
present	est	é	past haya	est ado
	est	emos	hayamos	est ado
	est	éis	hayáis	est ado
	est	én	hayan	est ado

			(or)	
	estuv	iera	(or)	iese
	estuv	ieras		ieses
imperfect	estuv	iera		iese
	estuv	iéramos		iésemos
	estuv	ierais		ieseis
	estuv	ieran		iesen

		(or)		
	hubiera	(or)	hubiese	est ado
	hubieras		hubieses	est ado
pluperfect	hubiera		hubiese	est ado
	hubiéramos		hubiésemos	est ado
	hubierais		hubieseis	est ado
	hubieran		hubiesen	est ado

	estuv	iere	hubiere	est ado
	estuv	ieres	hubieres	est ado
future	estuv	iere	future perfect hubiere	est ado
	estuv	iéremos	hubiéremos	est ado
	estuv	iereis	hubiereis	est ado
	estuv	ieren	hubieren	est ado

Imperative

est á
—
—
est ad

FIRST CONJUGATION : INFINITIVE ENDING IN -AR

CANTAR : to sing

Impersonal forms

Simple forms

Infinitive	— cant	ar
Gerundive (pres. part.)	— cant	ando
Past participle	— cant	ado

Compound forms

Infinitive	— haber cantado
Gerundive (pres. part.)	— habiendo cantado

Indicative

present		perfect			
cant	o	he		cant	ado
cant	as	has		cant	ado
cant	a	ha		cant	ado
cant	amos	hemos		cant	ado
cant	áis	habéis		cant	ado
cant	an	han		cant	ado

imperfect		pluperfect			
cant	aba	había		cant	ado
cant	abas	habías		cant	ado
cant	aba	había		cant	ado
cant	ábamos	habíamos		cant	ado
cant	abais	habíais		cant	ado
cant	aban	habían		cant	ado

preterite		past anterior			
cant	é	hube		cant	ado
cant	aste	hubiste		cant	ado
cant	ó	hubo		cant	ado
cant	amos	hubimos		cant	ado
cant	asteis	hubisteis		cant	ado
cant	aron	hubieron		cant	ado

future		future perfect			
cant	aré	habré		cant	ado
cant	arás	habrás		cant	ado
cant	ará	habrá		cant	ado
cant	aremos	habremos		cant	ado
cant	aréis	habréis		cant	ado
cant	arán	habrán		cant	ado

Conditional

	present			past			
	cant	aría			habría	cant	ado
	cant	arías			habrías	cant	ado
	cant	aría			habría	cant	ado
	cant	aríamos			habríamos	cant	ado
	cant	aríais			habríais	cant	ado
	cant	arían			habrían	cant	ado

Subjunctive

	present			past			
	cant	e			haya	cant	ado
	cant	es			hayas	cant	ado
	cant	e			haya	cant	ado
	cant	emos			hayamos	cant	ado
	cant	éis			hayáis	cant	ado
	cant	en			hayan	cant	ado

	imperfect			(or)	
	cant	ara	(or)	ase
	cant	aras		ases
	cant	ara		ase
	cant	áramos		ásemos
	cant	arais		aseis
	cant	aran		asen

	pluperfect		(or)			
	hubiera	(or)	hubiese	cant	ado
	hubieras		hubieses	cant	ado
	hubiera		hubiese	cant	ado
	hubiéramos		hubiésemos	cant	ado
	hubierais		hubieseis	cant	ado
	hubieran		hubiesen	cant	ado

	future			future perfect			
	cant	are			hubiere	cant	ado
	cant	ares			hubieres	cant	ado
	cant	are			hubiere	cant	ado
	cant	áremos			hubiéremos	cant	ado
	cant	areis			hubiereis	cant	ado
	cant	aren			hubieren	cant	ado

Imperative

cant a

—

—

cant ad

SECOND CONJUGATION : INFINITIVE ENDING IN -ER

COMER : to eat

Impersonal forms

Simple forms

Infinitive	— com	er
Gerundive (pres. part.)	— com	iendo
Past participle	— com	ido

Compound forms

Infinitive	— haber comido
Gerundive (pres. part.)	— habiendo comido

Indicative

present			perfect		
com	o		he	com	ido
com	es		has	com	ido
com	e		ha	com	ido
com	emos		hemos	com	ido
com	éis		habéis	com	ido
com	en		han	com	ido

imperfect			pluperfect		
com	ía		había	com	ido
com	ías		habías	com	ido
com	ía		había	com	ido
com	íamos		habíamos	com	ido
com	íais		habíais	com	ido
com	ían		habían	com	ido

preterite			past anterior		
com	í		hube	com	ido
com	iste		hubiste	com	ido
com	ió		hubo	com	ido
com	imos		hubimos	com	ido
com	isteis		hubisteis	com	ido
com	ieron		hubieron	com	ido

future			future perfect		
com	eré		habré	com	ido
com	erás		habrás	com	ido
com	erá		habrá	com	ido
com	eremos		habremos	com	ido
com	eréis		habréis	com	ido
com	erán		habrán	com	ido

Conditional

present	com ería	past	habría	com ido
	com erías		habrías	com ido
	com ería		habría	com ido
	com eríamos		habríamos	com ido
	com eríais		habríais	com ido
	com erían		habrían	com ido

Subjunctive

present	com a	past	haya	com ido
	com as		hayas	com ido
	com a		haya	com ido
	com amos		hayamos	com ido
	com áis		hayáis	com ido
	com an		hayan	com ido

		(or)	
imperfect	com iera		iese
	com ieras		ieses
	com iera		iese
	com iéramos		iésemos
	com ierais		ieseis
	com ieran		iesen

		(or)			
pluperfect	hubiera		hubiese	com ido
	hubieras		hubieses	com ido
	hubiera		hubiese	com ido
	hubiéramos		hubiésemos	com ido
	hubierais		hubieseis	com ido
	hubieran		hubiesen	com ido

future	com iere	future perfect	hubiere	com ido
	com ieres		hubieres	com ido
	com iere		hubiere	com ido
	com iéremos		hubiéremos	com ido
	com iereis		hubiereis	com ido
	com ieren		hubieren	com ido

Imperative

com e

—

—

com ed

THIRD CONJUGATION : INFINITIVE ENDING IN -IR

VIVIR : to live

Impersonal forms

Simple forms

Infinitive	— viv	ir
Gerundive (pres. part.)	— viv	iendo
Past participle	— viv	ido

Compound forms

Infinitive	— haber vivido
Gerundive (pres. part.)	— habiendo vivido

Indicative

present		perfect		
viv	o	he	viv	ido
viv	es	has	viv	ido
viv	e	ha	viv	ido
viv	imos	hemos	viv	ido
viv	ís	habéis	viv	ido
viv	en	han	viv	ido

imperfect		pluperfect		
viv	ía	había	viv	ido
viv	ías	habías	viv	ido
viv	ía	había	viv	ido
viv	íamos	habíamos	viv	ido
viv	íais	habíais	viv	ido
viv	ían	habían	viv	ido

preterite		past anterior		
viv	í	hube	viv	ido
viv	iste	hubiste	viv	ido
viv	ió	hubo	viv	ido
viv	imos	hubimos	viv	ido
viv	isteis	hubisteis	viv	ido
viv	ieron	hubieron	viv	ido

future		future perfect		
viv	iré	habré	viv	ido
viv	irás	habrás	viv	ido
viv	irá	habrá	viv	ido
viv	iremos	habremos	viv	ido
viv	iréis	habréis	viv	ido
viv	irán	habrán	viv	ido

Conditional

present	viv	iría	past	habría	viv	ido
	viv	irías		habrías	viv	ido
	viv	iría		habría	viv	ido
	viv	iríamos		habríamos	viv	ido
	viv	iríais		habríais	viv	ido
	viv	irían		habrían	viv	ido

Subjunctive

present	viv	a	past	haya	viv	ido
	viv	as		hayas	viv	ido
	viv	a		haya	viv	ido
	viv	amos		hayamos	viv	ido
	viv	áis		hayáis	viv	ido
	viv	an		hayan	viv	ido

imperfect	viv	iera	(or)	iese
	viv	ieras		ieses
	viv	iera		iese
	viv	iéramos		iésemos
	viv	ierais		ieseis
	viv	ieran		iesen

pluperfect	hubiera	(or)	hubiese	viv	ido
	hubieras		hubieses	viv	ido
	hubiera		hubiese	viv	ido
	hubiéramos		hubiésemos	viv	ido
	hubierais		hubieseis	viv	ido
	hubieran		hubiesen	viv	ido

future	viv	iere	future perfect	hubiere	viv	ido
	viv	ieres		hubieres	viv	ido
	viv	iere		hubiere	viv	ido
	viv	iéremos		hubiéremos	viv	ido
	viv	iereis		hubiereis	viv	ido
	viv	ieren		hubieren	viv	ido

Imperative

viv	e
—	
—	
viv	id

SPELLING CHANGES

Spelling changes required by certain verbs for certain persons do not in reality represent irregularities. In all these verbs they merely exist to retain the same sounds. It is therefore not a question of irregularity since, to the ear, nothing changes. Thus for example in "vencer" : to conquer, if we want to keep the same sound in the present we do not say *venco*, but *venzo* : I conquer.

Listed below are the equivalents :

Sounds ca - co become que - qui
Sounds ga - go become gue - gui
Sounds ja - jo become ge - gi
Sounds gua - guo become güe - güi
Sounds za - zo become ce - ci

A. — Changes in the first conjugation.

Verbs ending in **car, gar, guar, zar.**

Endings	Change	Infinitive	Preterite	Present subjunctive
car: c	becomes qu	*indicar* : to indicate	indiqué	indique, indiques, etc.
gar: g	becomes gu	*pagar* : to pay	pagué	pague, pagues, etc.
guar: gu	becomes gü	*averiguar* : to check	averigüé	averigüe, averigües
zar: z	becomes c	*izar* : to hoist	icé	ice, ices, etc.

Looking at this table we can establish that the change takes place when the ending begins with an "e". Therefore these changes only apply to the first person of the preterite and to the whole of the present subjunctive.

B. — Changes in the second and third conjugation.

Verbs ending in **cer, cir, ger, gir, guir, quir.**

Endings	Change	Infinitive	Present	Present subjunctive
cer ⟍ c	becomes **z**	*ejercer* : to exercise	ejerzo	ejerza, ejerzas, etc.
cir ⟋		*esparcir* : to scatter	esparzo	esparza, esparzas, etc.
ger ⟍ g	becomes **j**	*coger* : to take	cojo	coja, cojas, etc.
gir ⟋		*dirigir* : to direct	dirijo	dirija, dirijas, etc.
guir: gu	becomes **g**	*distinguir* : to distinguish	distingo	distinga, distingas, etc.
quir: qu	becomes **c**	*delinquir* : to commit a crime	delinco	delinca, delincas, etc.

CLASSIFICATION OF IRREGULAR VERBS

Group one

e – ie

These verbs have the diphthong *ie* when the *e* preceding the verb ending carries a tonic accent. This change thus only applies to the first three persons singular and the third person plural of the present indicative, the present subjunctive and the imperative.

PENS AR : "to think"

	Indicative	Subjunctive	Imperative
present	piens o piens as piens a pens amos pens áis piens an	piens e piens es piens e pens emos pens éis piens en	piens a pens ad

All the other forms of this verb – and of those belonging to the irregular verbs of group one – are regular and are conjugated like *cantar*.

PERD ER : "to lose"

Indicative	Subjunctive	Imperative
present pierd o pierd es pierd e perd emos perd éis pierd en	pierd a pierd as pierd a perd amos perd áis pierd an	pierd e perd ed

All other forms of this verb — and those belonging to the irregular verbs of group 1 — are regular and are conjugated like *comer*.

Discernir : "to discern", and *concernir* : "to concern", are the only verbs ending in **IR** belonging to group one and consequently follow the same irregularity. *Discierno* : I discern, *disciernes* : you discern etc. *Concierno* : I concern, *conciernes* : you concern, etc.

Group two

o – ue

These verbs have the diphthong *ue* when the *o* preceding the ending carries a tonic accent. This change therefore only applies to the first three persons singular and the third person plural of the present indicative, the present subjunctive and the imperative.

CONT AR : "to count, tell"

	Indicative	Subjunctive	Imperative
present	cuent o cuent as cuent a cont amos cont áis cuent an	cuent e cuent es cuent e cont emos cont éis cuent en	cuent a cont ad

All other forms of this verb – and of those belonging to the irregular verbs of group two – are regular and conjugate like *cantar*.

VOL VER : "to go home" (1)

	Indicative	Subjunctive	Imperative
present	**vuelv** o **vuelv** es **vuelv** e volv emos volv éis **vuelv** en	**vuelv** a **vuelv** as **vuelv** a volv amos volv áis **vuelv** an	**vuelv** e volv ed

All other forms of this verb – and of those belonging to the irregular verbs of group two – are regular and are conjugated like *comer*.

In this group there are only verbs of the first conjugation – ending in *ar* – and of the second conjugation – ending in *er*.

(1) *Volver* is a very important verb and we advise you to refer to lesson 70 note 1 to consult its other meanings.

Group three

c – cz

The verbs in this group take a z in the three forms of the present – indicative, subjunctive and imperative – in front of the c preceding the ending when the c must be followed by a strong vowel (a and o), i. e. when, phonetically, an ending takes the sound k (ca, co).

Verbs ending in acer, ecer, ocer, ucir belong to this group.

CONOC ER : "to know (a person)"

Indicative		Subjunctive		Imperative	
present	conozc o	conozc a	conoc e	
	conoc es	conozc as		
	conoc e	conozc a		
	conoc emos	conozc amos		
	conoc éis	conozc áis	conoc ed	
	conoc en	conozc an		

LUC IR : "to shine"

	Indicative	Subjunctive	Imperative
present	luzc o luc es luc e luc imos luc ís luc en	luzc a luzc as luzc a luzc amos luzc áis luzc an	luc e luc id

The other forms of this verb – and of those belonging to this group – are regular and are conjugated like *comer* and *vivir*.

Only verbs of the second and third conjugation are found in this group.

Exceptions :

Hacer : "to do" ; *placer* : "to please" ; *yacer* : "to lie down" – these three verbs have other irregularities and belong to a list of 24 verbs which we cannot classify here – *mecer* : "to rock" ; *cocer* : "to cook" and *escocer* : "to itch".

In addition to these six verbs, the "Real Academia" includes in the exceptions of this group verbs ending in *ducir*, since these verbs, in addition to the irregularities of group three, are also irregular in the preterite. These verbs form group four.

Group four

Verbs belonging to group four are those ending in *ducir*. In the present they have the same irregularities as verbs in group three. In addition to this – and this is why they form a group apart – the preterite ends in *duje* and consequently the imperfect subjunctive in *dujera* or *dujese* and the future subjunctive in *dujere*.

c – zc (present)
c – c j (preterite)

CONDUC IR : "to drive"

	Indicative	Subjunctive	Imperative
present	conduzc o	conduzc a	
	conduc es	conduzc as	conduc e
	conduc e	conduzc a	
	conduc imos	conduzc amos	
	conduc ís	conduzc áis	conduc id
	conduc en	conduzc an	

Indicative		Subjunctive			
preterite		**imperfect**		**future**	
conduj	e	conduj	era	conduj	ere
conduj	iste	conduj	eras	conduj	eres
conduj	o	conduj	era	conduj	ere
conduj	imos	conduj	éramos	conduj	éremos
conduj	isteis	conduj	erais	conduj	eréis
conduj	eron	conduj	eran	conduj	eren

(or)

conduj	ese
conduj	eses
conduj	ese
conduj	ésemos
conduj	eseis
conduj	esen

The other forms of this verb – and those ending in *ducir* – are regular and are conjugated like *vivir*.

Group five

Loss of i (preterite) (gerundive)

Verbs in this group lose the "i" in the preterite : past historic, imperfect as well as in the future subjunctive and the gerundive.

Verbs belonging to this group are those ending in *aner*, *añir*, *iñir*, *urir*, *eller* and *ullir*.

MULL IR : "to soften (wool)", "to break down (earth)"

Indicative		Subjunctive			
preterite		**imperfect**	(or)		**future**
mull í		mull era		mull ese	mull ere
mull iste		mull eras		mull eses	mull eres
mull ó		mull era		mull ese	mull ere
mull imos		mull éramos		mull ésemos	mull éremos
mull isteis		mull erais		mull eseis	mull ereis
mull eron		mull eran		mull esen	mull eren

Gerundive : mull endo

With the exception of the third person singular of the preterite, the imperfect, the future subjunctive and the gerundive, the other forms of this verb – and those sharing the same irregularity – are regular and are conjugated like *vivir* and *comer*.

*****

Group six

e – i

The "e" of the roots of the verbs in this group changes to "i" when the vowel must be tonic or if the ending begins with a diphthong or with an "a". This change applies in the present, the preterite and the gerundive.

In addition to *servir* : "to serve", verbs belonging to this group are those ending in *ebir, edir, egir, eguir, emir, enchir, endir, estir* and *etir*.

PED IR : "to ask"

Indicative		Subjunctive		Imperative	
present	pid o	pid a			
	pid es	pid as		pid e	
	pid e	pid a			
	ped imos	pid amos			
	ped ís	pid áis		ped id	
	pid en	pid an			

Indicative		Subjunctive			
preterite		**imperfect**	(or)		**future**
ped í		pid iera		pid iese	pid iere
ped iste		pid ieras		pid ieses	pid ieres
pid ió		pid iera		pid iese	pid iere
ped imos		pid iéramos		pid iésemos	pid iéremos
ped isteis		pid ierais		pid ieseis	pid iereis
pid ieron		pid ieran		pid iesen	pid ieren

Gerundive : pid iendo

The other tenses of these verbs are regular and are conjugated like *vivir*.

Group seven

Loss of "i" (preterite) (gerundive)

e → i

The verbs in this group assemble all the irregularities of groups five and six.

Verbs belonging to this group are those ending in *eir* and *eñir*.

RE IR : "to laugh"

Indicative	Subjunctive	Imperative
present		
rí o	rí a	
rí es	rí as	rí e
rí e	rí a	
re ímos	ri amos	
re ís	ri áis	re íd
rí en	rí an	

Indicative	Subjunctive	
preterite	**imperfect**	**future**
re í	ri era	ri ere
re íste	ri eras	ri eres
ri ó	ri era	ri ere
re ímos	ri éramos	ri éremos
re ístes	ri erais	ri ereis
ri eron	ri eran	ri eren
	(or) ese	
	eses	
	ese	
	ésemos	
	eseis	
	esen	

Gerundive : ri endo

Group eight

e – ie
e – i

The verbs of this group have firstly : in the present group – present indicative, present subjunctive and the imperative, the same irregularity as the verbs of group one, i.e. they have the diphthong *ie* when there is an "e" preceding the ending in the tonic persons.

Secondly, in the present, preterite and the gerundive, these verbs have the same irregularity as the verbs of group six, i.e. "e" becomes "i" when it must be tonic or if the ending begins with a diphthong or an "a".

Verbs belonging to this group are those ending in *entir*, like *sentir* : "to feel", *erir*, like *proferir* : "to utter" ; and *ertir* like *divertir* : "to entertain" : In short, all verbs having "r" or "nt" after the "e" of the root belong to this group. The only exception is *servir*.

Verbs ending in *uir* are regular in all other tenses, but the spelling changes which we have noted above must also be taken into consideration. This means that the unstressed *i* of the gerundive, the *i* of the third persons singular and plural of the preterite and consequently of the tenses derived from the preterite, situated between two vowels become *y*.

Indicative		Subjunctive			
preterite	constru i	**imperfect**	constru yera	(or)	yese
	constru iste		constru yeras		yeses
	constru yó		constru yera		yese
	constru imos		constru yéramos		yésemos
	constru isteis		constru yerais		yeseis
	constru yeron		constru yeran		yesen
		future	constru yere		
			constru yeres		
			constru yere		
			constru yéremos		
			constru yereis		
			constru yeren		

Gerundive : constru yendo

So we see that in the preterite group these verbs are not irregular as there is no addition of letters ; the *i* of the root simply changes to a *y*.

For verbs ending in *aer* like *caer* : "to fall" ; in *eer* like *leer* : "to read" ; in *oer* like *roer* : "to gnaw" ; and *oir* : "to hear", the unstressed *i* also becomes *y* in the preterite and the gerundive.

Moreover, *caer* : "to fall" and *oír* : "to hear" also belong to the group of 24 unclassifiable verbs.

Group eleven

Dormir : "to sleep" and *Morir* : "to die"

These verbs have the same irregularity as the verbs of group two ; thus they have the diphthong *ue (duermo :* "I sleep" ; *muere :* "he dies"). But in any other case the *o* becomes *u* in the same cases as group eight verbs when *e* becomes *i*.

DORM IR : "to sleep"

	Indicative	Subjunctive	Imperative
present	duerm o	duerm a	
	duerm es	duerm as	duerm e
	duerm e	duerm a	
	dorm imos	durm amos	
	dorm ís	durm áis	dorm id
	duerm en	duerm an	

Indicative	Subjunctive
preterite	**imperfect** (or)
dorm í	durm iera / iese
dorm iste	durm ieras / ieses
durm ió	durm iera / iese
dorm imos	durm iéramos / iésemos
dorm isteis	durm ierais / ieseis
durm ieron	durm ieran / iesen
	future
	durm iere
	durm ieres
	durm iere
	durm iéremos
	durm iereis
	durm ieren

Gerundive : durm iendo

Do not forget that the past participle of *morir* is irregular, thus *muerto* (not *morido*) : "dead".

Group twelve

Valer : "to be worth" and *salir* : "to go out"

These two verbs acquire the consonant *g* in gront of the ending in the present indicative when the ending begins with an *a* or an *o*. In the future and the conditional the vowel is lost and a euphonic *d* acquired.

In the imperative the last vowel is cut off.

	Indicative		Subjunctive		Imperative	
present	valg	o	valg	a		
	val	es	valg	as		
	val	e	valg	a	val	(ou) vale
	val	emos	valg	amos		
	val	éis	valg	áis	val	ed
	val	en	valg	an		

Indicative		Conditional	
future		**present**	
vald	ré	vald	ría
vald	rás	vald	rías
vald	rá	vald	ría
vald	remos	vald	ríamos
vald	réis	vald	ríais
vald	rán	vald	rían

SUMMARY OF IRREGULAR VERBS

Group	Verbs with this irregularity	Irreg.	Where it arises	Example
1	Numerous verbs having an *e* as the final vowel of the root	**e – ie**	present	*pensar, perder*
2	Numerous verbs having an *o* as the final vowel of the root	**o – ue**	present	*contar, volver*
3	Verbs ending in *acer, ecer, ocer, ucir*	**c – zc**	present	*conocer, lucir*
4	Verbs ending in *ducir*	**c – z** pret.: **duje**	present preterite	*conducir*
5	Verbs ending in *añer, añir, iñir, uñir, eller, ullir.*	loss of **i**	preterite gerundive	*mullir*

6	*Servir* and verbs ending in *ebir, edir, egir, eguir, emir, enchir, endir, estir, etir*	e – i	present, gerundive	*pedir*
7	Verbs ending in *eir, eñir*	loss of i e – i	present, preterite, gerundive	*reir*
8	Verbs ending in *entir, erir, ertir*	e – ie e – i	present, preterite, gerundive	*sentir*
9	Verbs ending in *irir* and *jugar*	i – ie u – ue	present	*adquirir, jugar*
10	Verbs ending in *uir*	+ y before **a, e, o**	present	*construir*
11	*Dormir, morir*	o – ue o – u	present, preterite, gerundive	*dormir*
12.	*Valer, salir*	+ g before **a & o.** vowel – euphonic **d.** final vowel removed in the imperative	present, future, imperative	*valer*

THE PAST PARTICIPLE

In general, the past participle ends in *ado* for verbs ending in *ar* and in *ido* for verbs ending in *er* and *ir*.

Irregular past participles generally end in *to, so* or *cho* : *abrir, abierto* : "opened" ; *imprimir, impreso* : "printed" ; *hacer, hecho* : "done".

The past participle is used with the verb *haber* to form the compound tenses. When it is put with the verb *ser,* it is used to form the passive voice of transitive verbs.

Some verbs have two past participles, one regular and one irregular.

The regular one is used to form the compound tenses and it is used with the verb *haber.*

The irregular one is generally used by itself as an adjective and may sometimes be used with *estar* or *tener.*

Only *frito* (from *freir* : "to fry"), *impreso* (from *imprimir* : "to print") and *provisto* (from *proveer* : "to provide") can be used in place of the regular participle to go with the verb *haber.*

List of current verbs having two past participles.

Infinitive		Regular Past Participle	Irregular Past Participle
Absorver	to absorb	absorvido	absorto
Abstraer	to abstract	abstraido	abstracto
Atender	to look after	atendido	atento
Bendecir	to bless	bendecido	bendito
Completar	to complete	completado	completo
Concluir	to conclude	concluido	concluso
Concretar	to concretise	concretado	concreto
Confesar	to confess	confesado	confeso
Confundir	to confuse	confundido	confuso
Convertir	to convert	convertido	converso
Corregir	to correect	corregido	correcto
Cultivar	to cultivate	cultivado	culto
Despertar	to waken	despertado	despierto
Difundir	to scatter	difundido	difuso
Distinguir	to distinguish	distinguido	distinto
Dividir	to divide	dividido	diviso
Elegir	to elect	elegido	electo
Exceptuar	to except	exceptuado	excepto
Expresar	to express	expresado	expreso
Extender	to spread	extendido	extenso
Fijar	to fix	fijado	fijo
Freir	to fry	freído	frito
Hartar	to satisfy	hartado	harto
Imprimir	to print	imprimido	impreso
Incluir	to include	incluido	incluso
Invertir	to invest	invertido	inverso
Juntar	to meet	juntado	junto
Maldecir	to curse	maldecido	maldito
Manifestar	to demonstrate	manifestado	manifiesto
Molestar	to annoy	molestado	molesto
Ocultar	to hide	ocultado	oculto
Omitir	to omit	omitido	omiso
Pervertir	to corrupt	pervertido	perverso
Poseer	to possess	poseído	poseso
Precisar	to specify	precisado	preciso
Proveer	to provide	proveído	provisto
Remitir	to put back	remitido	remiso
Soltar	to loosen	soltado	suelto
Suspender	to suspend	suspendido	suspenso
Sustituir	to substitute	substituido	substituto
Tender	to tighten	tendido	tenso

VERBS WITH THEIR OWN IRREGULARITIES

In Spanish there are 24 verbs which have their own particular irregularities and which, consequently, cannot be classified within the twelve groups which we have previously looked at.

Out of these 24 verbs, 19 are verbs which we can call "basic" inasmuch as one or several of them may be used to form the most elementary sentences used in everyday life.

Here you will only find their irregular forms. The omitted forms are conjugated normally according to the examples of verbs given ending in *ar*, *er* or *ir*. Spelling changes, not being considered as irregularities, will not be taken into account in this summary.

First you will find – in alphabetical order – the 19 verbs mentioned above ; then you will find the 5 remaining verbs – also in alphabetical order. This division has been established according to the usage of these verbs, the last 5 being very rarely used in current conversation.

ANDAR : "to walk"

Indicative		Subjunctive		

preterite
anduve
anduviste
anduvo
anduvimos
anduvisteis
anduvieron

imperfect
anduviera (or) anduviese
anduvieras
anduviera
anduviéramos
anduvierais
anduvieran

future
anduviere
anduvieres
anduviere
anduviéremos
anduviereis
anduvieren

SABER : "to know"

Indicative

present

sé

preterite

supe
supiste
supo
supimos
supisteis
supieron

future

sabré
sabrás
sabrá
sabremos
sabréis
sabrán

Subjunctive

present

sepa
sepas
sepa
sepamos
sepáis
sepan

imperfect

supiera
supieras
supiera
supiéramos
supierais
supieran

(or) supiese

future

supiere
supieres
supiere
supiéremos
supiereis
supieren

Conditional

present

sabría
sabrías
sabría
sabríamos
sabríais
sabrían

SER

See conjugation page 415.

TENER

See conjugation page 413.

TRAER : "to bring"

Indicative		Subjunctive	
present		**present**	
traigo		traiga	
		traigas	
		traiga	
		traigamos	
		traigáis	
		traigan	
preterite		**imperfect**	
traje		trajera	(or) trajese
trajiste		trajeras	
trajo		trajera	
trajimos		trajéramos	
trajisteis		trajerais	
trajeron		trajeran	
		future	
		trajere	
		trajeres	
		trajere	
		trajéremos	
		trajereis	
		trajeren	

VENIR : "to come"

Indicative

present

vengo
vienes
viene
–
–
vienen

preterite

vine
viniste
vino
vinimos
vinisteis
vinieron

future

vendré
vendrás
vendrá
vendremos
vendréis
vendrán

Subjunctive

present

venga
vengas
venga
vengamos
vengáis
vengan

imperfect

viniera
vinieras
viniera
viniéramos
vinierais
vinieran

(or) viniese

Conditional

present

vendría
vendrías
vendría
vendríamos
vendríais
vendrían

Imperative

ven

future

viniere
vinieres
viniere
viniéremos
viniereis
vinieren

VER : "to see"

Indicative		Subjunctive
present	veo	present	vea
		veas
		vea
		veamos
		veáis
		vean

imperfect
veía
veías
veía
veíamos
veíais
veían

past participle
visto

5 Verbs rarely used

ASIR : "to seize"

Indicative		Subjunctive
present	asgo	present	asga
		asgas
		asga
		asgamos
		asgáis
		asgan

ERGUIR : "to erect"

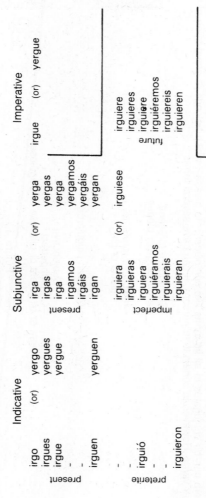

Indicative

present

	(or)	
irgo		yergo
irgues		yergues
irgue		yergue
—		—
—		—
irguen		yerguen

preterite

—
—
irguió
—
—
irguieron

Subjunctive

present

	(or)	
irga		yerga
irgas		yergas
irga		yerga
irgamos		yergamos
irgáis		yergáis
irgan		yergan

imperfect

	(or)	
irguiera		irguiese
irguieras		
irguiera		
irguiéramos		
irguierais		
irguieran		

Imperative

	(or)	
irgue		yergue

future

irguiere
irguieres
irguiere
irguiéremos
irguiereis
irguieren

Gerundive

irguiendo

PLACER : "to please"

This verb can be conjugated in all its forms like *complacer* : "to please", which belongs to group three of the irregular verbs. However, in certain third persons, it can have several forms :

Subjunctive (present)
plazca, plega or plegue

Indicative (preterite)
placio or plugo
–
placieron pluguieron

Subjunctive
Imperfect
placiera or pluguiera or placiese or pluguiese

Future
placiere or pluguiere

PODRIR or PUDRIR : "to rot"

For this verb it is advisable to use only the root *pudr.* except in the infinitive *(podrir)* and the participle *(podrido)*. This allows the verb to be converted to a regular verb and at the same time avoids any confusion with the verb *poder (podíra, podrias,* etc.).

YACER : "to lie down"

Present indicative		Present subjunctive			Imperative
yazco, yazgo (or) yago	yazca,	yazga	(or)	yaga	yace (or) yaz
	yazcas,	yazgas		yagas	
	yazca,	yazga		yaga	
	yazcamos,	yazgamos		yagamos	
	yazcáis,	yazgáis		yagáis	
	yazcan,	yazgan		yagan	

INDEX GRAMMATICAL

A